TENNESSEE IN TURMOIL

TENNESSEE IN TURMOIL:

Politics in the Volunteer State, 1920–1932

David D. Lee

Memphis State University Press

The author and Memphis State University Press are grateful for permission to quote from the following books:

Key, V. O. *Southern Politics in State and Nation.* New York: Vintage Books, 1949.
Lewison, Paul. *Race, Class and Party: A History of Negro Suffrage and White Politics in the South.* Copyright 1932, 1960 by Paul Lewison. New York: Russell & Russell, 1964.
McGill, Ralph. *The South and the Southerner.* Boston and Toronto: Little, Brown and Company in association with the Atlantic Monthly Press, 1964.

Copyright © 1979 by David D. Lee

All Rights Reserved. No part of this book may be reproduced or utilized in any form or by any means, electronic or mechanical, including photocopying and recording, or by any information storage and retrieval system, without permission in writing from the publisher.

Manufactured in the United States of America

Library of Congress Cataloging in Publication Data

Lee, David D   1948–
  Tennessee in turmoil.

  Bibliography: p.
  Includes index.
  1. Tennessee—Politics and government—1865–1950.
2. Elections—Tennessee—History. 3. Tennessee.
General Assembly—Voting. I. Title.
F436.L46   320.9'768'05   79-9264
ISBN 0-87870-048-X

This publication was made possible in part by a grant from the Tennessee Historical Commission.

To my parents

Contents

List of Tables	ix
Acknowledgments	xi
Preface	xiii
1. Tennessee in Transition	1
2. The Election of Austin Peay	19
3. Reform and Realignment	37
4. Boss	76
5. The Emergence of Crump	115
6. All Idols Were Clay	150
Appendix A: Definition of Urban and Rural	159
Appendix B: The Grand Divisions	161
Appendix C: Support Scores	162
Tables	178
Bibliography	193
Index	197

List of Tables

	Page
1. Raw Vote, 1922 Democratic Gubernatorial Primary	178
2. Percentage Vote, 1922 Democratic Gubernatorial Primary	178
3. Raw Vote, 1922 Gubernatorial Election	179
4. Percentage Vote, 1922 Gubernatorial Election	179
5. Support and Opposition for Austin Peay's Program, Sixty-third General Assembly, 1923 (Raw Totals)	179
6. Support and Opposition for Austin Peay's Program, Sixty-third General Assembly, 1923 (Percentages)	180
7. Raw Vote, 1924 Democratic Senatorial Primary	180
8. Percentage Vote, 1924 Democratic Senatorial Primary	180
9. Raw Vote, 1924 Presidential Election	181
10. Percentage Vote, 1924 Presidential Election	181
11. Raw Vote, 1924 Senatorial Election	181
12. Percentage Vote, 1924 Senatorial Election	182
13. Raw Vote, 1924 Gubernatorial Election	182
14. Percentage Vote, 1924 Gubernatorial Election	182
15. Support and Opposition for Austin Peay's Program, Sixty-fourth General Assembly, 1925 (Raw Totals)	183
16. Support and Opposition for Austin Peay's Program, Sixty-fourth General Assembly, 1925 (Percentages)	183
17. Raw Vote, 1926 Democratic Gubernatorial Primary	183
18. Percentage Vote, 1926 Democratic Gubernatorial Primary	184
19. Support and Opposition for Austin Peay's Program, Sixty-fifth General Assembly, 1927 (Raw Totals)	184
20. Support and Opposition for Austin Peay's Program, Sixty-fifth General Assembly, 1927 (Percentages)	184
21. Raw Vote, 1928 Democratic Gubernatorial Primary	185

x / List of Tables

22. Percentage Vote, 1928 Democratic Gubernatorial Primary	185
23. Raw Vote, 1928 Presidential Election	185
24. Percentage Vote, 1928 Presidential Election	186
25. Support and Opposition for Henry Horton's Program, Sixty-sixth General Assembly 1929 (Raw Totals)	186
26. Support and Opposition for Henry Horton's Program, Sixty-sixth General Assembly, 1929 (Percentages)	186
27. Raw Vote, 1930 Democratic Gubernatorial Primary	187
28. Percentage Vote, 1930 Democratic Gubernatorial Primary	187
29. Support and Opposition for Henry Horton's Program, Sixty-seventh General Assembly, 1931 (Raw Totals)	187
30. Support and Opposition for Henry Horton's Program, Sixty-seventh General Assembly, 1931 (Percentages)	188
31. Raw Vote, 1932 Democratic Gubernatorial Primary	188
32. Percentage Vote, 1932 Democratic Gubernatorial Primary	188
33. Raw Vote, Rural Faction, 1930 and 1932 Democratic Gubernatorial Primaries	189
34. Percentage Vote, Rural Faction, 1930 and 1932 Democratic Gubernatorial Primaries	189
35. Raw Vote, Antiadministration Faction, 1930 and 1932 Democratic Gubernatorial Primaries	189
36. Percentage Vote, Antiadministration Faction, 1930 and 1932 Democratic Gubernatorial Primaries	190
37. Raw Vote, 1932 Presidential Election in Tennssee	190
38. Percentage Vote, 1932 Presidential Election in Tennessee	190
39. Raw Vote, 1932 Gubernatorial Election	191
40. Percentage Vote, 1932 Gubernatorial Election	191

Acknowledgments

The assistance of many fine people, some of whom helped in ways they never realized, has made writing this study one of the most delightful experiences of my life. The staffs of the Tennessee State Library and Archives, the Memphis Public Library, and the Lawson-McGhee Library in Knoxville cheerfully and efficiently supplied materials for research. Robert McBride of the *Tennessee Historical Quarterly* and James Edmonson of the *West Tennessee Historical Society Papers* permitted me to include material previously published in those journals. Mrs. Cromwell Tidwell of Nashville, Tennessee, made available the papers of her father, Colonel Luke Lea, and showed me many kindnesses. Paul Bergeron, John Burnham, Dewey Grantham, Lee Greene, and Lowell Harrison all criticized various drafts and offered many useful suggestions. Professor Merton L. Dillon, who patiently supervised all of my graduate work, read the manuscript with his usual good judgment and pointed to numerous lapses of logic and style. Particular thanks must go to Professor Gary W. Reichard. Professor Reichard proposed this topic to me and guided my progress at every stage. His contributions, both as teacher and friend, have my deepest gratitude. Despite such talented assistance, some mistakes undoubtedly remain, and for those I claim responsibility.

Lengthy studies are often wearying of mind and spirit, and I would also like to thank the people who helped me to remember a world outside of libraries. Mrs. Maxine Stout of Nashville, Tennessee, graciously opened her home to an itinerant graduate student in a strange city. Good friends in Nashville and Columbus, Ohio, helped ease the tedium and frustration. Lastly, I must thank my parents, who have borne with grace and humor the difficulties of raising an over-educated son.

Publication of this book was made possible in part by a grant from the Tennessee Historical Commission.

Preface

"The South," V. O. Key wrote in 1949, "unlike most of the rest of the democratic world, really has no political parties. . . ."[1] In most democracies, political parties serve as a vehicle for the election of leaders and the creation of public policy. Shorn of this most basic institution of government by their one-party system, Southerners were forced to devise alternative methods for the resolution of public questions. This study examines the method that emerged in Tennessee during the 1920s. Factional politics in the Volunteer State were a loose, amorphous structure built around alliances of important and obscure figures throughout the state. What follows is an attempt to define the elements that comprised this political system, the ties that bound them together, the dynamics of coalition building, and the reasons why one faction eventually won preeminence in the state.

The backdrop for the clash of these factions was a state in the midst of a profound social transformation. The twin forces of industrialization and urbanization were relentlessly exposing the shortcomings of Tennessee's existing political institutions. As a result, Tennessee, like much of the South in the 1920s, was caught up in a movement that George B. Tindall has characterized as "business progressivism."[2] Its exponents sought to improve the efficiency of state government and expand public services to meet the needs of an increasingly industrial, urban-

1. V. O. Key, *Southern Politics in State and Nation* (New York, 1949), 16.
2. George B. Tindall, "Business Progressivism: Southern Politics in the 1920s," *South Atlantic Quarterly* 62 (1963), 92-106.

oriented society. Governor Austin Peay (1923-1927), in a far-reaching series of measures, did much to achieve these goals in Tennessee. Under Peay's supervision Tennessee built an extensive network of paved highways and upgraded its educational system at every level. The state government itself was reorganized from sixty-four uncoordinated agencies into a better managed operation under the guidance of eight commissioners.

Peay's program brought much needed reform to the state's administration, but the new structure also had two major impacts on the practice of politics in the state. First of all, the administration and funding of Peay's program brought a realignment of Tennessee politics. Since Tennessee's rural communities were in need of schools and roads, these areas benefited greatly from Peay's program. The money for these projects, however, came largely from Tennessee's more affluent urban areas. Gradually, through the mid-twenties, the cities of the state began to array themselves against the farm-backed administration faction. Secondly, in order to provide more efficient administration, Peay had concentrated power at the state level and in the hands of the governor. After his sudden death in 1927, Peay's political heirs, led by Luke Lea, publisher of the Nashville *Tennessean*, used this newly powerful governorship to build a statewide political machine. The machine was bound together by roads, school buildings, contracts, and other favors which the governor, thanks to Austin Peay's reforms, was now authorized to dispense.

Although this study is mainly a narrative interpretation of Tennessee in the twenties, I have also performed some simple analysis on voting returns in Tennessee elections and on selected roll call votes in the General Assembly. These techniques were used to provide a sharper picture of the membership of the state's two major factions. For the election analysis, I first separated Tennessee into its traditional three grand divisions and compared the strength of various candidates through raw votes and percentages. Working from the hypothesis that the growth of industry and cities was doing much to condition politics during the 1920s, I also divided the state arbitrarily into three groups based on the amount of urban population in each county. Counties with no urban population formed the first group; those with an urban population less than thirty percent of its total population made up the second group; and those with an urban population over thirty percent of its total population went into the third group.

In conjunction with voting analysis, I used these two factors—geography and urbanization—to study the behavior of the factions in the General Assembly. Tennessee's two governors from 1923 to 1933 were closely identified with the same faction. From the House and the Senate *Journals* I collected all items, regardless of issue content, on which the governor took a public position. I then constructed an index of support modeled on the *Congressional Quarterly's* index of support for the President. I divided the number of times a member voted with the governor's position by the total number of times he voted. This percentage, multiplied by 100 to give a whole number, was the index of support for each member. Again arbitrarily, I characterized legislators with scores of seventy or above as members of the administration faction, and those with scores below thirty as members of the opposition faction. Then I simply counted the number of legislators from each faction who fell into each of the urban and geographic categories and compared the totals.[3]

This procedure proved helpful in two ways. First of all, it gave important clues to the composition of the two main factions contending for leadership in Tennessee during the 1920s. Secondly, by analyzing roll call votes as well as popular votes, I was able, in effect, to "check" my results. Legislators who supported the administration, as anticipated, usually came from districts where the two governors ran well in the popular vote. Based on this research, I have concluded that the administration faction was centered in the farms and small towns across the state and in Republican East Tennessee. The opposition faction drew its strength from the large cities, especially Memphis and Nashville, and from Middle Tennessee.

Although I have paid some attention to presidential and senatorial races, this study is largely concerned with gubernato-

3. See Appendix C.

rial politics. William Goodman, a close student of Tennessee's political parties, has observed that the state's politicians have traditionally been more interested in the governorship than in federal offices. Governors, Goodman points out, are more closely involved with the daily interests of citizens than are congressmen, senators, and presidents. Goodman was writing in the early 1950s, but his remarks are even more valid for Tennessee in the 1920s, a time when the state was greatly expanding its public service role. Governors dominated the political landscape during those years and therefore deserve more extended analysis.[4]

Tennessee between 1920 and 1930 was attempting to bring increased organization to its public affairs. The motive behind this drive was to enable its governmental institutions to meet the problems created by the shift from a rural society toward an urban-industrial one. Ironically, however, the instruments of reform became the tools of renewed corruption. The climax of the struggle between the two dominant factions came in 1932: the leaders of the rural group were disgraced and Mr. Edward Hull Crump finally emerged as the "Boss."

---

4. William Goodman, *Inherited Domain: Political Parties in Tennessee* (Knoxville, 1954), 32.

TENNESSEE IN TURMOIL

1

Tennessee in Transition

It had been a long time coming, but by 1920 Henry Grady's dream was being realized. The industrial "New South" he had so zealously championed during the 1880s in the columns of his Atlanta *Constitution* was arriving at last. Across the South the face of the land was being altered by the expansion and diversification of industry. The South after the Great War was reaping the harvest and the whirlwind of an "industrial evolution." One of the states most deeply affected by this change was Tennessee. Industrialism burst across its wide expanse with varying impact, but no Tennessean completely escaped the coming of the new age.

Tennessee, like Caesar's Gaul, is divided into three parts. East Tennessee, its hazy peaks looming over the Great Valley of the Tennessee River, has been a land apart from the rest of the state. Unsuited by terrain to plantation-style agriculture, East Tennessee nursed an antebellum economy built around small farmers, while Middle and West Tennessee fell under the sway of the lords of cotton and slaves. At a time when most of the South was reacting violently against the possibility of emancipation, the first abolitionist newspaper appeared in East Tennessee. During the Civil War, the region opposed secession and became a bastion of Unionist sentiment. The legacy of the great conflict lingered in East Tennessee, as the mountain counties continued to return heavy Republican majorities in the years of the "Solid South." By 1920, its mountainous terrain was also setting East Tennessee apart from the state in another way, as its tumbling

2 / *Tennessee in Turmoil*

rivers and streams provided a virtually untapped source of water power to lure the prized industrial plants of the "New South."[1]

Middle Tennessee is separated from the East by the Cumberland Plateau, an area known for its deposits of timber and coal. The Highland Rim frames the fertile and productive Central Basin focused at Nashville. The limestone deposits of the Basin nourished grasses which produced excellent livestock, most notably the Tennessee walking horse. Huge tracts of available land gave rise to an extensive cotton culture by the mid-nineteenth century, and the vast plantations stood in sharp contrast to the small farms of the East. Middle Tennessee marched proudly with the Confederacy and was the scene of heavy fighting due to its strategic location. After the war, it became solidly Democratic.[2]

West of Nashville, the rolling hills give way to the broad Mississippi River bottom land. Here cotton ruled from the earliest settlement, and the plantation system became even more dominant than in Middle Tennessee. With cotton remaining the keystone of its prosperity in 1920, much of the state's black population lived in West Tennessee—another inheritance from antebellum times. Memphis dominated the West, its power springing from the immense white bales that crowded its wharves awaiting shipment. Although West Tennessee was bound politically to the rest of the state, in an economic sense the area was much closer to the Deep South and the Southwest than to East or Middle Tennessee. Thoroughly Democratic in its politics, the West was nonetheless aware of its minority position in the state and deeply suspicious of deals between the Eastern and Middle sections.[3]

1. Lee S. Greene and Robert S. Avery, *Government in Tennessee*, 2nd edition (Knoxville, 1966), 2-4. A third edition of this basic work by Lee S. Greene, David H. Grubbs, and Victor Hobday, *Government in Tennessee* (Knoxville, 1975) is also available. V. O. Key, *Southern Politics in State and Nation* (New York, 1949), 59. Wilma Dykeman, *Tennessee,* A Bicentennial History (New York and Nashville, 1975), 7.

2. Greene and Avery, *Government in Tennessee*, pp. 2-4. Key, *Southern Politics*, p. 59. Dykeman, *Tennessee*, p. 7.

3. Greene and Avery, *Government in Tennessee*, pp. 2-4. Key, *Southern Politics*, p. 59. Dykeman, *Tennessee*, p. 7.

By 1920, Tennessee, like much of the Upper South, was in the midst of an important socioeconomic transition. The sibling processes of urbanization and industrialization were gradually creating a new power base at the expense of the farmers and rural-oriented small town merchants and professionals. Manufacturing began a steady growth in Tennessee in the years after the Civil War, surpassing agriculture as a producer of wealth as early as 1890. Twenty years later, the value of goods manufactured in Tennessee was $180 million, topping the value of agricultural products by $69 million. In 1920, Tennessee factories turned out $556 million in goods, some $238 million more than Tennessee farms. Moreover, industry was employing an increasing percentage of the state's labor force. Farming still engaged fifty-four percent of Tennessee's male workers, but the percentage of men in manufacturing moved from thirteen in 1900 to twenty-two in 1920, a rate of growth higher than the national average.[4]

World War I greatly increased the pace of industrialization in Tennessee. Whereas the state's early industrial development was based on textiles, lumber, iron and steel, during the war the federal government sponsored four wood chemical plants in Tennessee, two explosives factories, and an aluminum smelter. After the Armistice, the two explosives factories shifted to the production of rayon, while three of the chemical plants and the aluminum smelter at Maryville continued operations. In addition to creating new war-related industries, the war stimulated local industries, particularly in East Tennessee. With its minerals, lumber, and the water power potential of the Tennessee River, the mountain region had long been attractive to industry, but the decade 1910–1920 saw spectacular growth. In 1910, Chattanooga had 192 factories producing $26.7 million in goods; ten years later it boasted 332 factories producing $136.6 million in goods.[5]

In these years the South as a whole was also experiencing

---

4. Joseph Macpherson, "Democratic Progressivism in Tennessee: The Administration of Governor Austin Peay" (Ph. D. Dissertation, Vanderbilt, 1969), 5-6, 26-28.
5. *Ibid.*

tremendous urban growth. During the twenties, the South's urban population climbed from 25.4 percent of the national total in 1920 to 32.1 percent in 1930, a higher rate of growth than in any other region. In Tennessee, cities across the state experienced a dramatic increase in size and influence. Between 1900 and 1920, the state's urban population nearly doubled, and the trend continued into the twenties. The urban percentage of the state's total population climbed from 16.2 percent in 1900 to 20.2 percent in 1910, to 26.1 percent in 1920, and to 34.3 percent in 1930.[6] Tennessee's urban population rose 46.7 percent during the decade 1920-1930, a rate three times the national average, and the ninth highest rate in the country. In 1900 only twenty-one of Tennessee's ninety-five counties included towns that exceeded 2500, but by 1920, thirty-nine counties claimed towns that large.[7]

As with manufacturing, East Tennessee cities were the fastest growing in the state. "The trend of urbanization," a contemporary observer noted, "is toward east Tennessee."[8] From 1900 to 1920 the population of Shelby (Memphis) and Davidson (Nashville) counties increased 6.1 percent and 4.7 percent respectively. In contrast, Hamilton County (Chattanooga) in East Tennessee grew 11.1 percent, and Knoxville a startling 24 percent.[9] Most spectacular was the growth of Kingsport. At the turn of the century it was a quiet mountain hamlet, but in 1909 with the completion of the Clinchfield Railroad through Holston Valley to the Eastern Kentucky coalfields, the boom was ignited. Brick and cement plants appeared by 1910, and on the eve of World War I the town had a power plant, a hosiery mill, and extract, pulp, and paper factories. A war-time cellulose plant grew into Tennessee Eastman Corporation. Over the next

---

6. *Ibid.*, pp. 26-27. C. E. Allred, "Human and Physical Resources of Tennessee," *Tennessee Agricultural Experiment Station Report* 50 (1937), 117-18. An urban area, in this stidy, is defined as it is defined by the United States Bureau of the Census: a town with a population of at least 2500 people.

7. Allred, "Human and Physical Resources," pp. 117-18. Frank B. Ward, "Industrial Development in Tennessee," *Annals of the American Academy of Political and Social Science* 153 (1931), 144-45.

8. Ward, "Industrial Development," pp. 144-45.

9. *Ibid.*

decade the city added the Kingsport Press, a foundry, and plants producing textiles, bookcloth, glass, and silk goods.[10]

Kingsport's East Tennessee rival, Knoxville, which John Gunther in the mid-1940s described as "the ugliest city I ever saw in America," also felt the impact of industrial growth. Economically dependent on manufacturing, Knoxville in 1920 had some 350 plants producing textiles, marble, and furniture. The Southern and the Louisville and Nashville Railroads maintained large car repair shops there. The city's population had exploded in the previous decade, increasing from 36,346 in 1910 to 77,818 in 1920. Despite this tremendous influx, Knoxville's population remained socially conservative and ethnically homogeneous. The percentage of blacks in the city declined from twenty-one to fifteen during the decade, and fewer than 2,000 Catholics lived there in 1920. As in most Southern cities, baseball and movies were prohibited on Sunday. Predominantly white and Protestant with a large working class, within a few years Knoxville was to become the center of Ku Klux Klan strength in the Southern Appalachians.[11]

The tenor of urban life beyond Knoxville was vastly different. Two hundred miles to the west lay Nashville, the self-styled "Athens of the South." Nashville's industry and population grew steadily during the early twentieth century, but the city escaped the harsh socioeconomic shocks that struck Knoxville and Kingsport. In the Roaring Twenties Nashville was a noisy, brawling city with a "Western spirit somewhat like that of Chicago." Gambling flourished and a sprawling red-light district prospered just a few steps from the Capitol. Forty years later Ralph McGill, a sportswriter for the Nashville *Banner* during those tumultuous years, exulted in the memory of it:

> What other town ever framed the governor of the state, put him drunk in bed at a sporting house, and then

---

10. George B. Tindall, *The Emergence of the New South, 1913-1945* (Baton Rouge, 1967), 96-107.

11. Louis Brownlow, *A Passion for Anonymity: The Autobiography of Louis Brownlow* (Chicago, 1958), 2:161-62. Kenneth Jackson, *The Ku Klux Klan in the City, 1915-1930* (New York, 1967), 59, 64.

6 / *Tennessee in Turmoil*

> raided it, taking him down to the station in a Black Maria?
> In what other city could a young and aesthetic reporter lie in the gutter under the wheels of a wagon loaded with watermelons in the old square while the bullets of two feuding political factions sang and ricocheted off the old stone buildings?[12]

Rowdiest and most sensational of all was Memphis, on the banks of the Mississippi. Memphis in 1920 was a violent city with a diverse population. Among its 162,000 inhabitants the city counted 10,000 Catholics and 10,000 Jews. Forty percent of its citizens were black. Much of its population was newly arrived from the rural South. Both white- and blue-collar wages were low and organized labor was weak. Not surprisingly, Memphis in 1920 had the highest homicide rate of any city in the world, more than fifty murders per one hundred thousand people. Liquor, gambling, and prostitution thrived under the benevolent care of the police department.[13]

Despite the rise of cities and industries, Tennessee in 1920 remained a state dominated by farms and rural influences. But although rural areas remained a potent force, they were experiencing a relative decline. The rural percentage of the state's population slipped from eighty-four percent in 1900 to seventy-four percent in 1920. Between 1900 and 1910 the gain in farm population was 2.9 percent, but between 1910 and 1930, movement away from farms surpassed the natural increase in farm population. The percentage of people engaged in agriculture declined from sixty-four percent in 1900 to forty-eight percent in 1920 and continued to drop in the following decade. Although the trend of such farm-related statistics was downward in these years, farming in 1920 was still the source of income for nearly three-quarters of the people of Tennessee. Its grip was slipping but by no means broken.[14]

12. Jesse C. Burt, *Nashville, Its Life and Times* (Nashville, 1959), 110. Ralph McGill, *The South and the Southerner* (Boston, 1964), 91-92. Harold W. Martin, *Ralph McGill, Reporter* (Boston, 1973), 26.
13. Jackson, *Ku Klux Klan in the City*, pp. 45-6.
14. John Knox, *The People of Tennessee: A Study of Population Trends*

One of the most important byproducts of this transition from a rural/farming state to an urban/industrial state was a growing pressure on state government. "Inescapably," James Thorogood has written, "new needs were appearing and neglected matters such as education, conservation, public health and inspection services were urgently pressing for solution." Tennessee's public services lagged conspicuously behind those of the rest of the nation. In 1920 fewer than one-fifth of the state's school children had access to an elementary school with an eight-month term; only twelve counties offered such a term, and the statewide average was only 126 days. Tennessee appropriated from the state treasury a fraction over thirty cents per white inhabitant for education, lowest among the thirteen Southern states. From the mountains to the Mississippi, Tennessee had only five hundred miles of paved roads. At the end of World War I, Tennessee stood forty-seventh among the states in per capita expenditure for all government services. As early as 1908, Governor Malcolm R. Patterson had called for "new policies befitting the dignity of a great state and commensurate with the needs and expectations of the people," but Tennessee's political dialogue was dominated through the mid-teens by the incandescent issue of prohibition. With the election of Thomas Rye to the governorship in 1914 the prohibition question was resolved at last, however, and attention was increasingly focused on the plight of state government.[15]

Most seriously, Tennessee's archaic tax structure was simply inadequate to meet the needs of an industrializing society. Although the state was becoming more urban and industrial, it continued to rely on a general property tax which frequently did not touch personal property. The burden of government was left mainly on farm lands and other real estate. As early as 1899, the state comptroller of treasury declared, "It is conceded by well-informed persons that the value of personal property is nearly, if

---

(Knoxville, 1949), 44-45, 75, 128. Macpherson, "Democratic Progressivism," pp. 26-27.

15. Tindall, *Emergence of the New South*, p. 312. Macpherson, "Democratic Progressivism," pp. 30, 59. James Thorogood, *Financial History of Tennessee since 1870* (Nashville, 1949), 90-91. Knoxville *Journal and Tribune*, July 30, 1922.

8 / *Tennessee in Turmoil*

not quite, equal to that of realty, yet the assessed value [of personalty] for 1899 was only 12.2 per cent of real estate." The rest of personalty remained "in hiding." In other Southern states, by contrast, the percentage ranged from 20.5 in Kentucky to 47.1 in Alabama.[16] The state thus depended for most of its revenue on its farm population, a group that was producing an ever shrinking percentage of the state's wealth. As the Rockwood *Times* observed, "The towns and cities of the state have become centers of commerce, trade, and industry. Hence, the wealth of the state has in large measure been withdrawn from the country and centered in the more populous areas." Moreover, fluctuations in the value of farm products reduced the value of realty and hurt the ability of farmers to pay taxes. The main source of revenue for the state government of Tennessee was actually rooted in an international market for farm commodities that the state could not control.[17]

Efforts to improve the efficiency of the existing tax system failed. Individual counties, rather than the state, held responsibility for assessment and collection of taxes. These assessments were made by elected officials, often with gross favoritism, and county administrators deducted "collection fees" before forwarding tax receipts to Nashville. In addition, each county tried to keep its own assessment as low as possible, throwing the tax burden on others. Seeking to mitigate these abuses, the legislature in 1907 passed the Back Tax Act, a law permitting state revenue agents to reassess property they considered to be undervalued. These reassessments could be retroactive for three years with interest. Intended to bring a measure of equity to the tax system, the Back Tax law instead became an effective political club. State revenue agents were closely tied to members of the legislature, and the threat of increased assessment could be very useful in dealing with obstreperous opponents. Business corporations were favorite targets of rural legislators.[18]

16. Thorogood, *Financial History*, pp. 68-69.
17. Macpherson, "Democratic Progressivism," pp. 10-13. Ernest J. Eberling, "Social Interpretation: Tennessee," *Social Forces* 1 (1926), 26. Rockwood *Times*, July 6, 1922.
18. Macpherson, "Democratic Progressivism," pp. 10-11.

With taxation emerging as a controversial statewide issue, Governor Thomas Rye in 1917 appointed a Committee to Investigate Assessments and Taxation. Noting that Tennessee's per capita expenditure for state government was only $1.88, second lowest among Southern states, Rye contended that the state system of taxation was so skewed that the largest amount of taxes was paid by those least able to pay, while those most able to pay were "virtually escaping taxation altogether." The committee's findings largely confirmed the governor's charges. It pointed to the evils of the general property tax clause of the constitution and urged an amendment to permit the classification of property for tax purposes. The committee also attacked the gross underassessment of realty and the competitive underassessment among counties. It complained bitterly of the breakdown of the equalization machinery and the failure to reach corporate personalty. Lastly, it recommended the creation of a permanent state tax commission armed with the power to enforce equalization and administer the tax system. A sweeping indictment of Tennessee's tax system, the report launched an eight-year reform effort that "produced more changes in administration and in revenue sources than any other previous period of the State's history."[19]

By 1920, then, taxation was emerging as a major source of discontent across Tennessee. City people as well as farmers were deeply dissatisfied with the system. The Davidson County Court spoke for many urban dwellers when, in April 1918, it complained that the four largest counties were most nearly conforming to the state tax laws and were thus bearing a disproportionate tax burden. Their complaint was justified because while intangibles escaped taxation, tangible property in cities, small property owners for example, was assessed fairly. Rural tax assessors were much less conscientious. Moreover, while tax collections were rising in urban areas, state spending for cities was declining. Farmers, for their part, were disgruntled over the property tax and the state's inability to tax intangible

19. Thorogood, *Financial History of Tennessee,* pp. 91, 101. Charles H. McCorkle, "Taxation in Tennessee" (M. A. Thesis, Vanderbilt, 1932), 27.

property. Virtually everyone resented the "back tax racket." The question could be delayed no longer and it burst violently over the political landscape in 1920.[20]

Politics in Tennessee has often taken on a factional character, but rarely was the state so thoroughly splintered as in 1920. The impact of history, geography, personal animosities, traditional rivalries, old issues and new issues had reduced both parties to little more than collections of feudal baronies. These petty lords played a cynical game, alternately joining and deserting each other, bidding for the stakes of power. Party lines virtually disappeared in some areas with groups nominally belonging to one party tipping the balance of power within the other. No effective statewide political leadership existed among either Democrats or Republicans, and governors and senators were selected by amorphous, highly personalized coalitions carefully nurtured by the individual candidates.

Within the Tennessee Democracy, several men exercised considerable—but not dominant—influence. The most colorful, most controversial, and perhaps most powerful was Colonel Luke Lea of Nashville. Born in 1879 to an established Middle Tennessee family, Lea first attracted attention in 1906 as a backer of Malcolm Patterson for governor. In the kind of flamboyant gesture that was to characterize his career, he seized the gavel in the midst of the chaotic state Democratic convention and restored order on the floor. Less than a year later, Lea broke with Patterson and founded the Nashville *Tennessean* to oppose him. In 1908, after Patterson defeated Edward Ward Carmack to gain renomination in the bitterest gubernatorial contest in Tennessee history, Lea hired the defeated candidate as editor of the *Tennessean*. Carmack's vituperative columns drew lightning in the tension-charged atmosphere, and the editor was killed in a gun battle on the streets of Nashville with two Patterson associates, Colonel Duncan Cooper and his son Robin. Again showing his flair for the dramatic, Lea made a point of person-

---

20. John Trotwood Moore and Austin P. Foster, *Tennessee: The Volunteer State, 1769-1923* (Chicago, 1923), 1:683. Gary W. Reichard, "The Defeat of Governor Roberts," *Tennessee Historical Quarterly* 30 (1971), 94-109.

ally assuming Carmack's duties as editor. Three years later, as the leader in a prohibition-inspired fusion movement between Independent Democrats and Republicans, his skill at coalition-building brought him a U.S. Senate seat. Lea rejoined the regular Democrats in 1914, but lost his Senate seat in 1916 to Kenneth McKellar in Tennessee's first direct senatorial election. The sound thrashing Lea received at the polls seems to have convinced him that he was more effective in smoke-filled rooms than on the public platform. Over the next decade and a half that he remained active in state politics, Lea never again ran for elective office. Instead he sought through his wealth, newspapers, and contacts to influence those who sat in places of power.[21]

The outbreak of World War I offered Lea a chance to recoup some of his lost prestige, and he played the opportunity like a master showman. He organized the all-volunteer 114th Field Artillery regiment and became its colonel. The regiment served with distinction in France, but Lea gained his greatest notoriety after the Armistice. In one of the most outlandish schemes ever concocted by an American military officer, Lea and a small group of men entered neutral Holland and bluffed their way into the castle housing the abdicated emperor, Wilhelm II of Germany. Their avowed purpose was to kidnap the monarch and "present him as a New Year's gift to President Wilson." Lea's military superiors were outraged and the colonel only narrowly escaped court-martial. AEF Adjutant General M. J. O'Brien reprimanded him, saying General John J. Pershing considered the episode "amazingly indiscreet." O'Brien's own words were somewhat harsher. "You had no right whatsoever," he said, "to present yourself at the chateau of the ex-Emperor of Germany without the authorization of the President of the United States first obtained." Lea's exploit, he concluded, "might have en-

---

21. William Waller, ed., *Nashville, 1900-1910* (Nashville, 1972), 90, 93, 326. Thomas Harrison Baker, *The Memphis Commercial Appeal: The History of a Southern Newspaper* (Baton Rouge, 1971), 272-73. Figuers Family Papers, Biographies, Miscellaneous Sketches, Box 1, File 2, Tennessee State Library and Archives. Joe Hatcher, interview with the author, February 18, 1976, Nashville, Tennessee.

tailed the most disastrous consequences." Unperturbed, Colonel Lea was soon in Paris trading alternately on his military rank, his Senate term, and his press credentials as he visited the Peace Conference. In an account of the affair written almost twenty years later, Lea quoted General Pershing as saying, ". . . I'm a poor man, but I'd have given a year's pay to have been able to have taken Lea's trip into Holland and to have entered the castle of Count Bentinck without invitation."[22]

By the time Lea returned to Tennessee the tone of his career had been set. He was an intelligent, charming man with an extraordinary ability to manipulate people. A close associate once remarked, "I always figured he could walk into a room of his enemies and in fifteen minutes be in complete control of them." He also had a gift for the dramatic and was a bona fide war hero. According to his friend Gordon Browning, Lea "was a man that had so much activity about him that you never could tell which direction he was going until he was there." But Lea's flaws were apparent also. In the Kaiser escapade he had risked an international incident for obscure and possibly personal motives. He avoided court-martial because he had carefully observed the letter if not the spirit of the law. An ambitious man with a taste for power, Lea could be reckless in pursuit of it.[23]

Lea's chief political opposition in Middle Tennessee was the Nashville machine controlled by Hilary Howse, Kit T. McConnico, and Edward Bushrod Stahlman. Howse, a political force of long standing in Nashville, had served frequently as mayor of the city. McConnico, a Nashville attorney, was generalissimo of the organization. The most influential of the three was Stahlman, publisher of the Nashville *Banner* and Lea's bitterest enemy. A German immigrant, he came to Nashville after the Civil War and bought the *Banner* in 1885. Over the next four

---

22. Baker, *Commercial Appeal*, pp. 272-73. Figuers Family Papers, Sketches, Box 1, File 2. Luke Lea, "Account of Effort to Kidnap the Kaiser," untitled manuscript in Tennessee State Library and Archives, pp. 9-12, 22, 52, 79-80.

23. *Governor Gordon Browning: An Oral Memoir* compiled by Joseph H. Riggs, March, 1966, Memphis Public Library, Memphis, Tennessee. Joe Hatcher Interview, February 18, 1976.

decades the paper acquired a well-earned reputation as one of the most outspoken in the South.

The reasons for the Lea-Stahlman enmity are uncertain. The two had not always been enemies and at times, during the prohibition struggles of the early twentieth century, Lea and Stahlman had cooperated politically. Part of their antagonism was undoubtedly rooted in the fact that they published rival newspapers in the same city. Lea himself said the two men had fallen out over the Senate contest of 1913. The state legislature chose William Robert (Sawney) Webb to fill the short-term vacancy created by the death of Robert Love Taylor. Writing in September 1931, Lea explained, "The night Senator Webb was elected, E. B. Stahlman, publisher of the Nashville *Banner,* and an old friend of mine, demanded that I go before the caucus and urge the re-count of Senator Webb and the election of him, Stahlman. This I declined to do and I have had the bitterest enmity of all the Stahlmans from that day to this." Whatever the reason, the hatred between the two men was very intense. In the midst of the 1914 gubernatorial campaign Stahlman wrote, "I have lived in Tennessee for fifty years and never during that long period of time have I been in contact nor have I heard of a more consummate traitor, liar, or all-around skunk than Luke Lea, whose course in life much better fits him for the garb of a felon than the toga of a United States Senator." Stahlman and the *Banner* could be expected to oppose Lea or anyone affiliated with him.[24]

The third major power center in the Democratic Party was the Edward H. Crump machine in Shelby County. Like many Tennessee political leaders, Crump was not a native of the state. Born and raised in Holly Springs, Mississippi, he came to Memphis as a young man, beginning as a clerk in a Memphis cotton company and moving on to become a bookkeeper with the Woods-Chickasaw Saddlery Company. When the company went bankrupt in 1902, Crump borrowed the money to buy it,

---

24. Paul Issac, *Prohibition and Politics: Turbulent Decades in Tennessee, 1885-1920* (Knoxville, 1965), 236. Luke Lea to Frank Earle Parham, September 12, 1931, Luke Lea Papers, unsorted, in the possession of Mrs. Cromwell Tidwell, Nashville, Tennessee.

14 / *Tennessee in Turmoil*

and soon became a prosperous businessman. Elected mayor of Memphis in 1909, he set about building an extensive political organization. As mayor, however, Crump ran afoul of the popular statewide sentiment for prohibition, and his dogged refusal to enforce the statute prompted Governor Rye to initiate legal proceedings that resulted in Crump's ouster as mayor in 1916.[25]

Despite his removal, Crump was determined to continue in politics. That same year he was elected county trustee and slowly began to consolidate his organization in Shelby County as well as in Memphis itself. Although Crump's machine did not enter a candidate in the 1919 mayoralty race, his shrewd last-minute declaration for Rowlett Paine made it seem the "Boss" was responsible for Paine's narrow victory. Although not yet absolute master of Shelby County, Crump in 1920 was still its single most important politician.[26]

The Tennessee Democracy was a party deeply riven by constant strife among amorphous, impermanent coalitions. Lea, Crump, and the Howse-McConnico-Stahlman group headed the three largest factions in Tennessee politics in 1920, but lesser factions existed all over the state. Mayor Ed Bass of Chattanooga was also a man to be reckoned with, but was not a mover and shaker on the order of the others. In addition, virtually every county Democratic organization was split into at least two groups, locked in continuous struggle for control. The party simply had no lasting organization or effective leadership.[27]

Writing in 1949 in the waning days of Democratic supremacy, V. O. Key observed that the Republican Party in the South "wavers somewhat between an esoteric cult on the order of a lodge and a conspiracy for plunder in accord with the accepted customs of our politics." The party served both functions but

---

25. Gerald Capers, "Memphis: Satrapy of a Benevolent Despot," in Robert S. Allen, ed., *Our Fair City* (New York, 1947), 219-21. Shields McIlwanie, *Memphis Down in Dixie* (New York, 1948), 360-63.

26. Capers, "Memphis," pp. 211-13, 220-21. William D. Miller, *Mr. Crump of Memphis* (Baton Rouge, 1964), 110-13, 117, 130.

27. Macpherson, "Democratic Progressivism," pp. 17-19.

particularly the latter in Tennessee. Republicans in Tennessee, as in most of the South, divided basically into two main categories, the Black-and-Tans, a racially mixed group, and the white supremacist Lily Whites. Each was further subdivided into smaller units based on patronage arrangements and geographic convenience. Through most of the 1920s the Black-and-Tan faction, headed by J. Will Taylor and Robert R. Church, controlled the party machinery. A Campbell County attorney, Taylor had long been a powerful figure in East Tennessee, but his election to Congress in 1918 from the second district secured his position as state boss. Two years later the Republicans returned to power in Washington, and Tennessee's first district also elected a new Republican congressman. Taylor, as national committeeman and now ranking congressional Republican, assumed control of federal patronage throughout the state. His position, however, was dependent on his remaining the only Republican of statewide influence. The election of a Republican governor or senator such as Governor Alf A. Taylor in 1920 would force him to share his patronage. As a result, Congressman Taylor showed a persistent willingness to deal with Democrats, especially in hotly contested primaries.[28]

An important element in Republican party support was the state's urban-based black vote. In 1920, Tennessee's black population was in the midst of an exodus from the soil. A decline in the total acreage of improved land operated by blacks, in the number of farms they operated, and in the black rural population revealed their diminishing tie with the agricultural system of the state. In 1920, 170,464 blacks lived in Tennessee's urban areas, representing 37.7 percent of the state's black population and 27.9 percent of its urban population. This shift of blacks to urban areas was politically significant for several reasons. As pointed out by Paul Lewinson, the leading student of black voting in the early twentieth century, most blacks who voted in the South lived in urban areas. The nature of cities, Lewinson

---

28. Key, *Southern Politics*, p. 227. Chattanooga *Times*, October 6, 15, 1926. Memphis *News-Scimitar*, October 5, 1926. *Browning Memoir*, p. 103. Joe C. Gamble, interview with the author, June 28, 1976, Maryville, Tennessee.

16 / *Tennessee in Turmoil*

says, contributed to the partial breakdown of the taboo against black voting. Change being a part of city life, city residents were already indicating, by moving there in the first place, their willingness to tolerate a degree of change. The size of cities also bred indifference, which permitted blacks to make small inroads into the South's urban politics. Cities also drew abler, better trained blacks, and their proximity to one another encouraged organization in the black community. As a border state, Tennessee had fewer laws limiting black voting than states farther south. A poll tax was levied, but since there was no white primary in Tennessee, blacks were able to play an important part in the primaries of both parties and in general elections.[29]

Even within this relatively open context, Memphis was unique in the extent to which it permitted and even encouraged black voting. According to Lewinson, in 1930 Memphis was the only place where blacks had made "a real breach" in the closed political system of the South. The presence of a sizable black middle class leadership in Memphis enabled the black community to organize and to become effective politically. The most important of the black leaders in Memphis was Robert R. Church, Jr. Having inherited a fortune and large business interests from his father, Church was gradually able to withdraw from these pursuits and devote himself to politics. His light skin and Caucasian features combined with his middle class manners to help him cultivate the network of personal friendships with high-level white officials that formed the base of his power.[30]

Church first entered politics in 1912, when he sought election as a delegate to the Republican National Convention. Because he was a Taft supporter, his election was contested by the white pro-Roosevelt members of the delegation. The incident convinced Church that the black community needed to organize to advance in the Republican Party, and he became a leader in the

29. Charles E. Hall, *Negroes in the United States* (New York, 1969), 53. Paul Lewinson, *Race, Class, and Party* (New York, 1964), 132-38. Eberling, "Social Interpretation," p. 27.

30. Lewinson, *Race, Class, and Party*, p. 162. David Tucker, *Lieutenant Lee of Beale Street* (Nashville, 1971), 69.

drive to establish Lincoln Leagues. These leagues helped to organize blacks in Shelby County by conducting voting schools to teach them electoral procedures. In 1916, Church used the Lincoln Leagues to register ten thousand voters and to pay the poll tax for the poor. While Church's candidates lost, they drew enough votes to impress Republican leaders, and he was named to the National Republican Advisory Board.[31]

With national recognition, Church entered the years of his greatest power. "His influence in the Republican Party," the Memphis *Commercial Appeal* observed in 1926, "is more extensive in the South than any man, white or black." Church had very close ties with Will Hays, Harding's campaign manager and Postmaster General from 1921 to 1922. During the Harding and Coolidge years, consequently, he enjoyed free access to the White House and was hailed as the "number one patronage dispenser of the South." Even the strident racist Senator J. Thomas Heflin of Alabama paid poetic tribute to Church's influence:

> Officers up a 'simmon tree
> Bob Church on de ground
> Bob Church said to de 'pointing powers
> Shake dem 'pointments down.[32]

Despite Church's power, he had only limited success in securing good appointments for blacks. In Memphis, 120 of 150 mail carriers, eleven of twenty-two special delivery boys, and twenty-two postal substitutes were black. No blacks, however, achieved a clerkship during Church's tenure. It was impossible to get a federal job in Memphis without Church's endorsement, but even his authority was circumscribed by the racial mores of the times.[33]

31. Mingo Scott, Jr., *The Negro in Tennessee Politics and Governmental Affairs, 1865-1965: The Hundred Years Story* (Nashville, 1964), 90. Tucker, *Lieutenant Lee*, pp. 70-71.

32. Scott, *Negro in Tennessee Politics*, pp. 91-92. George W. Lee, *Beale Street: Where the Blues Began* (New York, 1934), 254-55. Lewinson, *Race, Class, and Party*, p. 139.

33. Lee, *Beale Street*, p. 242.

18 / *Tennessee in Turmoil*

The Lily White wing of the state Republican party offered little opposition to the Taylor-Church axis. Fred Arn and Claudius H. Huston of Chattanooga fought Taylor in the East, and John McCall battled Church in Memphis. After his election to Congress in 1920, B. Carroll Reece also became a major figure in the Lily White group. The main conflict between the two groups was over control of the party and dispensation of patronage, however, rather than issues. The Lily Whites mounted several challenges to the Black-and-Tans, but because of the latter's ties to the national party, the Lily Whites never seriously threatened the Taylor-Church leadership.[34]

In 1920, Tennessee was approaching a major transition in its history. Geography had split the state into three distinct parts, each with a unique heritage. This fact, coupled with the state's rural social structure, had bred an intensely factional political system. In the early twentieth century, however, the state's economy was consolidating in cities and industries, power centers which demanded a state government that would be more efficient and more responsive to the public service needs of a growing society. By 1920, many Tennesseans were becoming concerned about the diverging natures of their political and economic systems, and were beginning to agitate for major reform in Nashville.

---

34. Chattanooga *Times*, July 19, August 6, 7, 1926. Columbia *Daily-Herald*, July 15, 1926. Nashville *Banner*, August 7, 1926.

2

The Election of Austin Peay

In 1919 Albert H. Roberts, backed by the Howse-McConnico-Stahlman faction, took office as governor of Tennessee. The new chief executive immediately turned to the pressing issue of the state's finances. Roberts and outgoing Governor Thomas Rye issued a joint recommendation for sweeping tax reform. "Our taxing system," declared Roberts in his Inaugural Address, "is among the weakest and worst of any state in the Union." He proceeded to lay before the legislature proposals designed to correct the inequities in the system and to broaden its revenue base. First of all, Roberts urged that the State Railroad Commission be expanded into a State Board of Equalization to oversee county assessors in a thorough-going reassessment of property values and equalization of tax rates. Secondly, he suggested a "sliding scale assessment" designed "to lure personalty (especially intangibles) from hiding. . . ." Under the proposed sliding scale, the ad valorem rate on total state assessments would drop in inverse proportion as the value of the total assessments increased. For example, on total state assessments of six hundred million, the ad valorem rate would be sixty-five cents but for a total assessment of two billion dollars, it would be thirty-five cents. In this manner, Roberts hoped to make Tennessee's tax system fairer and more efficient.[1]

The Roberts program sparked immediate controversy. Critics

---

1. Reichard, "Defeat of Gov. Roberts," pp. 95-96. McCorkle, "Taxation in Tennessee," p. 5. Thorogood, *Financial History of Tennessee*, pp. 102-4.

focused their opposition on the increased authority of the Railroad Commission and of the office of the governor itself. Together with the state comptroller and the state treasurer, Roberts held power of review over the Railroad Commission and, by extension, over the entire reassessment process. This brought Roberts under attack from both party conservatives who feared large concentrations of power, and local political leaders who realized that a shift in assessment authority toward Nashville would prompt a corresponding drop in their own strength.[2]

Other critics focused on the failure of the new scheme to achieve the desired ends. The sliding scale did not work. Total assessments increased but the bulk of intangible property and other personalty remained unlisted. The state's businessmen felt no particular need to declare personalty wealth that could so easily be hidden. Moreover, though the tax burden on property holders increased, the additional revenue still was not enough to balance the budget. Farmers were disgruntled about the impending reassessment of their holdings, accordingly their antagonism toward the governor began to build. The Paris *Partisan* editorialized, "It appears there is one source and one only . . . from which this additional revenue is to come . . . the smalltown property owners and the farm owners." The Trenton *Herald-Democrat* spoke for many when it charged that the law put "the burden of the tax on the farmers, while the big concerns of the state, the railroad and the corporations, bear even a lighter burden than usual." The agricultural slump that struck most of the nation in 1920 only enhanced this already considerable resentment.[3]

Roberts' inept handling of the tax issue had diminished his support by the spring of 1920, but potential candidates were

---

2. Gary W. Reichard, "The Republican Victory of 1920 in Tennessee: An Analysis" (M. A. Thesis, Vanderbilt, 1966), 13.

3. Reichard, "Republican Victory," pp. 14, 54. Reichard, "The Aberration of 1920: An Analysis of Harding's Victory in Tennessee," *Journal of Southern History* 36 (1970), 41. Truman H. Alexander, *Austin Peay, Governor of Tennessee: A Collection of State Papers and Public Addresses with a Biography by T. H. Alexander* (Kingsport, 1929) pp. xix.

reluctant to oppose him for the Democratic gubernatorial nomination. Such potentially formidable rivals as General Lawrence Tyson and Austin Peay decided that 1920 would be a good year to sit out the political wars because of the shattered condition of the Democratic Party and the mood of optimism among Republicans.[4] Finally a candidate emerged in the person of "Colonel" William Riley Crabtree, a Chattanooga realtor and ex-mayor of the city. The taxation issue quickly became the "supreme issue in the campaign for governor," as Crabtree attacked the state tax system, the expanded powers of the Railroad Commission, and the "financial extravagance" of the Roberts administration. His strongest press backer, the Chattanooga *News*, asserted that Roberts' reforms were merely a slick device for adding members of the legislature to the state payroll, since the law added the duties of a tax commission to the Railroad Commission and authorized it to hire tax statisticians. Most of the new employees, the *News* contended, were members of the legislature who voted for the act.[5]

Despite Roberts' unpopularity, Crabtree was not in a good position to exploit his opponent's weaknesses. In the first place, Crabtree had voted for the Rye tax plan while a member of the 1917 legislature, and the Rye proposals were similar to those of Roberts. More importantly, much of the antipathy toward Roberts came from farmers, and Crabtree, as an urban figure, could not effectively mobilize this sentiment. "Crabtree lives in the city of Chattanooga," observed the weekly Carthage *Courier*. "He is a rich man having married a wealthy lady. He never worked a day on the farm in his life, and he cares nothing for the farmers." Roberts, the *Courier* reminded its readers, "is a poor man having come up between the plow handles. Crabtree is a rich city man and never had a sympathetic impulse for the farmer in his life."[6]

In the August primary, Roberts took the nomination with 67,886 votes to his opponent's 44,853. Crabtree ran better against Roberts in the nonrural areas and carried the three

4. Reichard, "Defeat of Gov. Roberts," pp. 98-99.
5. *Ibid.*, 99-100.
6. Carthage *Courier*, July 15, 29, 1920. Alexander, *Peay*, p. 39.

largest Democratic counties—Shelby, Davidson, and Hamilton—by 12,295 to 8,768. Nevertheless, he polled only 32,558 votes to 59,118 for Roberts outside these major Democratic cities. In short, Crabtree was unable to take advantage of rural dissatisfaction with Roberts. The results suggested, however, that a candidate more attuned to Tennessee's rural majority might have defeated Governor Roberts.[7]

That autumn, Roberts faced such a candidate in Republican Alf A. Taylor of Happy Valley. "Uncle Alf," seventy-two years of age in 1920, had been a revered figure among East Tennessee Republicans for a generation. He had run for governor once before— in 1886 in the "War of the Roses" against his brother, Robert Love Taylor. Running again for the office he dearly coveted, Taylor easily defeated former State Agriculture Commissioner Jesse Littleton of Chattanooga in the primary and settled down to the serious business of defeating Roberts.

That goal was made easier to achieve by the late summer fight over the Nineteenth Amendment. President Woodrow Wilson and national Democratic leaders hoped the thirty-sixth state to ratify the amendment would be a Democratic one, and they urged Roberts to call a special session to pass the measure and formally affix it to the Constitution. The Governor concurred and the amendment was approved, but the struggle damaged his prestige still further. A large part of the Democratic press opposed woman suffrage and protest rallies were held across the state. There were even demands that Roberts be replaced as the head of the ticket.[8]

But the Taylor-Roberts campaign revolved around the Governor's tax scheme. Taylor decried the use of the Railroad Commission as an equalization board and instead suggested that a state tax commission be created. Unlike Crabtree, "Uncle Alf" shrewdly pitched his campaign to rural dissatisfaction. He was joined on the hustings by his celebrated foxhound "Old Limber" and a quartet composed of his sons and nephews. His rallies were like vaudeville shows, with the quartet singing and

---

7. *Fifty Years of Tennessee Primaries, 1916-1966*, compiled by Shirley Hassler (Nashville, 1967), 149-50. For a definition of terms, see Appendix A.

8. Reichard, "Defeat of Gov. Roberts," pp. 105-07.

the candidate accompanying them on the fiddle. The speaking consisted of anecdotes extolling the fox-hunting prowess of "Old Limber" interspersed with attacks on the sliding scale and with assertions that farm land should be more leniently taxed than corporate wealth because farming was "not purely a profit thing."[9]

The November elections brought a great victory for the Republicans. In the Presidential race, Warren Harding defeated James Cox and thus became the first Republican Presidential candidate to carry a Southern state since the end of Reconstruction. Taylor won a top-heavy victory, getting 55.2 percent of the vote. The lopsided margin was partly due to the huge turnout in East Tennessee where Taylor received 71.5 percent. Equally important was the striking success Taylor enjoyed in other rural areas across the state. "Taylor's appeal to farmers on the issue of taxation," writes a student of the election, "apparently paid off." Statewide Roberts got only 42.7 percent in rural counties compared to 71.6 percent in the primary against the city-bred Crabtree. Taylor ran nearly even with Roberts in the nonrural areas, splitting the vote 50.1 percent to 49.9 percent. He carried the four large urban counties, Shelby, Davidson, Knox, and Hamilton, 43,422 to 37,397.[10]

Roberts was the last Democratic gubernatorial nominee to be defeated for half a century. While several factors combined to unseat him, clearly the most important was the taxation issue. With the state falling further and further into debt after 1910, some kind of reform was inevitable, but Roberts' plan destroyed him politically. Crabtree hammered at him during the primary, and Taylor used the issue skillfully in the fall, winning rural support and riding it to the governor's chair.

Alf Taylor's two years as governor of Tennessee were frustrating and difficult ones for the elderly chief executive. The General Assembly was deeply riven by factionalism in both parties which shredded the governor's program. The legislature had hardly convened before the Democrats, who controlled both

9. *Ibid.*, 107. McGill, *South and the Southerner*, pp. 105-09.
10. Reichard, "Defeat of Gov. Roberts," pp. 103, 109. *Fifty Years of Tennessee Elections, 1916-1966*, compiled by Shirley Hassler (Nashville, 1967), 118-19.

houses, were planning to repeal the Tenure of Office Act which provided that a governor's appointments expired with his term. A second bill was introduced to deprive Taylor of power to appoint the heads of penal and charitable institutions. Under the constitution, the incoming Republicans could appoint a total of only 187 officials to remunerative and honorary positions, and the two bills threatened to freeze the executive machinery in the hands of the Democrats. The Tenure of Office Act was upheld, thanks to dissident Democrats who opposed the incumbent Roberts faction, but the Democrats did succeed in denying to the victors the spoils of the penal and charitable institutions.[11]

Not only were the Republicans the minority party in the legislature, but they also were weakened by factionalism. Taylor and his backers were opposed by a group organized around Jesse Littleton, whom Taylor had defeated in the 1920 primary. Littleton's backers in the legislature, led by John C. Houk of Knoxville, eagerly clutched at any opportunity to embarrass the new governor. The backbiting between the two factions flared into open warfare when Taylor nominated Thomas Peck to Littleton's old post as commissioner of agriculture. Peck's support had been instrumental in Taylor's primary victory, and Senator Houk ambushed the nominee in public hearings. Houk claimed that Peck had been guilty of fraud and misuse of public funds during his earlier tenure as commissioner of agriculture. Peck was eventually confirmed despite Houk's charges, but party harmony, such as it had been, was irreparably shattered.[12]

Against this backdrop of infighting, Taylor's legislative platform stood little chance. In his State of the State message issued shortly after his inauguration, Taylor addressed Tennessee's "Big Four" problems: rural schools, highways, economy in government, and taxation. Specifically, he suggested, as had Governor Rye, the creation of a state tax commission to oversee the revenue structure. Where Roberts had given the power of review to the already existing Railroad Commission, Taylor proposed to shift it to the new agency, which would supervise

---

11. Knoxville *Journal*, January 6, 7, 10, 13, 1921.
12. *Ibid.*, January 30, 31, February 2, March 16, 1921.

the county assessors and compel them to levy rates equitably. The three-man commission would be composed of a farmer, a manufacturer, and a business or professional man. In an effort to lessen the tax burden on farmers, property would be assessed in terms of its earning capability, rather than its actual value.[13]

Taylor's plans were frustrated by the combination of opposition in his own party, the sniping of Democrats, and the "Back Tax Machine," made up of legislators who profited politically from the existing structure. The Back Tax law of 1907 had permitted retroactive reassessment of property and created a new fund of jobs as state revenue agents. State legislators seized on the act as an ideal way of rewarding friends and threatening enemies. The machine exercised tremendous power in the state, and Taylor, hampered by a divided minority party, was no match for it. Mustering bipartisan support, it easily smashed Taylor's reform efforts.[14]

Plagued by party strife and opposed by powerful interests, the elderly governor simply could not provide the forceful leadership the situation required. "Someone must take the initiative," warned the Knoxville *Journal*, the state's only Republican daily. "The creaking of factionalism in the party machine is painfully evident."[15] By the time the legislature adjourned for a month-long recess on February 9, 1921, only one administration bill had been introduced. When Taylor finally did send over his program, the General Assembly destroyed it and passed over his veto both a miscellaneous appropriations bill and an increase in the legal interest rate.[16] With the failure of Taylor's program, landowners, in the second year of his administration, paid the largest land tax ever—$1,700,000 more than in 1919.[17] Like Roberts, Taylor had failed to tame Tennessee's tempestuous politics, and the state's problems continued to gather momentum.

By 1922 business and agriculture were joined in a broad-based

13. *Ibid.*, January 16, 19, March 8, 1921.
14. *Ibid.*, March 31, April 6, 11, 12, 1921.
15. *Ibid.*, January 25, 1921.
16. *Ibid.*, February 13, March 9, April 11, 1921.
17. Knoxville *Sentinel*, October 2, 1922.

movement for reform. The state's business organizations took an active role in that year's political battles, as the Chamber of Commerce and the Tennessee Manufacturers Association entered the fray under the banner "Good Government and Better Business." These groups were deeply concerned over the state's chronic inability to stay out of the red. The Chattanooga *News* stated their case in a succinct editorial:

> Tennessee government is not being conducted on the progressive lines that her best citizens desire and that are being followed in some of her sister commonwealths. Her financial affairs are in an unfortunate condition and heavy debts are becoming heavier. There is immediate need of a leadership which can rescue. Conditions which now obtain in Tennessee are a great handicap on its progress. They cannot be indefinitely continued without involving disaster.[18]

Business groups stressed the need for efficiency in government and economy in expenditures. Most of their political efforts were focused on races for the legislature because the General Assembly was more important than the governor in establishing the budget and overseeing state administration. Although businessmen took no overt part in the gubernatorial campaign of 1922 and endorsed no candidate, their emphasis on economy and efficiency did much to condition the atmosphere in which the election was conducted.[19]

A mass convention of farmers in Montgomery County voiced similar sentiments in calling for "the elimination of waste and extravagance in all departments of the state government, and the abolition of all needless offices or positions that only extract revenue from the pockets of the people, without giving adequate return." The Columbia *Daily Herald* reported that the farmers of Maury County solidly supported abolition of many

18. Chattanooga *News*, June 1, 1922.
19. Macpherson, "Democratic Progressivism," p. 36. Macpherson, "Democratic Progressivism in Tennessee: The Administrations of Governor Austin Peay, 1923-1927," *East Tennessee Historical Society Publications* 40 (1968), 53-54.

offices and bureaus and the reorganization of the state highway department. In addition to demanding economy and efficiency, farmers stressed their dissatisfaction with the tax system. The Montgomery County farmers called for "the proper and equitable distribution of the tax burden that now falls so heavily on the farmers and farming interests," while the Maury County farmers demanded the "extermination" of the back-tax system.[20]

The widespread discontent with Taylor and the general feeling that 1922 would again be a Democratic year in Tennessee prompted four candidates to stand for the Democratic gubernatorial nomination. Clarksville attorney and farmer Austin Peay was perhaps the strongest of the group. Born and raised in Kentucky, the son of a Confederate veteran, Peay took a law degree at Centre College in Danville, Kentucky, and moved to Clarksville, Tennessee, when he married. In 1900, at the age of twenty-four, he was elected to the legislature and promptly declared for speaker. The freshman was defeated but he battled the widely respected General Lawrence Tyson for one hundred ballots. Peay's opposition to prohibition allied him with Governor Malcolm Patterson, who named the rising young politician his campaign manager in the 1908 gubernatorial primary that climaxed in the shooting of Edward Ward Carmack. Stunned by the tragedy and closely linked to the discredited Patterson, who had pardoned one of Carmack's convicted killers, Peay withdrew from politics for nearly ten years. During this time his business activities not only brought him wealth but also helped shape his approach to public affairs. In addition to his law practice, Peay had a number of commercial investments and operated a large tobacco farm. This diverse background gave him a solid grounding in the techniques of business administration as well as an appreciation of the problems of Tennessee farmers. Peay's concern for economy and efficiency and for rural Tennessee became the hallmarks of his political career.[21]

Peay's main opponent for the Democratic nomination in 1922 was Benton McMillin, the "old war horse of Tennessee Democ-

20. Bolivar *Bulletin*, June 23, 1922. Columbia *Daily-Herald*, July 17, 1922.
21. Macpherson, "Administrations of Austin Peay," pp. 52-53.

racy." McMillin, like his Republican counterpart Alf Taylor, had a long and distinguished political record. He had served two terms as governor from 1899 to 1903, but more recently had been out of the country as minister to Peru and Guatemala. Although still an effective campaigner, he was seventy-seven years old in 1922 and his prolonged absence from the state had dimmed his appeal. Two other candidates played only minor roles in the contest. Harvey Hannah, a National Guard general and long-term member of the state Railroad Commission, had strength in East Tennessee, but lacked the statewide support necessary to make him a major candidate. L. E. Gwinn, a Memphis attorney, was making the obligatory and foredoomed first race to establish his name.[22]

The most striking aspect of the Democratic primary was the broad agreement among the candidates. Each of their platforms largely satisfied the criticism being offered by farmers and businessmen. Economy was the watchword. McMillin and Hannah called for "rigid economy" in administering the state's affairs, while Peay urged thriftiness with tax dollars. The Roberts tax laws and the back-tax scheme were repudiated. Peay declared that the sliding scale "should be promptly discarded" and pledged that if he were elected, "every vestige" of the back-tax system would go. McMillin and Hannah also attacked the back-tax system and Hannah urged the repeal of the "act . . . creating a tax commissioner and state board of equalizers." Both men favored reducing land taxes, lowering the eight percent ceiling on interest rates, and levying a gasoline tax for roads.[23] The nature of the contest prompted Chattanooga *News* editor George Fort Milton to observe, "all the candidates are vociferating daily that they will abolish the back tax machine. The candidates also assert solidly that they will change the present tax system. They also would unanimously hunt out the unfortunate holders of any notes, mortgages, or bonds. All of them would lend a substantial relief to Mr. Farmer."[24]

The important competition in the race was among rival

22. Alexander, *Peay*, pp. xix, xx.
23. *Sumner County News*, Gallatin, June 1, 8, 1922.
24. Chattanooga *News*, July 24, 1922.

political factions. Luke Lea threw his support to Austin Peay while the Howse-McConnico-Stahlman organization backed Benton McMillin. In Memphis E. H. Crump endorsed McMillin, and Clarence Saunders, founder of the Piggly Wiggly grocery chain, got his first taste of combat under the Peay standard. The primary was brutal in Middle Tennessee, fueled by the hatred between Lea and Stahlman, but the contest was not nearly so sharp in the West. Since Crump was in poor health and out of the city, the Peay forces, led by Saunders, had free run of Shelby County.

The senatorial contest of 1922 was nearly lost in the furor over the gubernatorial race. The senate was a secondary concern for most Tennesseans. Since the Republicans controlled the national government, Democratic senators had little federal patronage to dispense while state officials had a great deal. Congressman J. Will Taylor, Tennessee's most powerful Republican, had no desire to secure the election of a man who would become his rival. In addition, both party primaries promised to be one-sided. In the Democratic primary the incumbent, Crump associate Kenneth McKellar of Memphis, had only token opposition from Memphis attorney Guston T. Fitzhugh. The Republican primary pitted Newell Sanders, a Chattanooga manufacturer and former senator, against an obscure opponent named Harry B. Anderson.

In the August voting McKellar and Sanders swamped their respective rivals by better than two to one while Governor Taylor was renominated without opposition by the Republicans, but the Democratic gubernatorial primary was extremely close. McMillin ran well in East Tennessee and both McMillin and Peay were strong in Middle Tennessee, but the latter won the nomination in West Tennessee due to a top-heavy majority in Shelby County. "The farmers . . . had Governor McMillin nominated until he reached Memphis," Stahlman's Nashville *Banner* charged, but "Piggly Wiggly took the nomination away from the farmers and gave it to Mr. Peay."[25] The *Banner's* analysis was largely correct. Tables 1 and 2 show the impact of

25. Nashville *Banner,* October 20, 1922.

Shelby on the West Tennessee returns and on the final outcome. McMillin chalked up a 5,600 vote lead in the state's rural counties, leading Peay 20,660 to 15,073. Peay took a slight edge in the small-urban counties, but his margin of victory was provided by those counties whose population was more than thirty percent urban. Peay piled up a 6,300 vote lead in the large urban counties where his margin in Shelby County alone was 7,347. Peay won the nomination by 4,016 votes. Although he and McMillin were closely matched candidates, Peay's strength in Shelby slightly edged McMillin's strength on the farms and in East Tennessee.[26]

Since both candidates had stressed essentially the same issues in their campaigns, Peay's narrow victory, particularly among urban voters, can probably be attributed to McMillin's advanced age. In a race that centered on the need for imagination and innovation in state government, Peay's age (46 as opposed to McMillin's 77) and success as an attorney and businessman gave him an advantage among urban commercial interests who strongly felt the need for reform.

The general election paralleled the Democratic primary in several respects. Appeals for tax reform, efficiency, and economy in government dominated campaign rhetoric, and the candidates again agreed on the source and remedy of the state's problems. The Democratic Party still remained split into two antagonistic factions, the supporters of former Governor McMillin having deserted Peay and declared themselves "Taylor Democrats."

On the stump, Governor Taylor joined his opponent in denouncing the "back tax infamy," saying "the time has come to break it up." He called for revision of assessments and urged new laws to lighten the tax burden on farmers and small property holders. Taylor proposed a reorganization of the highway department and a general consolidation of state departments to increase efficiency and economy. The governor

---

26. *Fifty Years of Tennessee Primaries*, pp. 140-41. The item entries for each county often do not sum to the state total listed in the volume. I have arbitrarily assumed the county totals are correct and have adjusted the statewide totals accordingly.

stressed that the two percent increase in the ceiling on interest rates had been passed over his veto. Sounding much like his opponent, Taylor pledged the "conversion of the state capitol into a business instead of a political institution."[27] As the *Anderson County News* observed, "Mr. Peay and Governor Taylor favor many reforms in common. They both advocate economy in expending public funds, reorganizing the highway and tax departments, repeal of the eight percent law, abolishing the back tax system and other measures."[28] One editor wrote, "We do not recall a state election in which the two party leaders were so completely in agreement on the issues on which they were running."[29]

Peay's primary victory made renegades of two important Democratic chieftains, Stahlman in Nashville and Crump in Memphis. Stahlman's opposition was rooted partly in his intense hatred of Peay's patron, Luke Lea of the rival Nashville *Tennessean*, and partly in his fear that Peay's proposed reorganization of the state government would remove many of Stahlman's most powerful friends. Stahlman exercised power in the legislature, and the Peay plan would enhance the power of the governor. The *Banner* editor, therefore, bolted to Taylor, reasoning that a Democratic legislature was not likely to enact sweeping reform under the tutelage of a Republican governor. The *Banner* maintained a drumfire of criticism throughout the fall. In an effort to revive old issues, it charged Peay with being soft on prohibition and with befriending Duncan and Robin Cooper, the slayers of Carmack. The *Banner* reprinted editorials critical of Peay that had appeared in the *Tennessean* during the campaign of 1908. Describing Peay as the "minority nominee" with only 39 percent of the August vote, Stahlman accused him of being part of a "clique long out of power" that was merely using the tax issue. Peay sought "reform" of the tax and highway departments, Stahlman said, as a device to give power to his friends.[30]

27. Knoxville *Journal*, November 7, 1922.
28. *Anderson County News*, Clinton, October 7, 1922.
29. *Lawrence Democrat*, Lawrenceburg, October 27, 1922.
30. Macpherson, "Democratic Progressivism," pp. 98-99. Nashville *Banner*, October 2, 8, 11, 12, 17, 22, 1922.

Banner news stories on the campaign amounted to little more than anti-Peay propaganda. Even editorials endorsing Taylor usually became tirades against Austin Peay. Little pretense was made of objective reporting. Ralph McGill was assigned to cover Peay, and his dispatches were often very harsh. He counted the audiences and took note of embarrassing hecklers. One typical headline of a McGill item was, "Peay Poses as People's Friend." Peay was referred to in editorials and news stories alike as "Czar Austin," "autocrat," and "egotist." In contrast, the paper spoke of Taylor's "generous welcome," "fine crowd," "fine speech," and "enthusiastic applause." Realizing that Taylor's advanced age could be a handicap, the *Banner* emphasized his energy and referred to him as "iron man." On election day the front page headline was "Vote Early and Vote for Taylor."[31]

In West Tennessee, E. H. Crump's Shelby County machine was withholding its support. Crump, believing that Memphis was not getting its full share of state revenue collections, hoped to force concessions from Peay in exchange for his support. Crump said the Democratic candidate could expect "little enthusiasm" in Memphis unless he endorsed the repeal of the state public utilities law to bring about a reduction in rates and fares. Crump also demanded a "fair division of the automobile license tax and highway fund. Under the present law Shelby County has paid close onto a million and a half dollars and has received only $150,000. There is certainly no fairness in this division." On election eve, a full page advertisement appeared over Crump's signature in the Memphis papers:

> Shelby County is not getting a fair and square deal. This county has paid into the state treasury $812,625.97 in automobile taxes, and has received in return $21,257.83 and has paid out nearly $700,000 on the special highway fund, getting $130,000 back making a total of $1,512,625.97 paid out by the taxpayers and citizens of Shelby County, while they received back but $151,257.83. Is that fair?[32]

31. Nashville *Banner*, October 25, 27, 28, 31, November 1, 5, 7, 1922.
32. Knoxville *Journal*, October 31, 1922. Memphis *Commercial Appeal*, November 6, 1922.

With Boss Crump on the fence, Peay came to Memphis a week before election day. The candidate had emphasized his independence of bosses, and Peay's primary success in Memphis indicated he could carry Shelby County even without Crump. Moreover, Peay realized that returning auto license funds to the cities would hinder roadbuilding in rural areas and place more money at Crump's disposal. Instead of Crump, Peay again turned to his old friend Clarence Saunders, who had helped him in the primary. Crump later claimed that Peay first asked to see him and then changed his mind after meeting Saunders. The Peay backers said Crump requested a meeting. At any rate the two men did not confer. Before leaving the city, Peay issued a statement reiterating his refusal to make "any political trades or deals with anybody here or elsewhere" and announced that Clarence Saunders would be his campaign manager in Shelby.[33]

Clarence Saunders was like no other politician Tennessee had produced in all its turbulent history. He came from a farm family and had once clerked in a store belonging to Peay's father-in-law. In 1916 Saunders opened the first of his Piggly Wiggly grocery stores featuring a turnstile entrance and self-service shopping. The ex-dry goods clerk had wrought a merchandising miracle, and seven years later presided over an empire of 1,267 Piggly Wiggly stores. His power stemmed from his considerable fortune.

In 1922 Saunders became one of the first men to apply merchandising techniques to politics. In a word, he tried to "sell" Austin Peay. When the cold, withdrawn Peay returned to Memphis on the Monday preceding the election, he was met by an advertising campaign. Bands played, girls danced, and motorcars backfired along the downtown parade route. Slogans and pictures of the candidate sprouted from the pavement. As a final touch, Saunders cautioned Peay not to mention Crump in his speech. It was all reminiscent of a Piggly Wiggly grand opening, and Tennessee voters had never seen anything like it before.[34]

Faced with Peay's intransigence, Crump took his votes

33. Memphis *Commercial Appeal,* October 30, November 6-7, 1922.
34. McIlwanie, *Memphis Down in Dixie,* pp. 269-76. Nashville *Tennessean,* November 7, 1922.

34 / *Tennessee in Turmoil*

elsewhere. Rumors of a deal swept the state, and the suspicion grew that Crump would throw his machine's support to the Republicans. On November 6, the Memphis *News-Scimitar* published a telegram it had received from Governor Taylor calling for repeal of the public utilities act and redistribution of the state auto license tax revenue. Apparently Crump and the governor had reached an accord.[35]

The 1922 election restored the Democrats to power in Tennessee. Senator McKellar defeated Newell Sanders, his Republican challenger, by more than two to one. Despite the defection of Crump and Stahlman, Peay won an easy victory over Taylor. Peay took the rural and small-urban counties by small majorities, but the large-urban counties provided nearly two-thirds of his margin over Taylor (see Tables 3 and 4). Just as in the primary, he ran best in Tennessee's major cities. In winning, Peay thoroughly embarrassed his two main rivals. He carried Stahlman's home county of Davidson, 9,262 to 4,732 and Crump's Shelby County 7,368 to 5,707. Senator Kenneth McKellar, however, a Crump man, carried Shelby 11,348 to 942. The Memphis *Commercial Appeal* charged that Peay was "knifed" by four thousand votes, and Luke Lea's Nashville *Tennessean* observed that "without [Saunders'] intervention it is safe to assert that Mr. Peay would have been led to the political slaughter-pen by the Memphis Machinists." Austin Peay had won a resounding victory. He led in two of the state's grand divisions, carried the rural, small-urban, and large-urban counties and defeated his arch foes in the bastions of their greatest strength. It was an auspicious beginning for the Clarksville attorney and tobacco farmer.[36]

The 1922 gubernatorial election was a significant one in Tennessee history. It was the first election to be influenced by

35. Memphis *News-Scimitar*, November 6, 1922. Memphis *Commercial Appeal*, November 7, 1922.

36. *Fifty Years of Tennessee Elections*, pp. 112-13. Memphis *Commercial Appeal*, November 8, 1922. Nashville *Tennessean*, November 8, 9, 1922. As in *Tennessee Primaries*, the listed county votes often do not sum to the listed state totals. Again I have arbitrarily assumed the county totals are correct and have accordingly adjusted the statewide totals.

the mass communication revolution that was beginning to shake the nation. Besides Saunders' experiments in the use of merchandising techniques to "sell" Peay, radio was introduced to Tennessee politics. On October 28, Peay and Senator McKellar participated in "the first instance of the use of the wireless for political purposes in Tennessee." With a touch of awe, the *Sumner County News* reported:

> On the platform was set the wireless sending set of the General Telephone Company. The voices were carried to the local office of the company and there amplified and broadcasted to receiving stations in Putnam, White, Overton, Clay, and Jackson counties. In addition the speeches were put on the long distance telephone wires and subscribers in these five counties sat in their homes and heard the Democratic doctrines being expounded. . . . It is impossible to estimate how many people heard the speeches. More than 1,000 were in the court house, and possibly as many as 1500 at the receiving stations and telephones scattered over this section.[37]

Another salient characteristic of this election was the general sentiment for reform in state government that it revealed. Organized business took an active part in politics, and the state's farmers joined the clamor for economy and efficiency. There was much concern about the chronic lack of public services. Each of the four major candidates for governor, three Democrats and one Republican, voiced these grievances and proposed strikingly similar solutions.

The election also was a test among the political chieftains of the Tennessee Democracy. Here the clear winner was Luke Lea. The publisher had an extensive network of contacts, especially in Middle Tennessee, and Peay's victory gave him close ties to the governor's office. Clarence Saunders had also profited, but he had few political ambitions and lacked Lea's excellent con-

37. *Sumner County News,* Gallatin, November 2, 1922.

nections. The Howse-McConnico-Stahlman and Crump factions, both soundly beaten in their home counties, passed for the moment into eclipse.

Most importantly, the size of Peay's victory gave him wide latitude in shaping his program. His campaign had won favor with businessmen, and they seemed a likely constituency for the future, but Peay had also run well among farmers, establishing in the rural areas another potential source of strength. In his platform Peay had pledged a massive overhauling of the machinery of state government. His popular mandate suggested that he could shape his enterprise to appeal to several possible coalitions of the state's voters. A system that spoke more directly to the needs of the cities would permit him to build on the considerable strength he had shown in the large-urban counties. A more farm-oriented approach would permit the governor to exploit his smaller but still considerable strength in the state's small towns and rural areas. Thus the reform scheme he selected would have a profound impact on the political alignment of Tennessee.

3

Reform and Realignment

The 1920s was an era characterized by sounds—the Roaring Twenties, the Jazz Age, the Great Boom and the Great Crash. In the South, the hubbub centered around the Ku Klux Klan and the Scopes Monkey Trial. H. L. Mencken was shrilly castigating the "Sahara of the Bozart," and an army of evangelists exhorted a South repentant. In Birmingham and Kingsport, the clanging of machines accompanied by the sputtering of the Model T heralded the arrival of a new day. The South was a land in noisy ferment, but in the midst of it all, a quiet revolution was taking place. In a region better known for its outrageous, demagogic politics, a group of drab, statistic-spouting politicians trained as attorneys and businessmen was leading a movement for improved state government.

As George B. Tindall has pointed out, Southern state governments in the 1920s were taking steps to enhance administrative efficiency and to expand public services. Schools, roads, and governmental reorganization became the themes of a decade of Southern history. Alabama Governor Thomas Kilby established a state budget system and overhauled virtually every major state department between 1917 and 1921. He backed a $25,000,000 bond issue for roads and secured the highest appropriation for public schools in the state's history. North Carolina, under a series of governors between 1917 and 1926, revamped its tax system and approved a $50,000,000 bond issue for highways and a $6,750,000 issue for schools. In Virginia, from 1926 to 1930 Governor Harry F. Byrd supervised a reorganization of one hundred bureaus into fourteen departments and fought for higher taxes to finance highways.[1]

During his five years as governor, Austin Peay led the drive for efficiency and public services in Tennessee. When he took office in 1923, the state was beset by several very serious problems. Schools were stagnant, highways were lanes of mud, and the tax system weighed unjustly on property holders. Plagued by rising debts, declining revenue, and failing services, Tennessee was facing a crisis. Moreover, the state government had been unable to cope with the situation. Characterized by a weak chief executive, a parochial legislature, and a chaotic bureaucracy, Tennessee state government was a textbook study in futility.

As in most Southern states, the General Assembly dominated the government. The legislature controlled appointments to most state offices and staffed executive departments with the henchmen of individual members. The loyalties of Tennessee bureaucrats thus ran to their patrons rather than to their nominal chief, the governor. Moreover, since the state had no systematic approach to budgeting, that chore too fell to the legislature. Instead of submitting requests to a governor or some other central agency, each department head appeared before the legislature and presented his case for appropriations. The General Assembly, in turn, awarded funds to the supplicants as it saw fit, with no regard for an overall fiscal scheme. Grateful state departments geared their spending to the interests of legislators, and state projects were conceived with an eye for the political fortunes of those who voted the funds. The governor, by contrast, was virtually powerless. Members of the executive branch were hired and dismissed regardless of his wishes, and his subordinates owed neither place nor appropriation to him. With budgeting and appointments in the hands of the General Assembly, he had no tools other than his personal prestige to influence the actions of state departments.[2]

1. George B. Tindall, "Business Progressivism," pp. 92-106.
2. Franklin C. Rouse, "The Historical Background of Tennessee's Administrative Reorganization Act of 1923," *East Tennessee Historical Society Publications* 8 (1936), 104-21. Macpherson, "Democratic Progressivism," pp. 2, 15, 16.

Despite its position of prominence, the state legislature was not able to provide the kind of leadership that its place in state government demanded. The part-time nature of membership in the General Assembly was the main reason for this failure. Limited by the state constitution to a single seventy-five day session biennially, the legislators were out of touch with the situation in Nashville, and the short session did nothing to break down the intense parochialism for which the legislators were notorious. In addition, the turnover rate from session to session was very high because membership in the General Assembly was considered a boost to a man's "real" career, not a career in itself. Between 1921 and 1931, only once, 1929 to 1931, did as many as one-third of a single session return to the following session. Fledgling lawyers, for example, hoped a term or two in Nashville would give them the exposure and the contacts to further their practices. Preoccupied with the concerns of their constituents and their own careers, Tennessee's legislators were hardly equipped to provide the vigorous, ongoing leadership the state's problems demanded.[3]

Tennessee's confused and tangled system of bureaucracy was a major problem in itself. The Tennessee state constitution of 1870 had provided for four state administrative offices: governor, secretary of state, treasurer, and comptroller of treasury. Over the next half-century, administrative agencies multiplied tenfold. As each new situation arose, the legislature established an agency to deal with it. The process was carried out in ad hoc fashion with no thought to overlapping with or duplication of existing agencies. Often new agencies were assigned to departments only remotely concerned with their function. The commissioner of agriculture, for example, acted as commissioner of immigration. Both he and the secretary of state were designated in separate acts as the commissioner of internal improvements. The agriculture commission also supervised the state's chemical laboratory work although a separate state assayer also existed. By legislative fiat the commissioner served on the state board of

---

3. Macpherson, "Democratic Progressivism," pp. 153-55. Joe C. Gamble interview, June 28, 1976.

40 / *Tennessee in Turmoil*

health but exercised no control over the farm-related bureaus of game and fish and forestry. Lines of responsibility were blurred, confused, or nearly nonexistent. Agencies made no effort to communicate with others related to their concern. The bureaucracy functioned by fits and starts and appeared incapable of a coordinated effort.[4]

In 1923, then, Tennessee state government was plainly unable to generate effective leadership. The governor had no tools other than his personal influence to bring to bear in managing the executive branch. Very few options based on law or custom were available to him. The legislature, which actually held the power to manage the state, was of low quality, plagued by a high turnover rate, and was more interested in local concerns than in state matters. The bureaucracy was too much of a hodge-podge to spark orderly response to pressing needs. The state was sliding toward chaos as Austin Peay began to prepare his agenda for the 1923 session of the General Assembly.

The Sixty-third General Assembly, elected in 1922, stood in marked contrast to its divisive, quarreling predecessor. Only five members of the senate and eighteen members of the house, the lowest total of the decade, carried over from the Sixty-second legislature. Moreover, this general assembly had substantially less prior experience than did the members of its predecessor. Members of the 1921 session had served an average of .7969 terms in the legislature, but members of the 1923 session averaged only .5075 terms in prior service. The Sixty-third session was clearly a sharp break with the political past. The tenor of the new legislature was aggressive and determined. "The present general assembly does not appear to be made up of men who desire to stall or mark time while they wait for instructions," wrote Ralph Perry, legislative correspondent for the Nashville *Banner*. "It is very apparent there is a desire to make a record of accomplishment."[5] In January 1923, virtually assured a receptive audience, Peay sent the legislature a plan for

4. Rouse, "Historical Background," pp. 104-105.
5. Nashville *Banner*, January, 1923. *Biographical Directory of Tennessee Legislators*. This directory is incomplete for some counties.

sweeping reform of the state government, aimed specifically at improving economy and efficiency.

This package, known as the Administration Reorganization bill, was designed to bring order to Tennessee's convoluted bureaucracy and to enable the governor to act as the effective leader of the executive branch. Actually the Reorganization bill did not originate with Peay but with a group of Nashville businessmen who were concerned over the torpid economic climate in that city. The state's chronic inefficiency, they felt, was producing indebtedness and threatening increased taxes. Dan McGugin, a state senator, Nashville attorney and head football coach at Vanderbilt University; Graham Hill, president of Nashville Rotary; and Will Manier, secretary of the Nashville Chamber of Commerce, had begun to press for administrative reform early in 1921. Senator McGugin had introduced his own scheme in the 1921 legislature, but the bill drew little attention. Later that year, Arthur E. Buck of the New York Bureau of Municipal Research, had come to the city and conducted a thorough study. McGugin presented Buck's findings to the Chamber of Commerce in March 1922 and won a favorable response. By spring, the Tennessee Manufacturers Association was actively involved in the fight for reorganization, and McGugin keynoted its June meeting on the theme "Good Government and Better Business."[6]

In the fall of 1922, Buck returned to Nashville to draw up a definitive reorganization proposal to be presented to the winner of the Peay-Taylor gubernatorial contest. His expenses were paid by the Nashville and Knoxville Chambers of Commerce, the Tennessee Manufacturers Association, and a handful of private citizens including State Senator McGugin. After Peay's victory, Buck went to the home of the governor-elect in Clarksville, where the two men spent several weeks hammering out the details of the bill. As it emerged from these sessions, the bill proposed to condense Tennessee's sixty-four helter-skelter

---

6. Arthur E. Buck, *The Reorganization of State Government in the United States* (New York, 1938), 221. Macpherson, "Democratic Progressivism," pp. 150-52. Rouse, "Historical Background," pp. 109-111.

departments into eight commissions. The commission heads were to be named by the governor and were to serve at his pleasure. The commissioners would select all subordinates and employees, subject to the governor's approval. The legislature was to have no role in confirming any of these appointments. An orderly system of budgeting would be established, with the governor drawing up and submitting a comprehensive budget request for the state government. The measure would, in short, shift control of the state government from the General Assembly to the governor.[7]

With this detailed measure in hand, the new governor overwhelmed his prospective opponents. Hearings on the measure began immediately in the House Finance, Ways and Means Committee whose chairman, Sam R. Bratton of Obion County, was one of Peay's staunchest supporters. Criticism of the bill focused on the increased power it gave to the governor. Under its provisions, the governor could, so the critics charged, use his power to build a political machine. The Nashville *Banner* warned, "It turns over the state almost completely to one man to have and to hold," and "is sure, sooner or later, to develop a state machine." The proposed bill, the *Banner* stated, "creates a political machine so compact, so resistless, so immense and yet so simple, that, while it appears to be merely an incident of government, it may easily become the master of government, or even function as government itself."[8] Despite the *Banner's* attacks, however, the Administrative Reorganization Act of 1923 passed the General Assembly in less than a week with only four dissenting votes in the Senate and sixteen in the House. Sixteen of these twenty opponents were Republicans, and a seventeenth, Ingersoll Osea Remine of Loudon County, espoused no party but usually voted with the Republicans. Only three isolated Democrats out of 101 voted against Peay.[9]

Peay also dealt with inequities in the state tax structure. In a

---

7. Buck, *Reorganization*, p. 221. Macpherson, "Democratic Progressivism," pp. 150-52. Rouse, "Historical Background," pp. 109-111.

8. Nashville *Banner*, January 22, 25, 26, 1923.

9. Macpherson, "Democratic Progressivism," pp. 102-104, 152-53. *Tennessee House Journal*, p. 194. *Tennessee Senate Journal*, pp. 187-88, 191.

distinct break with the property tax method of raising revenue, Peay secured passage of a three percent tax on the net profits of corporations despite the threat it posed to his business support. This helped close the gap between tax receipts and expenditures and greatly increased the stability of state government. The value of farm property and the ability of farmers to pay their taxes depended on the price of agricultural products on the international market. Corporations functioned in a more stable environment, and a tax on their net profits offered a surer source of revenue for the state. The corporate excise tax made possible a drop in the land tax from thirty-six cents to thirty cents per one hundred dollars of evaluation.[10]

Peay intended to launch a major highway construction program but the method of financing the new roads stirred controversy. Cement companies which stood to profit from large state contracts and bankers who would receive the proceeds from bond sales urged a bond issue to finance the project. Peay, however, opposed any increase in the state's bonded indebtedness which, he believed, would have to be paid off by rural property holders. He opted instead for a gasoline tax, in effect a user's tax, and the General Assembly quickly approved his plan.[11]

The governor was thwarted only in his attempt to alter the composition of the State Board of Elections Commission. The board was composed of three members, two Democrats and one Republican, representing the three Grand Divisions of the state. Elected by joint convention of the House and Senate to staggered six-year terms, their principal duty was to appoint three local election officials in each county and to certify the honesty of elections. Through deals and trades with other members, the three state commissioners held sway in their own divisions and could pose a serious threat to any local bosses they opposed. When the West Tennessee seat, held by John C. Carey of Shelby County, fell vacant in 1923, Peay hoped to destroy the

10. Macpherson, "Democratic Progressivism," pp. 49, 362-63. Alexander, *Peay*, pp. xxv.
11. Macpherson, "Democratic Progressivism," pp. 209-210. Columbia *Daily Herald*, October 1, 1924.

Crump machine forever by securing the election of his own man to that seat and obtaining legislation to expand the membership of the commission from three to five with the governor designated to make the two interim appointments. These two appointments plus the West Tennessee seat would give Peay a majority on the powerful commission.[12]

The fight was a crucial one for Peay's foes, and Shelby County legislators led a solid contingent of Republicans and antiadministration Democrats against the commission bill. Such Peay backers as Senator Thomas Y. English of Maury County insisted the bill would aid in "purifying" the ballot box, but Senator Sam Breazeale of Roane County shook his fist as he barked, "It is factional politics, inspired by one faction to gain advantage over the other, and you know it." Across the Capitol in the House chamber, Representative Grover C. Peck of Overton County said it was a transparent attempt to transfer control of Shelby County from Ed Crump to Clarence Saunders. The *Banner* characterized the measure as an obvious power play and branded it the "greatest outrage of the legislative session." The bill passed the House 57-30, but failed in the Senate where it won a simple majority, 16-15, missing the constitutionally required seventeen votes when administration backer Senator William Overton of Jackson County stalked off the floor after a personal dispute with another senator.[13] The measure failed because eight of ten West Tennessee Democratic senators, three of them from Shelby County, opposed the administration. East and Middle Division Democrats endorsed it 14-3. Peay did manage to secure the election of his strong supporter Senator Sam Bratton to the West Tennessee seat, but the determined Carey sued on the grounds that the Tennessee constitution prohibited an individual from holding two state offices simultaneously. The court agreed, Bratton was ousted, and Carey claimed the seat.[14]

Austin Peay was elected with a broad base of support in 1922,

12. Macpherson, "Democratic Progressivism," pp. 173-74.
13. Nashville *Banner*, March 20, April 1, 2, 1923. *Tennessee House Journal*, 1089. *Tennessee Senate Journal*, p. 1040.
14. Macpherson, "Democratic Progressivism," p. 174.

and his strength was clearly reflected in the General Assembly of 1923. Fourteen of thirty-three senators and fifty-three of ninety-nine representatives had support scores of seventy or better for the governor (see Tables 5 and 6). (See Appendix C for an explanation of support scores.) His support came most consistently from the rural and small-urban representatives. Fifty percent of the members from rural areas and sixty-three percent of those from small-urban areas had high support scores for the governor. Among the three Grand Divisions, Peay was strongest in his native Middle Tennessee where sixty-five percent of the members had support scores of seventy or higher. Thirty-three of the thirty-six Peay backers in Middle Tennessee were from rural or small-urban districts.

Although Peay ran strongest in the large-urban counties in the elections of 1922, the big cities became increasingly wary of the governor during the legislative session. Only thirty-one percent of them can be counted as strong Peay backers and twenty percent as Peay opponents. About half of them, forty-nine percent, fell between these extremes. Large-urban representatives applauded his efforts for efficiency in state government, but they resented his rural oriented tax programs. Hence Tennessee cities neither endorsed nor rejected Austin Peay, but instead adopted a policy of watchful waiting.

Opposition to the new governor, defined as legislators with support scores of thirty or lower, came mainly from Republicans and a handful of dissident Democrats. Six senators and fourteen representatives can be described as anti-Peay, but only two of the senators and five of the representatives were Democrats. These seven men were scattered through Middle and West Tennessee, and their voting reflects no concentrated opposition to Peay. Peay was the master of the Sixty-third General Assembly. His implacable enemy, the Nashville *Banner*, could only grumble that, "The legislature of 1923 was thoroughly servile. He had but to command it acted." The elections commission bill, the *Banner* admitted, was the administration's only real failure.[15]

15. Nashville *Banner*, April 2, 1923, April 17, 1925.

With a solid record of legislative achievement, Peay moved to consolidate his backing for the 1924 campaign. The major threat to the governor's reelection once again was Shelby County, where financial woes had undermined Peay's leading backer, Clarence Saunders. Peay's opponents were carefully paying court to Shelby County and the unpredictable Mr. Crump. Mayor Ed Bass of Chattanooga wrote Crump in February 1924 to discuss the upcoming gubernatorial campaign, and E. B. Stahlman, through their mutual friend Senator McKellar, informed Crump that he expected Peay to have serious opposition in 1924. "Our course seems to me to be plain," McKellar told Crump, "namely to remain neutral for the present."[16] Peay finally won Crump's support, however. The participants in the bargaining are unknown, but in exchange for Shelby County support in the election and in the 1925 legislature, the administration agreed to endorse the Crump candidate for the state elections commission and to establish a medical school in Memphis. Campaigning in Memphis in the 1924 general election, Peay explained that "Mr. Crump and I are friends, have been friends for years, but we parted company for a while and let the people fight it out with the ballot."[17]

The arrangement with Memphis incorporated the last major anti-Peay stronghold in the Democratic Party. Peay's highway and tax programs had clinched his rural appeal, and Nashville had gone for him in 1922. Peay's enemies were left with no stronghold from which to attack him. Even organized business, although miffed by the three percent corporate excise tax, still professed admiration for the man who had secured passage of the Administrative Reorganization Act.[18]

Consequently, Peay's only opponent in the 1924 Democratic primary was John Randolph Neal, an East Tennessee attorney. Neal, a quixotic figure in Tennessee politics for several decades,

---

16. Ed Bass to E. H. Crump, February 29, 1924; Kenneth McKellar to Crump, January 5, 11, 1924, Container 2, McKellar-Crump Correspondence, Kenneth McKellar Papers, Memphis-Shelby County Public Library and Information Center, Memphis, Tennessee.

17. Nashville *Banner*, October 10, 1924, January 28, February 9, 1925.

18. Chattanooga *News*, February 14, 1923.

had a penchant for attacking aggregations of power. He especially resented Peay, who, he felt, had arranged Neal's dismissal from the University of Tennessee law school faculty. Almost a caricature of the absent-minded professor, Neal slept in his clothes and had to be forced to take baths, because he stored his books in the tub. A man of some wealth, he stuffed his paychecks in his pockets and then forgot them for months at a time. He gave simple exams and did not grade them, giving all his students a ninety-five. During his career, Neal lost nine gubernatorial elections, eighteen for the senate, and one for Congress. He was, in short, hardly a man likely to rally disgruntled Democrats.[19]

The 1924 Senate race was more hotly contested. Incumbent Senator John K. Shields was opposed by Judge Nathan Bachman of Chattanooga and General Lawrence Tyson of Knoxville. Tyson, an experienced politician with a distinguished record in World War I, was the more serious challenger to Shields. The outstanding issues of the campaign centered on Shields' alleged disloyalty to Woodrow Wilson and the Democratic Party. The senator had voted against the League of Nations and against a bonus bill for veterans. Shields defended himself saying that the League was the only issue on which he had opposed Wilson. Furthermore, Shields contended, he could see no reason to give taxpayers' money to able-bodied men such as veterans.[20]

Shields' position, however, made him vulnerable to a candidate like Tyson. The latter's military background gave him a strong following among the ex-servicemen of Tennessee. Newspapers supporting Tyson pointed out that Shields had voted for a bill to increase the pensions of Union veterans, "the soldiers who did their part to crush the southern Confederacy, the result of which it has required more than a half century to overcome, but he was so strong for it that he voted to pass it over

---

19. Bobby Eugene Hicks, "The Great Objector: The Life and Public Career of Dr. John R. Neal," *East Tennessee Historical Society Publications* 41 (1969), 39-41, 61-64.

20. Clarksville *Leaf-Chronicle,* July 21, 1924. Jonesboro *Herald and Tribune,* July 20, 1924.

the veto of a Yankee president." Tyson backers also blamed Shields for the farm depression, arguing that America's failure to enter into international agreements had cut foreign markets and ruined agricultural prices. Perhaps most effective was a full page newspaper advertisement with the caption "Lest We Forget" above a picture of Woodrow Wilson. The text described how Tyson had received the news of his son's death in combat, and then quoted a letter from Wilson as saying, ". . . I do not feel at liberty to say more than this: That I regarded Mr. Shields during my administrations as one of the least trustworthy of my professed supporters."[21]

In August, Austin Peay and Lawrence Tyson were easy winners at the polls. The Governor won ninety-three of Tennessee's ninety-five counties and defeated Neal by nearly five to one. Tyson won forty percent of the vote while Shields barely edged Bachman for a distant second (See Tables 7 and 8.). The returns showed Tyson was strong across the state. He ran slightly behind Bachman in East Tennessee, but took the Middle and West and won the rural, small-urban and large-urban vote. The primary indicated that factional strife in Tennessee was, for the moment, at a low point. Peay and Tyson won broad based victories while the Republican candidates, Thomas Peck for governor and Hal Lindsay for the Senate, were nominated without opposition.[22]

The fall election was quiet, with most attention focusing on the governor's race. A few of Peay's enemies, led by E. B. Stahlman and the Nashville *Banner*, bolted the party and staked their hopes on the Republican candidate, Thomas Peck. The *Banner*, which had ignored Peay in the primary, began to blast him in a series of daily front-page editorials printed under the headline, "The Indictment Stands." It persistently referred to him as the "so-called Democratic nominee" and in staccato criticism attacked his "autocratic tendencies." In early October, Stahlman introduced Illinois Governor Frank Lowden at a

---

21. Chattanooga *News*, July 31, 1924. Jonesboro *Herald and Tribune*, July 30, 1924.
22. *Fifty Years of Tennessee Primaries*, pp. 135-137. Neal carried White and Wilson Counties.

Republican rally in Davidson County, spicing his remarks with caustic references to Governor Peay.[23]

Peay and his friends were equally vituperative in their countercharges. In Fayetteville, participants in a "public rally" burned copies of the *Banner* and rebuked its "unfair, unjust and misleading propaganda against the state candidates and nominees of the Democratic Party." The meeting adopted a resolution stating, "We do not credit the *Banner* with Republican principles. . . . It is anti and contra to whatever powers that be—unless it can dictate. Its policy now and for years past is to rule or ruin; dictate or destroy. Its sordid purpose is to establish a Republican organ in Middle Tennessee."[24] The Nashville *Tennessean* argued that the Reorganization Act was at the root of the *Banner*'s campaign and said that Peay could have had the support of the "self-styled independent daily" had he not removed a *Banner* friend, Tax Assessor A. V. Louthan, from office. The candidate himself was more blunt. Peay called the *Banner* "that rotten Nashville newspaper" and continued, "It goes into Democratic primaries and supports some candidates but never has a shred of respect for the result. It is subject to no moral compunction. Is it a Republican newspaper? No, I think too much of my Republican friends to lay it at their door. It claims to be independent. But this means to be independent of all restraints which truth and morality impose on decent people."[25]

The Republican nominee for governor, Captain Thomas F. Peck of Monroe County, was a member of J. Will Taylor's Black-and-Tan faction and the man whose nomination to be commissioner of agriculture had stirred such turmoil in the 1921 legislature. Notwithstanding rumors that the Republicans had decided to concede the gubernatorial and senatorial races and to focus on the presidential contest, Peck made a strong effort, ridiculing the governor's endorsement of a Smoky Mountains

23. Nashville *Banner*, October 3, 6, 9, 10, 20, 1924. Chattanooga *Times*, October 9, 1924.
24. Fayetteville *Observer*, October 16, 1924.
25. Nashville *Tennessean*, November 9, 1924. Nashville *Banner*, October 30, 1924.

park as a "Peay shrine" and branding it the "hughest [sic] joke of the whole campaign." As a former commissioner of agriculture who was well-connected in the rural areas, Peck sought to portray himself as the friend of the farmer, and his starchy opponent as the defender of the big cities, but his demand for repeal of the three percent excise tax on corporate profits seemed to many farmers to be a prelude to higher property taxes. Peck's advocacy of a bond issue to replace the "pay as you go" method of financing road building also hurt him among farmers.[26]

The November balloting brought a great victory for the Democratic Party in Tennessee. John Davis won the state against Calvin Coolidge in the Presidential race, despite a large Republican turnout in East Tennessee where the President ran over 7,000 votes ahead of the rest of the ticket (See Tables 9 and 10.). Davis swept the Middle and the West and took the small-urban and large-urban vote. Coolidge led in the rural counties, thanks to his margin in East Tennessee. Robert LaFollette, running as a Progressive, received only three percent of the vote. In the Senate race, Tyson, like Davis, lost the East but ran strong across the state to win an easy victory over Lindsay (See Tables 11 and 12.).[27]

Peay was returned to the governorship in an election that resembled the Peay-Taylor race of 1922. The three Grand Divisions returned virtually the same percentages for Peay in both races although his percentages in West Tennessee increased slightly due in part to the support of Shelby County (See Tables 13 and 14.). Voting patterns in the 1923 legislature, however, suggested that the governor's strength was waning in large-urban areas and growing in small-urban and rural areas. This trend continued in 1924. Whereas Peay had won seventy-five percent of the vote in the large urban counties in 1922, his vote fell off to sixty percent in 1924. Peay's strength in small-urban counties increased from fifty-three percent in 1922 to sixty-three percent in 1924. The taxing and public service

---

26. Chattanooga *News*, October 8, November 3, 1924. Knoxville *Journal*, October 14, 21, 25, 30, 1924.
27. *Fifty Years of Tennessee Elections*, pp. 106-107.

policies of the administration were costing Peay votes among his original backers but were winning new support for him in the small towns and on the farms.

Peay's percentage of the rural vote declined slightly between 1922 and 1924, but this was due to the strong effort undertaken by Tennessee Republicans to carry the state for Calvin Coolidge. In 1924 Peay and Peck combined drew 33,349 more votes in East Tennessee than Peay and Taylor had earned in 1922. The turnout in the rest of Tennessee, by contrast, was much more stable, declining by 4,258 votes in Middle Tennessee and increasing by 10,542 in West Tennessee. The Republican turnout for Coolidge in East Tennessee gave Peck a 27,085 vote lead in the rural counties of the East that Peay could not overcome. Peck's service as commissioner of agriculture also helped his rural vote total. The governor did, however, carry the rural counties of the Middle and West by some ten thousand votes. The victory was an impressive one, and it was on a note of high optimism that Austin Peay looked toward the opening session of the Sixty-fourth General Assembly.[28]

Peay hoped to avoid making enemies by ignoring the struggle to organize the new legislature. With the administration taking no part, Lucius D. Hill of Sparta was chosen speaker of the senate and William F. Barry of Madison County speaker of the house by the Democratic caucus. But if the governor anticipated an orderly and responsive session, he was soon disabused of the notion. Neither Hill nor Barry was considered an administration follower, and Hill soon became a troublesome opponent. Moreover, the General Assembly had again experienced a high turnover in membership, as was customary in the 1920s. Only eleven of thirty-three senators and twenty-four of ninety-nine representatives returned from the cooperative 1923 legislature. Of these thirty-five members, twenty had been pro-Peay in 1923, four anti-Peay, and eleven independent.[29]

Peay also was beginning to reap the whirlwind of his newly

---

28. *Ibid.*, pp. 108-109.
29. Chattanooga *News*, January 3, 1925. Nashville *Banner*, January 4, 6, 1925. *Public Acts of Tennessee, 1923, 1925.*

created authority. If he had the power to make friends by selectively placing roads and schools, these same decisions could also make him enemies. One county faction, for example, through control of the county court might select one highway route. Subsequently a rival faction might win a majority on the court and select another route. Peay, through his highway commissioner, would be forced to choose between the two. Since the local factions in Tennessee were evenly balanced in most counties, the governor gained an enemy no matter how he decided. In addition, a large group of officeholders who had lost their jobs under Peay or who felt neglected by the parsimonious 1923 General Assembly was looking to the 1925 legislature to remedy the hard times. The state's financial condition was improving, which helped their case, and some legislators were becoming wary of the growing power of the governor. The General Assembly was not ripe for open revolt, but it clearly would have to be carefully led if revolt was to be averted.[30]

During the early weeks of the session, Peay was too preoccupied to provide that leadership. He was often away from the capital on extended trips to Knoxville and Washington, working for the Smoky Mountains park. With the governor absent, his program faltered, and by the end of January only one administration bill, the sales tax on tobacco products, had been enacted. After the legislature returned from its mid-February recess, Peay remained in Nashville and began to exert more effective leadership. During the second half of the session, the General Assembly passed a general education bill, gave the governor authority to acquire the property needed to establish the Reelfoot Lake and Smoky Mountains parks, and approved a substantial reduction in the property tax rate.[31]

The tobacco tax and the general education bill together brought major changes to Tennessee schools. Prior to the Peay Administration, state funds for education were turned over to county officials to spend as they saw fit. The state department of education took only a small part in supervising or coordinating education around the state, and the condition of Tennessee

---

30. Macpherson, "Democratic Progressivism," pp. 221-222.
31. *Ibid.*, pp. 65-66. Nashville *Banner*, January 25, 1925.

schools reflected the neglect. The General Education Act of 1925, designed to overhaul this sytem, also served to concentrate more power in Nashville. The bill established a state equalization fund to pay each county any additional revenue it might need to run its elementary schools for eight months and to pay its teachers according to the new state salary schedule. Furthermore, the act standardized the licensing of teachers, set statewide standards, and made education a state responsibility. This revamped system was partially financed by the sales tax on processed tobacco. Money derived from the tax provided the equalization fund. Together these two acts placed a floor under the quality of schools and made it possible for schools in even the poorest counties to maintain an eight-month term.[32]

Peay had secured the enactment of much of his program, but the effort had been difficult and unpleasant. Factional antagonisms, nearly dormant in 1923, were again awakened in 1925. The Nashville *Banner* noted with some satisfaction that, "in 1923, the governor's wishes were enough to pass a bill, but in 1925 the legislature was much less willing to respond." George Fort Milton of the Chattanooga *News* spoke for the administration in denouncing the "incompetent, factional legislature" and observed, "Times without number it was demonstrated that the purpose of the hostile faction was not constructive but wholly destructive." The assembly, believing Peay would not run again and unwilling to yield more power to him, adopted an independent attitude toward the governor (see Appendix C). Fewer members than in 1923—seven in the senate and thirty-seven in the house—had support scores of seventy or more, while the number of Peay's opponents—six in the senate and nine in the house—also declined slightly. The tendency of the legislators to cluster in the middle reflects the unsettled nature of Tennessee politics in 1925. Since Peay was a powerful man, his foes within the party were content to wait for the governor to retire without openly embracing him, or publicly repudiating him.[33]

32. Andrew David Holt, *The Struggle for a State System of Public Schools in Tennessee, 1903-1936* (New York, 1938), 349-55. Macpherson, "Democratic Progressivism," p. 65. Alexander, *Peay*, pp. xxvii, xxix.
33. Nashville *Banner*, February 15, 1925. Chattanooga *News*, April 18, 1925.

The shift in Peay's support from Middle to East and West Tennessee and from cities to small towns and farms continued in the 1925 legislature. Increasingly, the governor was drawing votes in the assembly from East and West Tennessee while his native Middle Tennessee became the center of his most important opposition (see Tables 15 and 16). Forty-one percent of the East Tennessee representatives and fifty percent of those from West Tennessee can be counted as strong Peay backers. East Tennessee Democrats were drawn to Peay because, as the minority party in their own section, they were forced to seek leadership at the state level. Six East Tennessee Republicans also joined in backing the governor as a result of his efforts to secure the Great Smoky Mountains park, to increase funds for the University of Tennessee, and to build roads in that isolated section. West Tennessee, made up largely of farms and small towns, was the kind of constituency the governor's program was designed to reach, and Peay's influence with legislators from west of the Tennessee River clearly shows its success. Forty-three percent of rural legislators and thirty-three percent of small-urban representatives had high support scores for the governor, while only twenty-two percent of the large-urban representatives did. Of twenty pro-Peay legislators in West Tennessee, seventeen came from rural or small-urban counties. Eleven of fifteen pro-Peay easterners came from similar counties, while three of the remaining four were from Hamilton County, where Peay had strong political connections.

Middle Tennessee, by contrast, was becoming the focal point of opposition to Peay. In 1923, thirty-six Middle Tennesseans were strong supporters of the governor, but in 1925, only nine were. This startling drop was due to several factors. First of all, Middle Tennessee was headquarters for the two most antagonistic factions in the Democratic party. Luke Lea and E. B. Stahlman were bitter enemies and through their newspapers, the *Tennessean* and the *Banner* respectively, they fanned the flames of political passion in the middle division. In addition, Middle Tennessee, as in 1918 and 1922, was usually the home of at least two candidates for governor. Both factions in Middle Tennessee were thus well-developed and maintained an almost constant combat that did not exist in West Tennessee. Given the strength of the factions, other variables such as urban/rural factors played little part in influencing Middle Tennessee legislators. Of nine Peay backers, five were from rural counties and four from small-urban ones. Of twelve Peay opponents, six were from rural counties, five were from small-urban counties, and one was from a large-urban county. Thirty-four Middle Tennesseans, including most of the Davidson County delegation, remained with the independents.

Despite the opposition he encountered in the 1925 legislature, Peay brought significant changes to Tennessee's political structure in his two terms as governor. His program had moved the center of power from local to state government and from the legislature to the governor. Peay himself remarked, "All governors before me were governors in name only."[34] His reshaping of the fundamental pattern of government caused a major political realignment in Tennessee. Armed with authority to appoint commission heads and, through them, to influence the spending of state money and the dispensing of state patronage, the governor of Tennessee became an effective statewide political leader for the first time since the Civil War.

Peay used this power to build a personal following in the small towns and rural areas of Tennessee. Tax reform and expanded public services were the basis of Peay's appeal to these groups. In 1923 the governor pledged a one million dollar reduction in the property tax. He achieved his goal by persuading the legislature to repeal the five-cent property tax levy for state fairs. To provide the extra revenue to pay for public services, Peay opted for such devices as a corporate profits tax, a gasoline tax, and a tobacco sales tax. As tax collections went down in rural areas, state expenditures there were going up. Peay's staunchest defender, Luke Lea's Nashville *Tennessean,* pressed this point with regard to the tobacco tax. "The tobacco tax," the *Tennessean* pointed out, "is largely collected in the centers of wealth and property; it is paid where the per capita assessment of property is high. But it is distributed to counties where per

---

34. Nashville *Banner,* July 18, 1926.

capita wealth is small. . . ." Moreover Peay had rejected bonds as a possible means of financing new roads. Interest payments on a bonded indebtedness could have increased property tax rates but the "pay-as-you-go" gasoline tax spread the cost of new roads more equitably.[35]

Peay was also working to build his support among farmers and small-town residents of Republican East Tennessee. This political step-child, ignored by Democratic governors in the past, received its share of the new services and the cherished Great Smoky Mountains park. East Tennessee had long sought to have the state purchase the Little River tract before loggers marred its natural beauty. Peay was the first governor actively to support their efforts and this fact was not lost on them. Peay also pushed the expansion of higher education in the East, being instrumental in expanding East Tennessee Normal School into East Tennessee State Teachers College, and substantially increasing appropriations for the University of Tennessee at Knoxville. The Knoxville *News-Sentinel* typified the Eastern reaction: "Perhaps no Governor has done more for East Tennessee than Gov. Peay," it wrote, "He has taken an unusual interest in her welfare and is a believer in her future prosperity."[36]

Peay's most important backer was Nashville publisher Luke Lea. The colonel was a shrewd and powerful politician whose opinion Peay respected, but the governor always remained fiercely independent. An observer who knew both of them has remarked, "Peay was not dictated to by anybody. Lea had considerable influence but there was never any claim he was running the Peay Administration." Lea himself best described the nature of their relationship in a letter to Peay shortly after the 1922 election:

> You will need as you have never needed before disinterested friends, and I want you to count the *Tennessean* and me in the class of your real disinterested friends.

35. Bolivar *Bulletin*, June 25, 1926. Nashville *Tennessean*, July 3, 11, 12, 1926.
36. Chattanooga *Times*, August 8, 1926. Knoxville *News-Sentinel*, July 14-15, 1926. Joe C. Gamble interview, June 28, 1976.

Reform and Realignment / 57

You are under no obligation either to the *Tennessean* or to me except that obligation a public officer owes to every one of his constituents. Not on account of lacking interest in you but due to the keenest interest in your administration will either the *Tennessean* or I under any circumstances make any recommendation to you for any one to fill any office that is appointed by you or elected by the General Assembly. . . .

We are, however, going to take the liberty of making certain suggestions to you as to matters of policy and general legislation . . . knowing . . . that you will accept or discard them as they may seem sound or unsound.[37]

The closeness between the two became most apparent as Peay's health began to fail. Suffering from chronic heart trouble, his treatment required an extended stay at a Battle Creek, Michigan, sanitarium in the summer of 1925. The governor asked Lea to "keep an eye on things" in his absence, and during Peay's confinement they exchanged several letters discussing policy and analyzing the political situation. Just six weeks before he died, Peay wrote, "Luke Lea has been like a brother to me."[38]

For both Lea and Peay, the most irritating event of the summer of 1925 was the celebrated Scopes Monkey Trial at Dayton, Tennessee. In early July, Lea wrote, "I have received several letters from Mr. Bryan and he has all the enthusiasm of a debutant over the approaching trial at Dayton. If Bryan . . . could be eliminated from the prosecution, it would be very much better for the State." In reply, Peay expressed his disgust with "that Dayton mess." Northern newspapers, he told Lea, "are running the Scopes trial in big leads on front page space and Tennessee is coming in for their ridicule until I fairly boil." Angered by "those boys who invented that jamboree,"

---

37. Lea to Peay, November 15, 1922, Container 6, File 6, Austin Peay Official Papers, Tennessee State Library and Archives, Nashville, Tennessee.
38. Lea to Peay, June 25, July 2, 7, 21, 25, 1925; Peay to Lea, June 25, July 12, 18, 26, 1925, Luke Lea Papers. Peay to Paul J. Kruesi, August 25, 1927, Container 72, File 6, Peay Official Papers.

Peay was afraid the storm over evolution would undercut all he had worked for. Despite the furor, however, the Scopes Trial never became an issue in Tennessee politics because most Tennesseans seemed to approve of the Monkey Law. As Lea observed, "with the exception of a little group that is dubbed by itself, the 'intelligensia' and regarded by the general public as the black sheep of the 'isms' family, public opinion is all one way."[39]

The major point of disagreement between Peay and Lea centered on the Highway Department. Peay adamantly opposed mixing highways and politics. The governor explained his feelings to a constituent who wrote requesting a job: "We had a slush of politics before the present administration, with the result that the people were securing no roads. Nothing is more sure than the disruption of highway activities by politics." Peay consistently refused to interfere with the location of Tennessee highways. "I must leave the road locations to the Highway Department," he wrote. "It is their business and for me to attempt it would be to demoralize our road building completely." When Mayor H. T. Boyd of Sweetwater suggested that votes might be forthcoming in the 1926 primary if the governor endorsed a certain highway project, Peay replied: "There is a little disposition to force action while I am a candidate on these things, and you know how that works with a man who respects his word and honor. I cannot make promises for the sake of votes. That has been the ruin of road building in many states."[40]

Colonel Lea, however, was more willing to involve himself in the affairs of the Highway Department. In July 1926 he wrote Tom Henderson, a leading Democratic politician, asking him to suggest to Peay the use of a rock asphalt called Kyrock on a road project in Roane County. Lea had no personal interest in Kyrock, but his business associate Rogers Caldwell did. Also in

---

39. Lea to Peay, July 7, 1925, Peay to Lea, July 12, 26, 1925, Luke Lea Papers.

40. Peay to Victor C. Stafford, May 25, 1926; Peay to S. T. Sparks, May 25, 1926; Peay to H. T. Boyd, June 16, 1926, Container 4, File 1, Peay Official Papers.

1926, Lea suggested that political contributions might be forthcoming for the primary struggle with Hill McAlister if the state purchased all of its cement from one concern, but Peay branded the proposal "unthinkable." When a measure was introduced in the 1927 General Assembly to shift two cents of the state gasoline tax from the state to the county governments, Lea asked Congressman Gordon Browning to pressure State Senator Dorsey Bramley of Carroll County to vote against it. Lea subsequently promised Browning that his district would receive a road and that the congressman could pick the contractor for the job. Peay, however, overrode Lea, telling Browning he would permit no such trades. Nevertheless, the differences between Lea and Peay in this area were minor and did not distract from the admiration and trust they had for each other.[41]

Peay was a controversial man, and his administration cemented a solid political alliance while generating a determined opposition. Among Peay's strongest foes were organized business and urban commercial interests. Business leaders, after backing Peay on the Reorganization Act, broke with him on his tax policies. The corporate profits tax and the tobacco sales tax turned commercial and manufacturing interests against him. Bankers were offended when the governor secured repeal of a 1921 law that had raised the ceiling on interest rates from six percent to eight percent. Peay's refusal to issue bonds for road building placed still another wedge between the governor and some elements of the business community. The Peay administration increased the tax load on business and spent the revenue on rural roads and schools. By 1925, therefore, organized business was leading the fight against the governor.[42]

Peay's loss of business support could be an important key to interpreting Southern progressivism in the 1920s. George B. Tindall has suggested that a group of "business progressives," primarily urban-oriented professional people, were pushing

---

41. Lea to Tom Henderson, July 7, 1926, Lea Papers. Memphis *Press-Scimitar*, April 18, 1931. *Browning Memoir*, pp. 99-101. Browning refers to "Representative" Bramley but he was actually in the state senate.

42. Macpherson, "Democratic Progressivism," pp. 207-10. Macpherson, "Administrations of Austin Peay," pp. 58-59.

Southern state governments toward more efficient operation and expanded public services. Events in Tennessee, however, show that the impetus for these reforms came instead from the state's rural and small-town areas. Tennessee urbanites, by contrast, seem to have had little interest in such things as roads and schools. Expanded public services, almost by definition, meant that the richer urban areas would be taxed to provide services for the poorer rural areas. Such may well have been the situation in other states of the heavily rural South, indicating that farmers rather than urbanites may have been the driving force behind "business progressivism."[43]

More potent opposition to Peay's program came from the local political fiefdoms, both urban and rural, whose power had been undercut by the Peay reforms. Since county political organizations in Tennessee were almost invariably split into at least two constantly warring factions, Peay's "usurpation" of local authority necessarily affected local power struggles. Factions that curried his favor were boosted by the largesse he could grant, while those who fought him felt the cool winds of gubernatorial indifference. By 1925, Peay had made a number of powerful enemies at the local level across the state.[44]

Peay found his most dangerous opponents in Tennessee's two leading cities, Nashville and Memphis. Each was dominated by a single boss, Hilary Howse in Nashville and Edward H. Crump in Memphis, who had the power to deliver the city's votes to the candidate of his choosing. The Peay reforms represented a threat to their local position, and they marshalled their potent forces against him. The much weaker administration faction could not counter the machine in either place. Peay had important backers in both cities in 1922, but his strength ebbed quickly during his years in office so that by 1926 the two cities were strongly opposed to the governor.

Nashville politics were torn by the constant warfare between two ruling factions, one led by Mayor Hilary Howse and

43. Tindall, "Business Progressivism," pp. 92-106.
44. Macpherson, "Democratic Progressivism," p. 19. Macpherson, "Administrations of Austin Peay," pp. 58-59.

publisher E. B. Stahlman, and a second group following Colonel Luke Lea, by now the *eminence gris* of Tennessee politics. Lea was influential with Peay, and the wide circulation of his Nashville *Tennessean* made him a power particularly in the rural areas of Middle Tennessee. The colonel controlled some Davidson County offices, most notably that of attorney general, but his strength was concentrated at the state rather than the municipal level. Howse, for his part, bossed the capital city while Stahlman kept up a steady barrage of criticism against the governor and his programs. The new power center the governor was creating in the state and his rural-oriented tax and public service plans were the primary targets of Stahlman's criticism. In extremely vituperative language, the publisher excoriated the two Peay administrations. He attacked the Reorganization Act as giving too much power to the governor. Peay, he charged, was using highways for political purposes and was trying to incorporate school boards into his personal machine. Moreover, the *Banner* charged, he was manipulating education funds to pad the state employee list and pressuring new employees for campaign funds. The paper also attacked Peay for redistributing revenue from richer counties to poorer ones and branded the Great Smoky Mountains park "ridiculous" and "preposterous." Clearly the concentration of power at the state level was worrying the Nashville bosses and the upward trend of state taxes and expenditures was making the situation still more unpalatable.[45]

Another urban boss who, by 1926, was beginning to worry about his position was E. H. Crump of Shelby County. Despite their past political differences, Peay and Crump were actually very similar in their approach to government. Crump as Mayor of Memphis and Peay as Governor of Tennessee both used techniques of business administration to fight inefficiency and waste. Just as Peay worked for schools and roads, Crump expanded such basic municipal services as the fire department and health department. Both men also were concerned with

---

45. Nashville *Banner*, October 3, 6, 7, and November 3, 1924; August 1, 3, 1926.

developing a more equitable tax scheme. They were thrown into conflict, however, by the shifting balance between state and local authority that the Peay reforms prompted.[46]

Crump showed little concern for state politics earlier in his career, but a series of events forced him to take stock of his position in terms of statewide events. Memphis, as Gerald Capers has written, belonged more to Mississippi-Arkansas than to Tennessee. It could be seriously hurt by a state administration that favored East and Middle Tennessee. Peay, a Clarksville resident with strong support in Middle Tennessee, had assiduously courted the Republican mountaineers to the east. Most tangibly, Peay was taxing Shelby County wealth to aid the state's economically depressed rural areas. This fact especially rankled Crump. He pointed out that from 1923 to 1926 the state had collected $1,909,263.34 in auto license taxes from Shelby County yet paid back for roads only $23,579.10. The state maintained a paltry twenty-four miles of highway in Shelby, all built before Peay's election. The gasoline tax and the tobacco tax seemed to be further proof of Peay's "Robin Hood" instincts.[47]

Like Peay's opponents in Nashville, Crump was intensely concerned with the threat the governor posed to his own power base in Memphis. His 1915 ouster taught him that in Tennessee the city is the creature of the state and that to hold power locally he had to control the Shelby delegation to the General Assembly and dominate the state Democratic Party. When in the mid-twenties he began to consolidate his control of Memphis and Shelby County, Crump realized he could not afford to ignore the state. Crump's close relationship with Tennessee's senior senator, Kenneth McKellar, was another factor in his opposition to Peay. The governor's popularity and machine could make him a formidable candidate against McKellar in 1928. Crump hoped to forestall Peay's candidacy by upsetting the governor's bid for reelection in 1926. Austin Peay was in a position to break

---

46. Allan H. Kitchens, "Ouster of Mayor Edward H. Crump, 1915-1916," *West Tennessee Historical Society Papers* 19 (1965), 118-19.

47. Capers, "Memphis," p. 227. Stanley J. Folmsbee, Robert E. Corlew, and Enoch L. Mitchell, *History of Tennessee* (New York, 1960), 2:348. Memphis *News-Scimitar*, August 3, 1926.

Crump. The Boss had to defeat him or deal with him, and Peay was not an easy man to bend.[48]

Aware of the gathering opposition to him after 1924, Peay had mixed emotions about a third term. No Tennessee governor since Isham G. Harris during Civil War days had served three terms, and Peay already was under heavy fire as an "autocrat." Despite his relative youth (he was fifty in 1926) Peay was in very poor health and an arduous campaign might prove too much for him. At the same time, however, he feared that a change in administration would result in the destruction of the reforms he had so laboriously achieved. Possibly Peay, as Crump feared, was eyeing McKellar's Senate seat and hoped to use a third term to keep himself visible, although the governor repeatedly denied interest in going to Washington. Peay summarized his feelings about the race in a letter to a supporter:

> I ousted a political crowd in this state but they have never gone to work in good faith. Most of them have been sitting about waiting to take charge when I quit and they have their lines and plans all made to begin mulcting this state again. . . . There is no way to get me into a race for another term unless the people order it themselves and they will have to make their wishes in the matter very clear and plain. That, I am not expecting them to do. They usually wake up too late.[49]

In January 1926, Peay issued a statement inviting the voters of Tennessee to express their opinion on his pursuit of a third term. The response was overwhelmingly favorable, though it is hard to say how many telegrams were the product of genuine sentiment and how many were sent by the members of the state machine who were concerned about their own political fu-

---

48. Macpherson, "Administrations of Austin Peay," pp. 57-58. Greene and Avery, *Government in Tennessee,* p. 52.
49. Knoxville *News-Sentinel,* July 29, 1926. Austin Peay to Judge John Y. Peete, August 21, 1925, Container 3, File 1, Austin Peay Official Papers.

64 / *Tennessee in Turmoil*

tures.[50] A few months later Peay announced his candidacy and began a whirlwind speaking tour around the state.

Peay's opponent for the Democratic nomination was State Treasurer Hill McAlister of Nashville. McAlister, a lawyer, had long experience in politics, having served as city attorney of Nashville and as a member of the state senate. In 1919 he had been elected to the first of four terms as state treasurer. Backed by the Howse-Stahlman machine in Nashville and the Crump machine in Memphis, McAlister concentrated his attacks on the centralization of power during the Peay years. He promised to maintain the existing pace of public services yet simultaneously restore local control. McAlister's platform consisted largely of amendments to the Reorganization Act and the General Education Act. He pledged an eight-month school term, but promised repeal of the tobacco tax that financed the extended sessions. He also proposed the creation of a board of regents to replace the governor as supervisor of the state's education system, thus divorcing public schools from politics. McAlister promised more highways, built without political considerations, and, mindful of his big city backers, the return of a larger part of automobile license taxes to the counties that paid them. Furthermore, he urged that the governor's nominations for executive department commissioners be made subject to senate confirmation and that the state comptroller be given control of public revenues. In summary the candidate demanded the amendment of the Reorganization Act to "eliminate all autocratic power and to restore the principle of democratic government in Tennessee."[51]

McAlister's urban backing was a valuable asset, but it made him an easy target for barbs from the proadministration press in a mostly rural state. Peay was a country lawyer and tobacco farmer, while McAlister was city born and bred. McAlister had a reputation as a health faddist and was given to dieting. When he became ill on a tour of rural counties the Peay forces speculated that "possibly Mr. McAlister had eaten an egg that had been boiled five minutes instead of three. It sat ill on his delicate urban

---

50. Austin Peay Official Papers, Container 34, File 3.
51. Nashville *Banner*, July 15, 1926. Macpherson, "Democratic Progressivism," p. 74.

stomache [sic]." McAlister had trouble relating to rural problems, a handicap that plagued him throughout his campaign. In addition, he lacked the driving energy of Austin Peay. "McAlister is a fine fellow with a good record," wrote E. H. Crump, "but oh my, he certainly needs push and pep."[52]

Peay, for his part, was vulnerable on the third-term issue, which alienated important backers around the state. Most serious was the defection of Clarence Saunders in Memphis, who angrily protested the third term. The grocery magnate had given a tremendous boost to Peay in Shelby during the 1922 campaign. Since then, Saunders had lost Piggly Wiggly in an ill-starred move to corner the company's stock, but he had rebounded quickly with another food marketing scheme. He advertised himself as "Sole Owner of My Name" and so christened his new grocery chain. His media blitz against Peay in 1926 focused on Peay's alleged arrogance in seeking another term and took as its slogan, "GIVE US A HUMAN MAN! One in Whom Warm Blood Flows." He branded Peay the "great-I-Am-Ness" and said two terms as governor was honor enough for any man. Saunders attacked his old friend as a cold and unfeeling politician who played sleight of hand with the state's taxes and cynically created a political machine out of state employees.[53] Perhaps Saunders harbored some resentment that Peay had not been sufficiently helpful in his recent tax troubles, but the governor had written several letters in his behalf, and no evidence exists to suggest this caused Saunders' change in attitude. The newspapers of the period invariably mention the third-term issue in rationalizing Saunders' defection. Moreover, in 1928 the Memphian again supported the Luke Lea faction, indicating that the third term was the only reason for his defection in 1926.[54]

---

52. Crump to McKellar, January 8, 1926, Container 2, McKellar-Crump Correspondence, Kenneth McKellar Papers. Macpherson, "Democratic Progressivism," p. 74.

53. Memphis *News-Scimitar,* July 23, 1926. Memphis *Commercial Appeal,* August 3, 1926. Chattanooga *Times,* July 17, 24, 28, 1926.

54. Austin Peay to U.S. Representative Edwin L. Davis, August 3, 1923, Container 1, File 1; Luke Lea to Austin Peay, July 28, 1923, Container 9, File 5, Peay Official Papers. Memphis *Commercial Appeal,* July 31, 1926.

Peay's strategy in 1926 was to appeal to Tennessee's rural voters, emphasizing the benefits his programs had provided the farm and small-town population. He particularly stressed his role as Tennessee's "good roads governor." In his opening speech at Trenton, the governor underscored the point, saying he was willing to make roads the sole issue of the campaign. In 1922, he reminded his listeners, the state had constructed and was maintaining 382 miles of highway. By midsummer of 1926, he said, the figure was approximately 6,000 miles.[55]

Peay played on his success in shifting the tax burden and upgrading public schools. Large advertisements appeared in rural papers, showing the ratio of taxes collected to state expenditures in 1922 and in 1926 for that county. An advertisement in the Camden *Chronicle*, for example, explained that in 1922 the state collected $14,072.80 in property taxes from Benton County and spent $17,066.12, whereas in 1926 the state took out $8,099.77 while spending $25,704.44. The Nashville *Tennessean* noted that property holders paid $1.5 million less in taxes than when Peay had taken office. Peay defended the tobacco tax by comparing richer counties to poorer ones. Davidson County, for example, had an assessed wealth of $5254.78 per child and levied 30¢ per $100 to maintain an eight-month school. In contrast, Overton County had an assessed wealth of only $603.24 per child and the revenue from its 55¢ levy had barely kept the schools open five months. Therefore, McAlister's promise to end the tobacco tax while sustaining a statewide eight-month term was, Peay concluded, nonsense.[56]

"The tobacco tax," the *Tennessean* explained, "is a part of that progressive principle of taxation that would get away as far as possible from the unfair and unscientific property tax, that imposes the burden of government upon farms and homeowners." Tennessee, the paper continued, had finally learned that education is not a civil or county responsibility but a state responsibility. A property tax to support this effort would be confiscatory. Peay repeatedly told his audiences that he took full

---

55. Columbia *Daily Herald*, July 7, 1926. Nashville *Tennessean*, July 12, 1926.
56. Nashville *Tennessean*, July 12, August 1, 1926. Camden *Chronicle*, July 2, 1926.

responsibility for the tax, urging his listeners not to blame local senators and representatives who had voted for it because of their confidence in him.[57]

Peay bound all this together with a campaign rhetoric that played on rural suspicions of the large cities. He repeatedly hurled defiance at the city bosses, shouting, "Crump of Memphis can't beat me. Howse of Nashville and Bass of Chattanooga can't beat me. This I know because the people of the state are with me." He expressed confidence that the "solid, unselfish, and dependable citizenship of Tennessee will see to it that the city gangs do not take this election." The city machines, he warned, "do not understand the rural problems. They never have and never will. They are only concerned with their local matters. They do not know the great things that affect state development. Tennessee has never progressed when the state government was under their control and never will."[58]

As in 1922 and 1924, Peay faced virulent opposition from Stahlman and the Nashville *Banner* in Middle Tennessee. Now more than two months before the 1926 primary Stahlman began a series of daily front page editorials attacking the governor. He accused Peay of manipulating figures to present himself in a good light, and a *Banner* reporter systematically rebutted every Peay speech after it was delivered. Many Banner attacks focused on Peay's alleged use of state agencies for political purposes. The paper renewed old charges about roads and schools in politics and gave extensive coverage to statements by State Geologist Hugh D. Miser that the Peay campaign had solicited contributions from state employees, even specifying cash payments instead of checks. The *Banner* said Highway Commissioner James G. Creveling had been fired for resisting such efforts. The paper identified State Commissioner of Labor Ed M. Gillenwaters as the moving force behind a $350,000 slush fund. When Highway Commissioner C. Neil Bass wrote to the *Banner* denying the accusations, Stahlman billed him for adver-

57. Nashville *Tennessean*, July 3, 11, 1926. Memphis *Commercial Appeal*, June 30, 1926.
58. Knoxville *News-Sentinel*, August 2, 1926. Memphis *Commercial Appeal*, August 4, 1926.

68 / Tennessee in Turmoil

tising saying the letter was "Peay propaganda." The newspaper also accused Peay of transferring money from the school fund and using it to hire additional state employees. The *Banner* also joined the chorus against the third term and denounced the increase in state expenditures over the previous four years. It branded as hypocrisy Peay's claims that he had lowered property taxes, arguing that cuts in the state property tax had been offset by increases in the local tax to meet obligations the state should have assumed.[59]

Peay fought back savagely against Stahlman by questioning his loyalty during World War I. An unsigned advertisement in the *Tennessean* charged that in 1918 the *Banner* was "trying to spread German Kultur instead of inspiring patriotism." The advertisement went on to describe the war records of Peay appointees, charging that as state treasurer, McAlister had never appointed ex-servicemen to office and had consistently opposed them as candidates for public office: "Hill McAlister is the avowed and unrelenting opponent of the former soldier. Why? The principal newspaper support of Hill McAlister was pro-German during the war and has consistently fought the former serviceman since the war." When 50,000 copies of the *Banner* were sent out across Tennessee paid for by "a friend," the Peay forces wondered aloud whether the donor had been a "friend" of America during the World War. The governor's supporters claimed that German Foreign Minister Zimmerman had sent $300,000 to Tennessee during the war to influence the press and that the *Banner* was the only pro-German paper in the state. Other possible donors of the free papers, the Peay people speculated, were the Tobacco Trust and the Republican Party.[60]

The Peay forces denied that the *Banner* had a legitimate role to play in a Democratic Party primary, arguing that the newspaper had not supported a Democratic Presidential nominee since 1882 and only Albert H. Roberts among Democratic gubernatorial nominees since 1908. The *Banner* was "meddling" in the

59. Nashville *Banner*, July 2, 3, August 1, 3, 4, 1926.
60. Bolivar *Bulletin*, July 23, 1926. *McNairy County Independent*, Selmer, July 30, 1926. Nashville *Tennessean*, July 24, 1926.

"His Master's Voice," the *Tennessean*, July 31, 1926.

Democratic primary, said the Peay forces, and would refuse to accept the verdict if the winner failed to submit to the dictates of E. B. Stahlman. In a cartoon entitled "His Master's Voice," the *Tennessean* caricatured McAlister as "Little Nipper" listening to the Victrola. The candidate wore a "Back Tax Gang" collar and the phonograph was labelled "The Banner." Another, less imaginative cartoon showed McAlister as a dummy seated on the knee of a ventriloquist labeled A. V. Louthan.[61]

If the battle was fierce in Nashville, it rose to a white heat in volatile Memphis. Crump, now completely opposed to Austin Peay, was in the midst of a final drive to consolidate his hold on Shelby County and the city of Memphis. The core of his new machine was composed of public employees and the black, nominally Republican, Robert Church machine. Also important to Crump's power were his links to the Shelby county underworld. Clark Porteous, a Memphis reporter, testified that "Vice provided a sort of slush fund, . . . the political organization could call on these people for money and did." Frank Rice, "generalissimo" of the organization, kept the "boys" in line and tended to the details. The public employees controlled by Crump provided a ready reserve of ward and precinct leaders across the county. Deductions from their salaries helped finance candidates. The extensive vice and liquor interests that flourished in the city during the Roaring Twenties also supplied money for the organization with "voluntary" donations. Racketeer Jim Mulcahy often spent up to a thousand dollars paying poll taxes for the machine. The teeming black wards gave Crump a pool of some forty percent of the city's population which he could vote as he desired through arrangements with the black leader Church.[62]

---

61. Bolivar *Bulletin*, July 16, 1926. Chattanooga *News*, July 14, 1926. Memphis *Commercial Appeal*, July 27, 1926. Nashville *Tennessean*, July 31, August 3, 1926.

62. Lamar Whitlow Bridges, "Editor Mooney versus Boss Crump," *West Tennessee Historical Society Papers* 20 (1966), 104. Tucker, *Lieutenant Lee*, p. 98. Nashville *Tennessean*, July 12, 31, August 3, 1926. Clark Porteous in an untitled collection of reminiscences of E. H. Crump in the Memphis-Shelby County Public Library and Information Center, Memphis, Tennessee, p. 5. No evidence suggests that Crump profited personally from these transactions.

Reform and Realignment / 71

Each of these groups in turn received something from Crump. Public employees could expect raises and promotions while other loyal spear carriers could rely on the machine for government jobs if the need arose. Memphis vice dispensers believed that no other city leader would be as tolerant of them as Crump and they considered their contributions a good investment. Blacks too stood to benefit from Crump rule. The Boss opposed police brutality in the black community and made some sincere efforts to improve the quality of life along Beale Street. Crump fought the Ku Klux Klan in 1923 and was the Memphis politician most likely to listen to black demands.[63]

As the 1926 campaign warmed up, the Peay newspapers began to exploit the race issue. The Nashville *Tennessean*, with its large rural circulation in Middle Tennessee, reported that the Orange Mound Booster Club, a black civic organization, had endorsed McAlister and that the Crump machine had engineered the registration of 10,000 blacks in the Shelby Democratic primary. The pro-Peay Memphis *Commercial Appeal* in a long editorial a few days before the primary declared that, "This Is a White Primary, Colored People Can Vote in County Elections, But Not in the Governor's Race. The Democratic Primary is a Democratic Primary. It is a white man's fight. The colored people will have their chance to vote for governor in November. . . . There are no colored Democrats." The *Tennessean* pointedly reminded its readers that any man who urged another to vote fraudulently was guilty of a crime.[64]

Peay faced opposition from both Crump and Saunders in Shelby, but the governor still had powerful friends there. Mayor Rowlett Paine, a Crump enemy, tried to use the police force to limit illegal voting though he met with only limited success. Paine was in serious political trouble himself, however, and Peay got more valuable assistance from Charles P. J. Mooney, editor of the Memphis *Commercial Appeal.* Mooney was a colorful Irishman with a rich brogue and a quick temper. A native Kentuckian, he had had broad newspaper experience

63. William D. Miller, *Mr. Crump,* pp. 204-05, 212-13.
64. Memphis *Commercial Appeal,* August 3, 1926. Nashville *Tennessean,* August 4, 1926.

before he came to the *Commercial Appeal* in 1908. The paper was owned by several prominent Memphis families who also held large interests in privately owned utilities. Crump feuded with these utilities throughout his career and believed, with some reason, that they were responsible for his ouster as mayor. Crump and Mooney were allied on certain major issues, such as the switch to commission government in Memphis and opposition to the Klan, but basically the two men were in deep conflict. Crump saw government as a kind of benevolent despotism, while Mooney was aghast at Crump's "total disregard" for the electoral process and his tendency to ignore laws that got in his way. Thus in 1926 the *Commercial Appeal* was giving Austin Peay vital editorial support in Mr. Crump's backyard.[65]

In addition to his political foes in Nashville and Memphis, Peay had also incurred the enmity of two important organized economic groups, business and labor. Businessmen resented the thrust of Peay's tax policies, especially his efforts to tax industrial wealth. The Tennessee Manufacturers Association, headed by John E. Edgerton, was particularly vocal in its criticism. Organized labor, though divided, was also inclined to oppose the governor. George L. Berry, president of the International Printing Pressman's Union of America, strongly endorsed Peay, because he "has been fair to organized labor." The Tennessee Federation of Labor made no overt endorsements, but it issued a comparison of the labor record of the two candidates that was decidedly partial to McAlister. The Federation described the Nashvillian as "friendly to labor" and remarked that as a state senator "he voted for every bill introduced by the Tennessee Federation of Labor." Peay, in contrast, had selected Ed M. Gillenwaters as his commissioner of labor, an appointment the TFL branded "unsatisfactory," and had denied a TFL request that he be removed. Furthermore, the governor had increased the use of convict labor and had not pushed a

---

65. Turner Catledge, *My Life and The Times* (New York, 1971), p. 33. Lamar W. Bridges, "The Fight Against Boss Crump: Editor C. P. J. Mooney of Memphis," *Journalism Quarterly* (Summer, 1967), 245-49. Bridges, "Editor Mooney," p. 106. Memphis *Commercial Appeal*, July 25, 30, 31, 1926.

child-labor amendment in the General Assembly. McAlister was clearly the TFL choice in 1926.[66]

Tempers were short and violence flared as Tennessee Democrats filed to the polls. The Friday before the primary, at a meeting in the office of Shelby County Trustee Frank Gailor, Boss Crump had given his orders: "Boys, we're going down the line for Hill McAlister; get out and go to work." During that weekend the followers of Robert Church canvassed the black wards of Memphis, instructing the troops to vote for McAlister. On Tuesday, members of the machine smoothly shuttled black voters to the polling places. Mooney's reporters from the *Commercial Appeal* swarmed about as Memphis police smashed cameras and arrested "loiterers." Turner Catledge, a *Commercial Appeal* reporter and later editor of the *New York Times*, described the events: Crump's men, according to Catledge, took blacks who voted in the Republican primary, gave them phoney poll tax receipts, and revoted them in the Democratic primary. Catledge had stationed himself at a polling place when several Crump "hoods" climbed out of a long Packard owned by the sheriff's department and beat him "rather badly."[67]

Despite Crump's efforts, Peay won the nomination by some 8,000 votes. Victory was sweet, and Mooney's *Commercial Appeal* rhapsodized:

> . . . tears, idle tears, interspersed with oathladen sobs came from the orphan boys yesterday when they looked about the field strewn with the fragments of a once mighty machine.
>
> They rubbed their eyes, bleary with seeing double in the count, and wondered how it all happened. . . .
>
> "They just naturally outstole us" was the way one of the fatherless put it yesterday.

The newspapers on the day after the election proclaimed the

---

66. Macpherson, "Administrations of Austin Peay," p. 59. Chattanooga *Times*, July 18, 1926. Nashville *Tennessean*, August 3, 1926.

67. Catledge, *Times*, pp. 45-46. Nashville *Tennessean*, August 2, 6, 1926.

Peay victory and filled the air with cries of fraud. The *Commercial Appeal* headlined:

> NEGROES GANG POLLS FOR HILL MCALISTER IN RAPE OF BALLOTS/ORGY OF DEBAUCHERY HITS BOTTOM IN PRIMARY
> In an orgy of negro herding . . . the machine smashed through yesterday for Hill McAlister in Shelby County with a majority of more than 12,000. . . . They voted them by the thousands. No literacy test was applied. It was not even necessary for the negroes to mark their ballots. . . . Carloads of the dusky skinned McAlister Democrats made the polling places with clock like regularity. Many of the cars were driven by white men.

The Bolivar *Bulletin* echoed the *Commercial Appeal*:

> In Shelby County, . . . the most disgraceful scenes were enacted since the Civil War. Reporters for the press were arrested, beaten, their cameras broken and other indignities suffered. Negroes were herded in droves and voted by the thousands.

The Chattanooga *Times* ran a counter-volley from W. W. Courtney, McAlister's campaign manager, charging fraud in Peay's majorities in East Tennessee. The Nashville *Banner*, for its part, kept a sullen silence.[68]

Peay achieved a glowing success. He carried the rural counties 33,533 to 22,597 and trounced McAlister in East Tennessee, 29,731 to 13,831. His narrow eight-thousand vote margin in the final tally clearly came from these areas (see Tables 17 and 18). Peay's winning coalition in 1926 stood in sharp contrast to the alliance that had first nominated him four years earlier. In 1922, Peay won twenty-seven percent of the vote in East Tennessee, a

---

68. Memphis *Commercial Appeal*, August 6, 7, 1926. Bolivar *Bulletin*, August 3, 1928. Chattanooga *Times*, August 7, 1926. Nashville *Banner*, August, 1926.

weak third in a four man field; four years later, the governor trounced McAlister in the East carrying sixty-eight percent of the vote. The results in Middle Tennessee were close in both elections, but the Peay percentage in West Tennessee fell off in 1926 due to the heavy Shelby vote against him. In addition to East Tennessee, Peay demonstrated strength in the state's farms and small towns. Having won only thirty percent of the vote in rural counties in 1922, he won sixty percent against McAlister in 1926. In small-urban counties, he ran well in both elections, taking forty-one percent of the vote against three opponents in 1922 and fifty-five percent against one opponent in 1926. The large-urban counties, however, turned sharply against Peay during his two terms in office. The large-urban vote, which had tipped the nomination for Peay in 1922, gave him only forty-two percent of the vote in 1926. Nominated by the large cities in 1922, Peay had by 1926 become the candidate of the farms and small towns.[69]

The effect of the Peay governorship was to polarize Tennessee politics, arraying the state's major urban areas against the farms and small towns. The Peay machine was built around usually Republican East Tennessee and rural-oriented Democrats of Middle and West Tennessee. Opposed to the Governor were the local city machines in Memphis and Nashville. The administration faction proposed measures that concentrated power at the state level and in the hands of the governor, and the opposition faction worked for local control and maintaining power in the state legislature. As a result, the struggle between Peay and his opponents became two dimensional. On one level, it was a fight for control of the state, but on another, it was a battle to shape the course of reform in Tennessee. The clash between these groups would, over the next five years, shake the Volunteer State to its foundations.

69. *Fifty Years of Tennessee Primaries*, p. 131.

4

Boss

Austin Peay won an easy victory over the Republican nominee, Walter White, in the 1926 general election, but the primary had been a divisive and difficult one for the Democratic Party. Since the battle between administration and antiadministration factions promised to carry into the newly elected General Assembly, Peay decided to intervene in the organization of the House and Senate. Peay backers had a heavy majority in the House and their candidate, Seldon Maiden of Weakley County, was chosen speaker without opposition. The race for Senate speaker attracted several candidates, but the opposition faction could not settle on one man. Crump conferred with Kit McConnico and E. B. Stahlman of the Nashville machine, but the three could not agree. "The whole situation is pretty chaotic and confusing to me at this time," McConnico wrote to Crump in early December.[1] While the opposition vacillated, the Senate finally chose Henry Horton, a first-term pro-Peay member from Marshall County.

The General Assembly then proceeded to the selection of state officers. The winners were all strong Peay men except Treasurer John Nolan.[2] The governor quickly won another important victory when he succeeded in placing his candidate, Henry

---

1. K. T. McConnico to Crump, December 7, 1926; McKellar to Crump, December 24, 1926; Crump to McKellar, January 20, 1927, McKellar-Crump Correspondence, Container 2, McKellar Papers.
2. Macpherson, "Democratic Progressivism," p. 176. Nashville *Banner*, January 4, 6, 1927. Memphis *Commercial Appeal*, January 23, 1927.

Colton of Nashville, in the Middle Tennessee seat on the State Elections Commission. Ed Crump favored the incumbent A. D. Curtis of Shelbyville, who seemed assured of reelection until the Davidson County delegation switched to the local candidate Colton. Peay's shrewd choice of a nominee split the big cities and deprived Crump of an important ally in the pliable Curtis.[3]

From that point on, however, the General Assembly became a nightmare for Austin Peay. His enemies, led by the Shelby delegation, attacked his program unmercifully. Peay's main goal was a constitutional amendment to facilitate the taxing of personalty. Farm possessions, under this amendment, might be taxed at only sixty percent of their worth. Bankers bitterly fought the provision that permitted a tax on bank accounts and finally forced Peay to withdraw that section. Even with the bankers appeased, the governor still faced a formidable task. The most determined opposition to the measure, the *Commercial Appeal* observed, was "being led by the senators and representatives of the big cities." An advertisement in the Memphis papers, written by E. H. Crump and signed by the entire Shelby delegation, complained that the city's tax burden was already too large and warned, "YES, PEAY IS TRYING TO CLEAN MEMPHIS." As the issue reached its climax in mid-February, Peay suddenly fell gravely ill with pneumonia, and the legislature took a six-week recess to await his recovery.[4]

When the assembly reconvened, Peay, still weakened by his near-fatal illness, was not able to supply his customary vigorous leadership. While he secured most of his program—an extension of the tobacco tax, expansion of the Smoky Mountains park, and other items—the governor also sustained some galling defeats. In the House, thirty-six members spread a resolution on the *Journal* stating their unqualified opposition to the constitutional amendment Peay had proposed. Their action meant the needed two-thirds vote could not be won in the ninety-nine

---

3. Nashville *Banner*, January 18, 19, 1927. Memphis *Commercial Appeal*, January 18, 20, 1927.

4. Memphis *Commercial Appeal*, January 27, 30, April 13, 1927. McKellar to Crump, February 2, 1927, McKellar-Crump Correspondence, Container 2, McKellar Papers.

78 / *Tennessee in Turmoil*

member House and spelled the death of tax reform in Tennessee. The opposition to the amendment closely paralleled the opposition to Peay himself in the recent primary. Nineteen of the thirty-six House opponents came from large-urban counties, and fifteen of the thirty-six were from Middle Tennessee. In all, twenty-eight of the thirty-six came from either the large-urban counties or from Middle Tennessee. Clearly the large cities and the taut political divisions of the middle section were the main sources of anti-Peay sentiment.[5]

In the wake of Peay's worst setback, the legislature passed an appropriation bill which included a $750 bonus for its members. When Peay replied with an angry veto, the assembly quickly overrode him. The governor was further chagrined when the assembly, led by the Shelby delegation, approved a one-cent increase in the gasoline tax. Tennessee's urban counties had fought this tax since Peay first introduced it in 1923, and representatives from Davidson, Knox, and Hamilton counties voted against it once more. Since Peay opposed a further increase in the tax, Shelby's support for it was clearly calculated to embarrass the governor. This time, however, his veto was sustained.[6]

By 1927, the Tennessee Democratic Party had largely resolved itself into two discrete factions. The Sixty-fifth General Assembly reflected the rising acrimony in Tennessee politics. The administration could claim thirty-five backers and the opposition, thirty-three. As in the 1925 legislature, Peay's support was strongest in East and West Tennessee where thirty-one percent and twenty-seven percent of the members could be classified as strong supporters, as indicated by Tables 19 and 20. Rural and small-urban Tennessee, as in the previous session, continued to back the governor enthusiastically—thirty-two percent of rural members and twenty-eight percent of small-urban members voted with the governor at least seventy percent of the time.

5. Nashville *Banner*, March 31, 1927. *Tennessee House Journal*, pp. 626-27.
6. Nashville *Banner*, April 25, 1927. Memphis *Commercial Appeal*, April 11-12, 1927.

Twenty-eight of the thirty-five Peay backers came from rural and small-urban constituencies. The governor's links to East Tennessee Republican boss J. Will Taylor are reflected in voting in the General Assembly. Nine of Peay's thirty-five supporters were East Tennessee Republicans, six of them from Taylor's Second Congressional District. A seventh was from Hawkins County which adjoined Taylor's district and often opposed his rival, First District Congressman B. Carroll Reece. As it took final form, the Austin Peay-Luke Lea faction thus was composed mainly of small-town and rural legislators from Middle and West Tennessee, together with members of the Republican J. Will Taylor machine.

The opposition faction had no well-defined state leadership. Made up mostly of members from the large-urban counties and from Middle Tennessee, it included seven from the East (but only three Republicans), fifteen from the Middle, and eleven from the West. The figure for the West is somewhat misleading, however, because eight of those anti-Peay people came from Crump-controlled Shelby County. Fifteen of the thirty-four Peay opponents came from counties more than thirty percent urban and eleven more came from the combative Middle division. Thirty-nine percent of large-urban legislators and twenty-nine percent of the Middle Tennessee members opposed Peay. These two groups formed the core of the opposition, although their numbers were increased by personal enemies of the governor scattered around the state.

On October 2, 1927, Austin Peay died suddenly of a cerebral hemorrhage. In an instant, Tennessee's political configuration was thrown into turmoil. Peay had been the strongest political figure in the state, and his passing left a tremendous power vacuum. The new governor was the Speaker of the Senate, sixty-one year old Henry H. Horton of Marshall County, owner of a large farm south of Nashville. Horton had virtually no political experience; he had held a few local offices and had served a term in the Tennessee House in 1903, but had not been active on the state level until his election to the Senate in 1926. Horton identified himself as a Peay backer, and the governor had welcomed his support but had carefully kept him at arm's length. In a letter addressed to "Gov. Austin Pea" [sic], Horton had solicited his backing in the speaker's race.

> My Dear Govenor [sic]:-Since the clearing away of the clouds of the recent political baddle [sic] I find myself the Democratic nominee for State Senator. . . . I also find myself feeling that I could the better serve my District and the State at large by being Speaker of the Senate. I hope that you will be open minded at least, to my candidacy, and that you will with hold any desission [sic] that you may make as to my fitness for the job until I can see you and have a talk with you. I have always supported you and have been in hearty sympathy with your administration of the affairs of the State. And should I be selected as Speaker of the Senate I confidently believe that you and I could work together for the good of the people of the greatest State in the Union.[7]

Peay's reply, while cordial and gracious, stopped far short of a Horton endorsement: "I had known of your nomination and for several days have been straining for an opportunity to write you and many others. . . . You are so well qualified to be a Senator and will render such splendid service that I am most delighted that the State will have the benefit of your membership. Come in to see me at your first opportunity and let me have a talk with you."[8] When a constituent wrote to ask Peay's choice for speaker, the governor said he hoped for "some strong administration man," but Horton's was only one of five names he suggested. Horton also tried to "inlist [sic]" Luke Lea in his campaign, but the colonel too was noncommittal. After Horton's election as speaker, there were persistent but unconfirmed

---

7. Horton to Peay, August 18, 1926, Container 74, File 5, Peay Official Papers.
8. Peay to Horton, August 20, 1926, Container 74, File 5, Peay Official Papers.

reports that Peay had extracted a promise from the new speaker to resign if the governor's office fell vacant.[9]

Horton simply lacked the strength to fill the void created by Peay's death. He had no political base and little talent for administration. As Joe Hatcher observed, "He wasn't a politician at all. . . . He wasn't cut out for governor and the rough and tumble of politics." Chosen speaker as a compromise candidate, his success as governor would depend on the assistance he could muster from more powerful people.[10]

The man Horton came to rely on most was Luke Lea. Lea's friendship with Austin Peay had given him access to the highest councils of government, and he held a thick batch of political IOUs. Already a wealthy man through inheritance and business dealings, Lea was in the process of acquiring the Memphis *Commercial Appeal* and the Knoxville *Journal*. These two papers, combined with his Nashville *Tennessean*, gave him a firm grip on the state's most important communications medium. Lea's banker in these and other transactions was Nashville businessman Rogers Caldwell. Caldwell and Company was an early-day conglomerate, operating everything from banks to baseball teams. In the 1920s it was the most powerful private financial institution in the South, with interests and investments extending from Texas to Georgia. Lea's political sagacity and Caldwell's money made the pair a formidable force in Tennessee, and Horton soon fell under their influence.

Very quickly rumors began to circulate that Lea and Caldwell were using their influence with Governor Horton for personal gain. Added to the old charges that state departments were being managed in the interest of the incumbent administration were new allegations that state officials were throwing contracts to Caldwell and Company enterprises. The most frequent charge was that Highway Commissioner C. Neil Bass was being pressured to specify the use of rock asphalt exclusively in certain

---

9. Peay to John R. Snow, December 13, 1926, Container 74, File 5, Peay Official Papers. Horton to Lea, August 19, 1926, Lea to Horton, August 20, 1926, Lea Papers.

10. Joe Hatcher interview, February 18, 1976.

state road building projects regardless of lower bids from the producers of other kinds of surfacing materials. Kentucky Rock Asphalt Company, a Caldwell and Company subsidiary and the makers of a rock asphalt called Kyrock, stood to profit by such a directive because the proximity of its quarries to Tennessee would enable it to underbid its rock asphalt competitors.[11]

Kentucky Rock Asphalt representatives had lobbied state officials since the beginning of Tennessee's road building campaign, but Austin Peay was wary in dealing with them. For example, in April 1924, company representative Horace Carr wrote to Governor Peay asking him to look into a "misunderstanding" between the Highway Department and Kentucky Rock Asphalt. Peay refused to involve himself in the dispute and instead referred the matter to a federal expert for arbitration. After Peay's death, the company increased its pressure on the government and convinced Horton to specify rock asphalt. However, Commissioner Bass refused, possibly because the material had occasionally proven unsatisfactory.[12]

Horton hoped to win Bass over because the commissioner, as a Peay appointee, was a visible link between the governor and his popular predecessor. Horton approached his old friend Doctor D. R. Neil, Bass' father-in-law, and suggested Neil discuss with the commissioner the notion of directing the department in ways more compatible with Horton's political needs. Doctor Neil indignantly refused the request. The governor then proposed to split the duties of the highway commissioner, making Bass chief engineer and appointing a new administrator to act as commissioner. When Bass refused the deal, Horton replied, "I do not feel that public interest can best be served by your continuation as Commissioner. I am, therefore, . . . asking your resignation."[13] Bass stiffly complied two days later in a private letter, reminding Horton that Peay had

11. Nashville *Banner*, July 11, 1928.
12. Horace Carr to Peay, April 22, 1924, July 23, July 29, 1924, Container 13, File 7, Carr to Peay, April 12, 1926, Container 22, File 5, Peay Official Papers.
13. *Second Report of the Special Legislative Investigating Committee of the 67th General Assembly, State of Tennessee*, pp. 19-20. Horton to Bass, February 13, 1928, Container 47, File 8, Henry Horton Official Papers, Tennessee State Library and Archives, Nashville, Tennessee.

suggested combining the two jobs. As chief engineer, Bass bluntly observed, "I could not proscribe and enforce a rule that our employees should take no part in politics. I would not have the power to select the road materials to be used by the Department."[14] Significantly, when reporters asked Bass if he had had a disagreement with Horton, the ousted commissioner replied, "No, not with the governor." Pressed as to whom he might have quarreled with, Bass answered, "I would rather not say."[15]

The quarrel was probably with Luke Lea. The colonel had long felt that state departments could be useful in building power, but Austin Peay had always been reluctant to use his departments in that fashion. Horton, however, was more receptive. In a letter to the new governor, Lea explained

> The greatest obstacle that you had to overcome was lack of loyalty in several of your departments, noticeably in the Engineering Department. . . .
>
> I am not asking anything for myself, but I am asking on behalf of all of your loyal friends that disloyalty be punished and loyalty rewarded. May I not at your earliest convenience discuss with you men who were continuously and openly opposed to you and who were filling high positions in your administration.

Bass had refused to cooperate and Lea recommended his dismissal. The new commissioner was Colonel Harry S. Berry, a long-time friend of Lea and wartime comrade-in-arms. Lea informed Berry that Horton's chances for victory in 1928 were negligible unless the Highway Department became more helpful. Shortly thereafter, rock asphalt was specified for certain Tennessee road projects.[16]

Lea's motive in this maneuvering was probably political. He

---

14. Bass to Horton, February 15, 1928, Container 47, File 8, Horton Official Papers.
15. Knoxville *News-Sentinel*, February 15, 1928.
16. *Second Report*, pp. 19-24. John McFerrin, *Caldwell and Company: A Southern Financial Empire* (Nashville, 1969), 103-04. Lea to Horton, no date, 1928, Lea Papers.

seems to have had no personal connection to Kentucky Rock Asphalt or any other rock asphalt company. Kentucky Rock Asphalt was a Caldwell and Company holding, but Rogers Caldwell's empire was vast, and his rock asphalt interests were only a small part of it. A close friend of both Lea and Caldwell has remarked, "They weren't getting rich out of the state. That was small potatoes." Caldwell certainly stood to profit from the use of Kyrock, but the political benefits to Lea, especially in terms of campaign contributions, would be substantially greater.[17]

In building his power, Lea also hoped to capitalize on the new fluidity Peay's death introduced to Tennessee politics. The perceptive George Fort Milton of the Chattanooga *News* advised Horton:

> It has been suggested to you, I know, that it is desirable for you to inherit the enmities as well as the friendships of the Peay administration. I am not at all sure this is true . . . as there were some enmities toward Peay which were toward Peay personally, and not toward the policies he sought to maintain. If any of these are willing to support the Peay policies with you as their executive, it seems to me that you could quite readily accept this support, and that it might be beneficial to the state in reducing to small proportions a factionalism which undoubtedly is not for Tennessee's good.

In closing, Milton added a word of caution for the new chief executive:

> Austin Peay at times sharply checked the ambitions and desires of some of his friends. He was the governor not of one man, but of the people of the state. No more dangerous report could be spread about any governor than that he listened to the advice of only one man or

---

17. Joe Hatcher interview, February 18, 1976.

clique. From my conversation with you, I have complete assurance that no such report can truthfully be spread about our new governor.[18]

Even as Milton was suggesting a new flexibility in state politics, Luke Lea and E. H. Crump were making overtures to each other. In late 1926, Memphis *Commercial Appeal* editor C. P. J. Mooney died, and Lea, in association with Rogers Caldwell, began to negotiate for the purchase of the *Commercial Appeal*. The deal was closed in May 1927. Through the paper, Lea now acquired new influence in Shelby County. As a measure of this, in August, Watkins Overton, Crump's candidate for Mayor of Memphis, solicited Lea's endorsement. Lea's reply was very favorable although stopping short of actual endorsement. With the main issue "boss rule," meaning Crump, the *Commercial Appeal* was conspicuously silent as Overton and the Crump machine retook the city of Memphis. In March 1928, Crump wrote to McKellar that "Lea is extremely anxious for Governor Horton to get Shelby's vote. It has been suggested that he put up a bond for the permanence of his recent conversion to Shelby." That summer, with the gubernatorial primary only a month away, Lea and Caldwell obtained controlling interest in the Manhattan Savings Bank and Trust Company. The Memphis *Press-Scimitar*, a pro-Crump paper, welcomed the pair to the Memphis business community and expressed hope that the new bank would prove "a splendid investment."[19]

Rumors of a major political deal grew in early summer, 1928. Hill McAlister again entered the primary as the candidate of the antiadministration faction, and Lewis Pope represented those former Peay supporters who opposed Lea and Horton. But with

---

18. George F. Milton to Horton, October 6, 1927, Container 50, File 3, Horton Official Papers.

19. Baker, *Commercial Appeal*, p. 278. Robert Talley, *One Hundred Years of the Commercial Appeal: The Story of the Greatest Romance in American Journalism, 1840-1940* (Memphis, 1940), 67, 278. Overton to Lea, August 23, 1927, Lea to Overton, August 26, 1927, Lea Papers. Crump to McKellar, March 6, 1928, Container 2, McKellar-Crump Correspondence, McKellar Papers. Memphis *Press-Scimitar*, July 7, 1928.

the primary just weeks away, the gubernatorial race remained in a state of suspended animation. On July 6, the *Press-Scimitar* reported a clandestine meeting between "a Memphis political leader and a prominent publisher." Exactly what Lea and Crump offered each other is uncertain. Crump later admitted that Lea had suggested a package of business and political connections, but the Memphis boss said he "declined."[20]

Each of the bosses was a threat to the other. Austin Peay had won the 1926 primary because with his large support in other parts of the state he was able to negate the big Shelby vote, but Henry Horton, Lea's candidate in 1928, seemed unlikely to pile up Peay's majority outside of Shelby. In a bid to expand his influence, Lea was sponsoring veteran Congressman Finis T. Garrett against Crump's man Kenneth McKellar in the Senate race. Lea apparently offered Crump a free hand in the Senate race if he would stay out of the gubernatorial primary. Crump, realizing it would be difficult to unseat Horton and fearing Garrett's appeal, was clearly interested in the bargain. The idea of dividing Tennessee into machine districts may also have been on the agenda. Abruptly, however, on July 20, Mayor Overton, speaking for the Crump machine, endorsed Hill McAlister for governor. Why the Lea-Crump bargain failed to materialize has remained obscure, but the effect of its failure was clear—the Lea and Crump factions were immediately thrown into a brutal primary struggle.[21]

The 1928 gubernatorial primary campaign revolved around control of the power center which Austin Peay had created. Crump, Stahlman, and Hill McAlister, the opposition nominee, concentrated their fire on Lea and Caldwell and their alleged manipulation of Governor Horton. The Nashville *Banner*, no friend of the late governor, conceded that at least Peay had been his own man, whereas Lea was dominating Horton to secure "political control of the state." The *Banner* featured a fictional series of letters written between Governor-in-Name Henry Horton and Governor-in-Fact Luke Lea, and printed daily

20. Memphis *Press-Scimitar*, July 6, 26, 1928.
21. *Ibid.*, July 21, 1928.

"More Truth than Poetry," The Nashville *Banner*, July 30, 1928. Reproduced here by permission of the publisher.

88 / *Tennessee in Turmoil*

cartoons depicting Caldwell as Kid Kyrock and the "Governor-in-Fact" as "Musso-LEA-ni." The main issue, Hill McAlister told a Kingsport audience, was whether "unseen forces" should continue in power. In a scathing two-hour attack McAlister charged that "Senator Lea is the real governor of Tennessee! It is he who aspires to retain his control over Tennessee's Chief Executive. . . ."[22]

The opposition press around the state echoed similar themes. Horton, the Knoxville *News-Sentinel* said, was a "mere puppet," and the Memphis *Press-Scimitar* wrote him off as the "maniken [sic] of Luke Lea and Rogers Caldwell." The Carthage *Courier* editorialized against the "invisible administration" which was running the state to further its selfish interests. Openly contemptuous of the incumbent, the *Courier* said

> Governor Horton could no more accomplish these ends [Governor Peay's] than a ribbon clerk could watch a blacksmith shoe the left hind foot of a mule and then shoe the right foot.[23]

Horton's handling of the state highway department was the focus of these attacks on the "invisible government." In the midst of a swirl of innuendo about favoritism and misconduct, Neil Bass issued a public statement explaining his dismissal as highway commissioner. A month before Austin Peay's death, Bass remembered, Lea and Caldwell met with the commissioner and asked him to specify rock asphalt as the only surfacing material contractors could bid on for completing a forty-mile stretch of highway from Huntingdon to Jackson. Bass firmly refused. In January 1928, Herbert Carr, president of Kentucky Rock Asphalt, renewed the request, and Bass again refused. Within two weeks, the new governor had asked for his resignation. In a separate statement, Doctor D. R. Neil, Bass's father-

---

22. McFerrin, *Caldwell and Company*, p. 105. Nashville *Banner*, July 1, 8, 9, 1928. Kingsport *Times*, July 11, 1928. Chattanooga *Times*, July 31, 1928.
23. Knoxville *News-Sentinel*, July 17, 1928. Memphis *Press-Scimitar*, July 17, 1928. Carthage *Courier*, July 19, 26, 1928.

in-law, confirmed that Horton had asked him to speak to Bass about more closely coordinating highway department projects with Horton's political needs. His dismissal, Bass asserted, was due to his refusal to specify rock asphalt.[24]

Neil Bass had detonated a bomb and the self-assured Lea was plainly shaken. In a rare public statement Lea denied any financial interest in rock asphalt companies. He admitted attending a meeting with Bass and Caldwell but insisted that Bass called the session and simply told Caldwell of new specifications for rock asphalt and of the department's decision to use more of it. Never, the colonel stated, had he asked anyone to specify rock asphalt or to fire Neil Bass. Caldwell gave his first newspaper interview the day after Bass's statement. He denied any improper conduct and said he never discussed rock asphalt with "anyone now connected with the Highway Department." He added that Hill McAlister and Lewis Pope had both sought his support. Governor Horton, for his part, said he wanted only to transfer Bass, not to fire him. The Lea newspapers began a campaign to discredit Bass; just three days after his statement both the Knoxville *Journal* and Memphis *Commercial Appeal* published identical items reporting a deal between Bass and McAlister to make Bass highway commissioner if the latter won election as governor.[25]

The Lea-Caldwell-Horton defense had some interesting holes. As the Nashville *Banner* pointed out, Caldwell denied discussing rock asphalt with "Governor Horton, Commissioner Berry, or Chief Engineer McEwen, or anyone else *now* connected with the Highway department [*Banner's* italics]." More significantly, neither Lea nor Caldwell referred to Bass's encounter with Herbert Carr in January 1928. The statements of the three men were carefully worded denials which stopped short of a sweeping refutation of the charges against them. An East Tennessee supporter warned Lea, "The two things that hurt

---

24. Knoxville *News-Sentinel*, July 21-22, 1928. Nashville *Banner*, July 21, 1928. Chattanooga *News*, July 23, 1928.

25. Nashville *Tennessean*, July 22, 23, 1928. Chattanooga *Times*, July 23, 1928. Knoxville *Journal*, July 24, 1928. Memphis *Commercial Appeal*, July 24, 1928.

Horton over this way more than any other, are the dismissal of Bass and the rock asphalt argument. I think more attention should be paid to some of these charges that are hurled at Horton—too many charges of a serious nature seem to go unanswered." By late July, the Horton candidacy was staggering from two hard blows delivered just days apart—the opposition of Crump and the Bass disclosures.[26]

With the race tight, Shelby County once again became the center of attention. For the third time in six years Crump and Clarence Saunders, who backed Horton, were engaged in a flamboyant struggle for local control. Past masters of the art of generating publicity for themselves and their candidates, Crump and Saunders conducted an extravagant shouting match in the pages of the city's newspapers. In a series of full-page ads, Saunders attacked Crump's personal integrity, accusing Crump of using his influence to secure contracts for his insurance company, Trezevant and Crump, and then collecting large fees for them. Another Saunders advertisement headlined "SHAME! SHAME! SHAME! Crump the Oath Violator has no shame," said Crump personally engaged in election fraud. When the Memphis *Press-Scimitar* endorsed McAlister, Saunders branded the editorial "A COWARDLY SURRENDER!" and added that "this publication is ever ready with the assassin's knife to strike when it suits its purposes."[27]

Crump was no more restrained in his replies. "Asking "Who Is This Fresh Upstart?" Crump denounced the "Kyrock twins," and continued, "This is not the first time that some little squirt has sought to make me the issue." Alluding to Saunders' Piggly Wiggly troubles, Crump declared, "When Henry Ford declares automobiles dangerous, John Barleycorn denounces whiskey, Gilda Grey opposes dancing, and the leopard changes his spots, The Upstart may talk of HONESTY." He accused Saunders of giving money to the Republican Party and characterized him as a

26. Nashville *Banner*, July 23, 1928. Mitchell Long to Lea, no date, Lea Papers.
27. Memphis *Commercial Appeal*, July 31, 1928. Chattanooga *News*, July 26, 1928.

smart-aleck, cheat, fraud, and embezzler. In summary, he concluded, Saunder's campaign consisted of "all the slime and filth that could emanate from a totally depraved mind."[28]

At times the campaign in Shelby approached the level of farce. Crump organized a McAlister rally in Covington and gave Shelby officeholders the day off to attend. As McAlister began his remarks an airplane flew over dropping leaflets reading "HORTON IS THE MAN SAYS CLARENCE SAUNDERS." Crump howled with outrage and Saunders responded in an advertisement: "MR. CRUMP GETS MAD! and the buzz of a little airplane did it." Saunders teased: "Now I say a man's got to be red-headed if he will get mad at a harmless little airplane sporting in the air." The plane "made Mr. Ed Crump red-headed mad," said Saunders, but *"Nothing herein is to be construed as a reflection on red hair as I like red hair and wish mine was red."*[29]

Saunders also exploited the race issue in the Shelby County campaign. In an advertisement headed "YOUR BACKBONE! *Let it be good and strong,"* Saunders charged that if McAlister won "there will go out to the world the story of a beaten and subdued white race." In another layout labeled "BOB CHURCH-CRUMP! That's the vote getting gang," he said, "The stench of such a combine of politicians and negroes is enough to stop every decent man's nose in Tennessee from taking a single breath." Calling Crump a "traitor to his race," Saunders said a victory for Crump and Church would spark race warfare in the streets of Memphis.[30]

Crump's well-known reliance on black votes in Memphis also prompted Lea, through his newspaper chain, to try to turn the race issue against Crump and his candidate McAlister. Lea particularly played on fears of "negro domination" and the use

---

28. Chattanooga *News,* July 30, 31, 1928. Memphis *Commercial Appeal,* August 1, 1928.
29. Chattanooga *News,* July 23, 1928. McFerrin, *Caldwell and Company,* p. 106.
30. Memphis *Commercial Appeal,* August 1, 2, 1928. Chattanooga *News,* July 27, 1928.

of Memphis black votes to override the "white majority" outside Shelby. The *Commercial Appeal* insisted that

> The practice of voting negroes in white primaries in Memphis and Shelby County is an outrage. It is unfair to the white Democratic men and women in the other 94 counties in Tennessee.
>
> The Democratic nominee for governor of Tennessee ought to be the choice of white Democrats. . . .
>
> It will be unfortunate for Tennessee if at anytime the negroes of Memphis and Shelby County should hold the balance of power in the Democratic party.[31]

In Knoxville, the *Journal* talked of those who sought to "establish in Tennessee the negro as the political balance of power." On July 31, reporting that white Democrats were deserting McAlister in great numbers, the *Journal* asked rhetorically whether "any democratic voter can now vote for McAlister, knowing that to do so is leaving the decision in the hands of this illegal group of colored voters." The *Tennessean* echoed this message. "Will the honest voters of 93 counties permit the white Democratic party to be made black and tan by the city machines of Shelby and Davidson?" asked a *Tennessean* editorial. "The Democratic party, which restored the white man's rule in Tennessee, must and shall be preserved as the white man's party." "A vote for Horton," the paper explained, "is a vote for white supremacy. A vote for McAlister is a vote to give the negro the balance of power in Tennessee with all its attendant horrors." The issue, said the *Tennessean* was, "THE PERPETUATION OF THE WHITE MAN'S SCHOOL AND THE PROTECTION OF THE WHITE WOMAN."[32]

While the battle raged in the state's newspapers, the candidates themselves worked the hustings. Horton conducted a bland campaign stressing his fealty to the Peay program and his

---

31. Memphis *Commercial Appeal*, August 2, 1928.
32. Knoxville *Journal*, July 31, August 1, 1928. Nashville *Tennessean*, July 28, August 2, 1928.

concern for home and church. His slogan was "Let Horton Finish the Job," and his friend William Brock, a Chattanooga candy manufacturer, quoted Peay as having said, "I don't believe I'll live through my third term. But it is a great comfort to me to know that my mantle will fall upon the shoulders of my friend Henry Horton. I know that he will carry out my program." Speaking in Knoxville, Horton came out solidly "for the home, for the church, and for the immediate development of East Tennessee." He frequently referred to himself as a "dirt farmer," piously intoning that the "invisible government" behind him was the "spirit of eternal truth."[33]

In both substance and tactics, the Horton effort was a repeat of Peay's 1926 campaign. His platform, as put forth by the *Tennessean*, called for the end of the state land tax, the continuance of the excise and tobacco taxes, the development of roads and water resources, and the continued improvement of the state school system. A mysterious Land Tax Repeal League appeared which conducted an extensive campaign for Horton in the small weeklies. The *Banner* accused the LTRL of bribing the weekly papers to support Horton but the editors hotly denied this, explaining the advertisements were "routine business." The LTRL, one of them retorted, had a "worthwhile message for the readers of country newspapers," while McAlister had "nothing whatever that he can tell the people through the weekly newspapers that will get him votes."[34]

Horton's "Me and Peay" message was undermined in late July when the governor began to attack Neil Bass, alleging waste and extravagance during his tenure as highway commissioner. While campaigning in Clarksville, Horton received a hand-delivered letter from Mrs. Austin Peay expressing her resentment at Horton's charges against Bass. She publicly declared her support for Lewis Pope, her husband's commissioner of institutions, and scoffed at Horton's assertion that he was Peay's

---

33. Knoxville *Journal*, July 21, 1928. Bolivar *Bulletin*, July 27, 1928. Nashville *Banner*, July 19, 1928.

34. Nashville *Tennessean*, August 2, 1928. Manchester *Times*, July 19, 1928. Maryville *Enterprise*, July 25, 1928. Camden *Chronicle*, July 13, 1928.

chosen successor. The embarrassed governor promptly tempered his remarks.[35]

Hill McAlister, recognizing the widespread acceptance of Peay's reforms, modified his position from the one he held in 1926, hoping thereby to win support from ex-Peay voters who were disenchanted with Horton. The Chattanooga *News* remarked that McAlister had virtually adopted the program he opposed in 1926, while the Knoxville *News-Sentinel* wrote, "Regardless of what he may have stood for two years ago, Hill McAlister today represents a truly progressive movement in the state." McAlister mainly directed his attacks on the "invisible government." He wrote off the Lea papers as house organs and demanded to know how Horton planned to make up the $3,000,000 in revenue the state would lose by repealing the land tax. As a measure of how far he had come since his 1926 campaign, McAlister said he feared that the lost income would close the University of Tennessee and shorten county school terms.[36]

The unknown quantity in the 1928 primary was Lewis Pope. Pope commanded wide respect in Tennessee, having served as commissioner of institutions under four governors over a ten-year period. A man of rock-ribbed integrity, he lasted only three weeks under Horton. Luke Lea, he said, demanded his dismissal because he refused to permit his department to play politics. Peay was known to have held Pope in high regard, and some said the late governor had extracted a promise from Horton not to oppose Pope in 1928 if Horton should succeed Peay. Whatever the specifics of the arrangement, Peay probably did favor Pope as his successor. Pope argued more effectively than McAlister did that Horton was not Peay's legitimate heir but rather a pawn of Luke Lea. He ridiculed Horton's proposal to abolish the land tax and accused him of firing the most capable people in the government because they refused to take orders from Luke Lea. His own successor as commissioner of institu-

35. Knoxville *News-Sentinel*, July 28, 1928. Nashville *Banner*, July 31, 1928.
36. Chattanooga *News*, July 21, 1928. Chattanooga *Times*, July 20, 1928. Knoxville *News-Sentinel*, July 11, 31, 1928.

tions, Pope said, was a man Horton had never met. Pope hardly mentioned McAlister, concentrating his fire on the state machine.[37]

Pope's effort elicited mixed responses around the state. The Clarksville *Leaf Chronicle*, Knoxville *News-Sentinel*, Memphis *Press-Scimitar*, and Chattanooga *News* all expressed a preference for him but, concluding that he had no chance, endorsed Horton or McAlister. His appeal was strong among the Peay stalwarts disenchanted with Horton and Lea, but since he lacked organizational backing, his prospects seemed minuscule. In a close election, however, it seemed that he might hold the balance of power.[38]

Tennessee businessmen were divided in their sentiments on the primary. Some—such as Joe Fly, the president of the Mr. Bowers stores in Memphis—preferred McAlister, believing that Horton's election would mean higher taxes on such luxury items as gasoline, cigarettes, and movie tickets. Others, like John Edgerton of the Tennessee Manufacturers Association, were attracted to Horton because of his opposition to labor legislation.[39] Labor, for its part, had largely healed its divisions of 1926. Horton had made himself anathema by his stand against legislation favoring railroad workers, and Pope, reluctant to reduce the state's use of convict labor, was equally unpopular. The Tennessee Federation of Labor probably spoke for most union members in endorsing McAlister, so that, unlike 1926, McAlister could now count on the solid support of organized labor.[40]

By the end of July, it was obvious that Horton was in serious trouble. Pope threatened to pull needed votes from the Peay coalition, the Crump deal had fallen through, and the letter from Mrs. Peay had seriously compromised him. Confronted with a

---

37. Knoxville *News-Sentinel*, July 14, 31, 1928. Chattanooga *News*, July 13, 1928. Chattanooga *Times*, July 13, 1928.
38. Clarksville *Leaf-Chronicle*, July 19, 1928. Chattanooga *News*, July 31, 1928. Knoxville *News-Sentinel*, July 17, 1928. Memphis *Press-Scimitar*, July 30, 1928.
39. Memphis *Press-Scimitar*, July 24, 1928. Knoxville *News-Sentinel*, July 11, 1928.
40. Chattanooga *Times*, July 9, 1928. Knoxville *Journal*, July 7, 1928.

nearly desperate situation, Lea and Caldwell began to pressure their business subsidiaries for more campaign contributions. Exactly how much was raised and where it was spent is, of course, not recorded, but three Caldwell and Company cement firms are known to have given $65,000 and the parent company itself advanced $27,500 in notes. Contributions from other Caldwell enterprises, such as Kentucky Rock Asphalt and the newspaper chain, were probably of similar magnitude.[41]

Primary day, 1928, was a violent, chaotic affair, climaxing one of the state's bitterest campaigns. The anti-Crump press was indignant about the conduct of the election in Shelby County. The headline of the Chattanooga *News* screamed "Crump Hoodlums Create Reign of Terror at Polls." Horton poll watchers and *Commercial Appeal* reporters were jailed and beaten as "police, bootleggers, sheriff's deputies and ex-convicts seized the election machinery in the boldest steal the Crump boys ever attempted." The assistant attorney general for Shelby County, Will Gerber, assaulted a reporter; and Jim Mulcahy, a Memphis racketeer under federal indictment for bootlegging, stalked the precincts of the eleventh ward personally disposing of troublesome "snoopers." The Chattanooga *News* branded the day's activities "the most enormous act of political brigandage the state has known for many years." The *Press-Scimitar*, pro-Crump, carried no stories of intimidation at the polls, but conceded there should be an investigation, preferably independent of the police department.[42]

In the Horton camp, Luke Lea was seeking the votes to offset the Crump machine. After Shelby reported its vote and closed early in the evening, Lea began telephoning Horton backers across the state, telling them how many votes the governor needed from their area. One of Lea's assistants later remembered, "I don't know the mechanics of how they got them but they got them. . . . We just stayed up later than they did."[43]

---

41. McFerrin, *Caldwell and Company*, p. 107.
42. Chattanooga *News*, August 3, 1928. Memphis *Press-Scimitar*, August 2, 3, 1928. Memphis *Commercial Appeal*, August 3, 1928. Nashville *Tennessean*, August 3, 1928.
43. Joe Hatcher interview, February 18, 1976.

The winners in the primary were Kenneth McKellar and Henry Horton. McKellar defeated Congressman Garrett by two to one to win renomination to the Senate while Horton managed to hold together the Austin Peay coalition. East Tennessee gave Horton fifty percent of its votes, and he received over fifty percent in the rural and small-urban counties (See Tables 21 and 22.). The Middle Tennessee results, as usual, were close, although Horton had a slight edge. Lewis Pope drew nearly twenty-seven thousand votes, most of them apparently from the old Peay alliance. Of the eleven counties in which Pope won at least thirty percent of the vote, most of them surrounding his home county of Bledsoe, Peay in 1926 carried eight with over sixty percent of the vote. In addition, 20,004 of Pope's 26,849 votes came from rural and small-urban counties. The Pope candidacy was plainly a serious threat to the Peay coalition that Horton was struggling to maintain. McAlister, for his part, again drew his strength from Tennessee's large-urban counties, totaling 47,998 of his 92,047 votes. His strength there, plus his votes in hotly contested Middle Tennessee, made the 1928 primary one of the closest in Tennessee history.

Comparison of the election of 1928 with the Peay-McAlister returns of 1926 highlights some significant trends in Tennessee voting patterns. Tables 18 and 22 indicate that Horton was following in Peay's electoral footsteps. In 1928, Horton and Pope together polled sixty-four percent in the East as compared to Peay's sixty-eight percent in 1926. The Lea faction was obviously still strong in the mountains, but Peay's death had weakened its grip in that section. In Middle Tennessee, the Horton-Pope percentage was sixty-two percent against Austin Peay's fifty percent. This change, however, is due largely to the fact that Pope, a Middle Tennessean, was in the race and pulling additional votes in his native Bledsoe and adjacent counties. In West Tennessee, Horton and Pope ran four percentage points better than Peay due to the machine's growing strength west of the Tennessee River. The results in rural and small-urban areas reflect the rising power of the administration faction among these voters also. Horton and Pope outpolled Peay seventy percent to sixty percent in rural areas and sixty-seven to fifty-five percent in small-urban areas. Pope's own rural background doubtless helped to raise these percentages over the 1926 totals.

McAlister's strength too continued the trends that emerged in 1926. Confronted with two opponents in 1928, his percentage declined slightly in West Tennessee (although his raw vote totals increased in that division) and more markedly in Middle Tennessee under the impact of the Pope candidacy. He lost ground heavily in rural and small-urban areas, but most importantly, his percentage of the large-urban vote stabilized. This is explained by the tremendous increase in the Shelby County vote since 1926. In that year, Shelby cast 19,303 votes, 15,646 of them for McAlister. In 1928, however, Shelby cast 28,072 (an increase of 8,769), of which McAlister won 24,069 votes. Such a top-heavy vote for McAlister in this large county explains why McAlister outpolled Horton and Pope in West Tennessee, although the rest of that division supported them. In summary then, the strength of the state machine seemed anchored where Austin Peay had left it, in East and West Tennessee and in the farms and small towns. McAlister's strength was increasingly based in large-urban areas. As these areas were casting an ever increasing percentage of the state's Democratic vote, however, their candidate posed a continued threat to the dominance of the rural state machine.[44]

Democratic candidates on the state level encountered little opposition in the fall election. Horton met a nominal challenge from Raleigh Hopkins and Senator McKellar faced James Fowler, but neither Republican had a chance. The Presidential race between Herbert Hoover and Al Smith was much closer. Tennessee had gone for Harding in 1920, and the state seemed likely to go Republican again in 1928. Smith, a Catholic, a product of Tammany Hall, and an opponent of prohibition, was generally unpopular in Tennessee. Nevertheless, the Democratic factions reluctantly united behind the candidate. Smith was endorsed by every state official, both senators, the entire

---

44. *Fifty Years of Tennessee Primaries*, pp. 126-27.

congressional delegation, and most of the major newspapers. Lea and Crump also backed Smith.[45]

The Smith supporters fell back on the Lost Cause and racism in an attempt to maintain party loyalty. The Chattanooga *Times* editorialized, "The 'old Confederate soldiers' . . . are rallying to the standard of Gov. Smith with rare unanimity and characteristic fidelity to principles for which they fought." Luke Lea's Memphis *Commercial Appeal* reported that a poll taken at the Jefferson Davis Soldiers Home in Beauvoir, Mississippi, showed a heavy majority for Smith. The *Sumner County News* reminded its readers that five Confederate generals, the defense attorney for Jefferson Davis, and Daniel Decateur Emmett, the composer of "Dixie," had all been Catholics. The campaign climaxed in a full page advertisement, signed by ten Confederate veterans, run across the state the week before the election. Under the headline "Lest You Forget," the copy recounted the alleged horrors of Reconstruction and concluded: "This is perhaps the last national election for most of us. . . . God forbid that in our final years we shall see even one state in our sacred south land unfaithful to its trust. Stand by Democracy. Vote for Alfred E. Smith. To You From Failing Hands We Throw the Torch."[46]

Some Smith backers tried to offset religious prejudice with racial prejudice. Senator McKellar asked if Hoover believed in the "intermingling of the white and colored races in terms of equality." The *Commercial Appeal* said Southerners should be informed if Hoover "proposes to create new social relations in defiance of traditions over the objection of both white and colored." Hoover, the paper charged, favored antilynch laws and would permit blacks, namely Robert Church, to continue to influence patronage in Tennessee.[47]

Despite these efforts, Tennessee went heavily for Hoover in the November voting. The voting returns indicate that neither of

45. Chattanooga *Times*, October 1, 1928. Nashville *Banner*, November 1, 1928. Miller, *Mr. Crump*, pp. 144-47.
46. Chattanooga *News*, November 3, 1928. Chattanooga *Times*, October 7, 1928. Gallatin, *Sumner County News*, October 25, 1928. Memphis *Commercial Appeal*, October 29, 1928.
47. Memphis *Commercial Appeal*, October 4, 15, 1928.

100 / *Tennessee in Turmoil*

the two factions really exerted themselves for Smith. He received a smaller percentage of votes than had John Davis, the 1924 nominee, in all three grand divisions and in both urban and rural areas. He lost Davidson County despite the support of both Luke Lea and E. B. Stahlman. Smith won in Shelby County by some 6,000 votes, but Horton and McKellar carried it by over 16,000. The two also carried Davidson County by comfortable margins. In short, the two factions, whatever their public positions, did not make a strong effort to deliver Tennessee for Smith.[48]

Factional strife stirred again, however, when the state legislature convened in January 1929. "We will whip them before it is over," Crump wrote to McKellar, "for there will be no cessation of hostilities for seventy-five long days."[49] Charlie Love of Springfield, Horton's campaign manager, easily won election as House Speaker, but the two factions deadlocked in the struggle to elect a Speaker of the Senate. Crump and Stahlman supported James Bean of Moore County, while the administration picked William Abernathy of McNairy County.

The third candidate was Sam Bratton of Obion County, a close friend of the late Austin Peay but an avowed enemy of Luke Lea. In early December Bratton had written McKellar offering to back the Senator's choice for West Tennessee elections commissioner and offering general support: "On any matters pertaining to your interest that comes [sic] before the next State Senate, advise me thoroughly and I assure you it will be treated strictly confidential." McKellar relayed Bratton's letter to Crump, who suggested that McKellar "preferably over the telephone" indicate to Bratton that "Shelby would much prefer voting for him rather than some man that Luke Lea would put up." When the legislature did indeed deadlock, Crump threw the speakership to Bratton. Bratton's first move was to combine with the Shelby delegation to defeat Luke Lea's choice for secretary of state. Lea won one important victory, however, when the Democratic

---

48. *Fifty Years of Tennessee Elections*, pp. 97-98.
49. Crump to McKellar, January 7, 1929, McKellar-Crump Correspondence, Container 2, McKellar Papers.

caucus chose Grover Keaton for the West Tennessee seat on the State Board of Elections Commission, giving the administration a majority at last on that crucial body. Bratton, as he had promised, backed the Crump candidate, Thomas Hughes of Jackson.[50]

Keaton's victory was the administration's single bright spot in an excruciating session. Virtually every Horton proposal was solidly rejected by the General Assembly. One of the sharpest fights came on an administration measure to create a state water power commission to oversee development of Tennessee's water resources. The new commission would be separate from the already existing Railroad and Public Utilities Commission, and opponents were quick to charge that the bill was merely a scheme to give privately owned utilities companies control of the state's water power potential. Horton could not control the existing public utilities commission, they explained, so by creating a separate board, appointed by himself, he hoped to place this valuable natural resource in his own hands. Horton's opponents were buttressed by the fact that Representative Jake Levine, the bill's leading sponsor, was an attorney for the Tennessee Electric Power Company, which was trying to secure eleven dam sites in East Tennessee. The close link between Luke Lea and Thomas Greer of the Southern Utilities Corporation also fueled suspicions, and prompted Senator Bean to accuse Lea of conspiring with Greer's patron, Samuel Insull, to rob Tennessee of its water power.[51]

Facing certain defeat on its water power program, the administration looked for aid to J. Will Taylor and the Republicans. Lea had cultivated Taylor for years through occasional campaign contributions. "As I have written you heretofore" he reminded Taylor in 1928, "you may feel free to advertise in the [Knoxville] *Journal* and when the statement is sent you, please send it to

---

50. Sam Bratton to McKellar, December 8, 1928; Crump to McKellar, December 18, 1928, McKellar-Crump Correspondence, Container 2, McKellar Papers. Memphis *Commercial Appeal*, January 3, 4, 6, 8, 24, 25, February 5, 1929. Memphis *Press-Scimitar*, January 7, 9, 1929.

51. Memphis *Commercial Appeal*, February 5, 1929. Memphis *Press-Scimitar*, January 18, 23, February 5, 6, 1929.

102 / *Tennessee in Turmoil*

me." Now Lea offered a redistricting of the state beneficial to the Republicans. The bill as it was submitted to the legislature, cosponsored by all Republicans and administration Democrats, cut the size of the Shelby and Davidson County delegations and gave Republican areas in East Tennessee three additional senators and ten additional representatives. In exchange, the Republicans agreed to vote for certain administration bills, particularly those related to water power, and agreed to make no serious effort to elect a governor in 1930.[52]

Democrats across Tennessee were shocked and outraged, but Davidson and Shelby counties naturally led the protests. Senator Scott Fitzhugh of Shelby denounced the bill as a measure "designed to guarantee election of a Legislature which will jump to the crack of Colonel Luke Lea's whip." Crump cancelled plans for a trip to California and rushed to Nashville, bringing Senator McKellar with him. Davidson County businessmen began pressuring rural legislators to desert the administration. Rural Democrats in East Tennessee were aghast at their betrayal. Polk County Democrats branded it "vastly unfair," and embittered party members in Sullivan County telegraphed the governor, "It means all hope forever vanished Stop All the Democrats of Sullivan and Hawkins as well as your friends are up in arms against this Stop." The State Democratic Executive Committee called it "a severe blow to the welfare of the Democratic Party." The administration attempted to justify its action, calling the measure a "bipartisan" redistricting, but even T. H. Alexander, one of Luke Lea's favorite reporters, conceded that the bill would not appeal to "partisans." Confronted with such general opposition, the redistricting proposal was soon pigeon-holed. Taylor, for his part, was careful to cultivate both Democratic bosses. While dealing with Lea, the Republican boss was feeding information through Senator McKellar to Ed Crump.[53]

52. Knoxville *News-Sentinel,* July 28, 1930. Chattanooga *Times,* July 28, October 2, 1928. Miller, *Mr. Crump,* p. 153. Lea to J. Will Taylor, July 12, 1928, Lea Papers.

53. Memphis *Commercial Appeal*, February 13, 15, 1929. Memphis *Press-Scimitar*, February 9, 13, 1929. Polk County Democrats to Horton, no date;

The closing days of the session brought a steady series of defeats to the administration. The Senate created a steering committee to regulate the flow of legislation to the floor, and Bratton named three opposition members to the five-man panel. Horton's proposal to replace the land tax with a sales tax was voted down in the House, and his veto of a bill to place motor buses under the supervision of the Railroad and Public Utilities Commission was easily overridden. In its post-mortem, Lea's *Commercial Appeal* admitted that while "The administration's highway program was changed slightly and adopted with little opposition, . . . virtually all other strictly administration bills were materially altered or killed outright."[54]

Much of the opposition stemmed from the controversy around Luke Lea and his relationship to the state government. Lea, a shadowy figure since his return from the war, was being mentioned more frequently in the newspapers. One senator called him the "black hand that is guiding the ship of state to hell," and State Senator Sam Bratton, still fiercely loyal to the memory of Austin Peay, muttered darkly about those who had "an arm around Horton and a hand in the state treasury." To all this was added the continuing tension between the Lea and Crump factions. A Crump senator pulled a knife on a Lea backer during one exchange in the Senate, and Speaker Bratton, perhaps somewhat melodramatically, began to suggest his enemies had marked him for assassination. The struggle between state boss and city boss seemed to be building to a showdown.[55]

Crump had blocked his adversary in the General Assembly, but Lea, as a result of his influence over Horton and the power

---

State Democratic Executive Committee to Horton, no date; State Democratic Executive Committee to Horton, no date; Walter F. Moody to Horton, February 11, 1929, Container 51, File 1, Horton Official Papers. McKellar to Crump, February 17; Crump to McKellar, February 23; McKellar to Crump, February 23, McKellar-Crump Correspondence, Container 2, McKellar Papers.

54. Memphis *Commercial Appeal*, March 18, 19, 21, 22, 27, 30, April 2, 3, 15, 1929. Memphis *Press-Scimitar*, February 15, 1929.

55. Memphis *Commercial Appeal*, January 20, February 15, 16, 1929.

Austin Peay had built for the governorship, still held the trump card. Over Horton's signature, Lea had the ability to appoint a criminal court judge in Shelby, and the election of Grover Keaton gave him a majority on the State Board of Elections Commission. Crump, with his links to the Memphis vice rings, could ill afford hostile judges in Shelby. Moreover, through his control of the Shelby County Elections Commission, which supervised election machinery, Lea could enter an opposition slate in the county that might have a chance of challenging Crump. As the *Press-Scimitar* observed, "the Colonel had something on the ball that was too hot for the home team to handle." Through spring and summer 1929, Lea began to pressure the Shelby County leader. In early July 1929, the two bosses at last struck a bargain. Crump would be permitted to select a favorable judge and a friendly election commission. In exchange he would support Horton for governor in 1930 and throw Shelby delegation support behind a series of measures that Luke Lea wanted passed in the impending special session of the legislature. Crump bluntly assessed the situation for Senator McKellar. "We lost the elections commissioner in 1926 when we went for Hill McAlister," Crump explained. "Another fight in 1928 produced the same result."[56] Crump obviously did not feel his position would survive a state investigation.

The special session of the Sixty-sixth Tennessee General Assembly convened in Nashville on December 2, 1929. The first clue to Shelby County's changed policy came when Crump's three state senators skipped a meeting of the opponents of Horton's tax plan. The next day, Shelby voted solidly for Item 20, a Horton-sponsored measure permitting the Funding Board to borrow $10,000,000. A week later, the *Press-Scimitar* wrote, "During the first week Shelby solons have gone down the line for Gov. Horton at every turn." At the end of the session, the paper observed, "Col. Lea must be having a good laugh up his sleeve at the way Shelby has come to terms and is eating out of

---

56. Chattanooga *News*, May 19, 1931. Memphis *Commercial Appeal*, July 3, 1932. Memphis *Press-Scimitar*, July 15, 29, 1930, July 14, 15, 1932. Crump to McKellar, June 8, 1929; Crump to McKellar, June 8, 1929, McKellar-Crump Correspondence, Container 2, McKellar Papers.

his hand."[57] With Crump's help, the administration program, shattered in April, passed easily in December.

Of the nearly forty items on the governor's agenda, the most significant were Items 19, 20, 21, 23, 29, and 33. These measures added the commissioner of finance and taxation to the state funding board, authorized the board to borrow $10,000,000 through sale of bonds for highways, extended the period of maturity for the bonds from five to ten years, and permitted the board to borrow money to meet interest payments if there were no available funds. The bills also created a "Rent Account" in the state treasury and delegated to the funding board the power to select depositories for state highway funds. Luke Lea and Rogers Caldwell benefited directly from passage of these acts. The special session repealed most of the safeguards on the deposit of state money and gave the funding board wide powers over state bond revenue. The new addition to the board, the commissioner of finance and taxation, was a friend of Lea and Caldwell, giving them a voting majority. The funding board now channeled $9,000,000 into the Caldwell-controlled Bank of Tennessee. This amount was over and above the large deposits the state already had in such Caldwell banks as Holston-Union National and the Fourth and First National. During the next year and a half, Caldwell and Company thus had wide access to the income of the state of Tennessee.[58]

The performance of the 1929 legislature provides a startling indication of the extent to which Luke Lea had been able to establish himself as the Boss of Tennessee. Seventy-three members had support scores over seventy for Horton compared with only thirty-five for Austin Peay in 1927 (see Tables 25 and 26). Eighteen members, thirteen from Shelby and Davidson Counties, had support scores below thirty compared with thirty-three for Peay just two years earlier. The main sources of support for both governors were strikingly similar. Horton won the backing of seventy-six percent of East Tennessee members, sixty-four percent of rural members, and sixty-three percent of small-

57. Memphis *Press-Scimitar*, December 3, 4, 7, 10, 1929.
58. *Second Report*, pp. 64-65. Miller, *Mr. Crump*, p. 153. McFerrin, *Caldwell and Company*, pp. 107-115.

urban members, essentially the same coalition that Peay had built. In addition, however, Horton drew strong support from forty-seven percent of Middle Tennessee members and forty-six percent of West Tennessee members, compared with twenty-two percent and twenty-seven percent respectively for Peay. This tremendous surge is clearly due to the political arrangements that Luke Lea, no longer operating under the restraints imposed by Austin Peay, was making around the state.

The opposition to Horton was also similar to that which confronted his predecessor. Votes agains Horton came predominantly from large-urban members. Thirty-nine percent of large-urban members opposed Peay in 1927 and thirty-five percent of them opposed Horton in 1929. Middle Tennessee, however, where twenty-nine percent opposed Peay in 1927, was largely subdued by Lea's influence and only thirteen percent of that division's members fought Horton in 1929. This shift in Middle Tennessee is illustrative of the kind of power Lea and Horton were acquiring in state politics. In the opening days of the 1929 session administration proposals were severely mauled, but Lea carefully wooed the opposition and gradually built a formidable backing. His two most important bargains were with East Tennessee Republican boss J. Will Taylor and with E. H. Crump. By the time the special session convened in December 1929, Lea and Horton dominated the General Assembly.

With Crump appeased and the government in his pocket, Luke Lea entered his glory days as Boss of Tennessee. The Lea machine, the Chattanooga *Times* noted, sprawled across the entire state, including Taylor's East Tennessee Republicans, the Crump-Church apparatus in Memphis, and the emerging Cummings machine in Chattanooga. Crump henchmen found themselves with state jobs, the highway department began road construction in Shelby, and Lea newspapers lavished praise on Ed Crump. A new memorial highway wound through the mountains to Republican Knoxville, and the Boss's native Nashville received a branch of the University of Tennessee, a state armory, a highway department building, and a hospital plant. Road crews widened major highways coming into the capital city to a width of thirty-six feet. At least twelve members of the General Assembly joined the state payroll and approximately four others profited handsomely from state contracts. When Governor Horton offered to appoint Lea to the Senate to fill the unexpired term of the late Lawrence Tyson, the Boss graciously refused, explaining, "In my case I am convinced that officeholding does not afford the greatest opportunity for civic work. I believe I can be of more service to Tennessee, working in the ranks as a private citizen."[59]

One of the most important components of Lea's power was his newspaper chain. By 1928 he owned a large paper in each of Tennessee's three major cities and he carefully coordinated their views on political questions. During the 1928 primary, for example, Lea went into conference every afternoon and wrote editorials for the papers. He told his editors which candidates to support and suggested specific stories designed to help those candidates. On election day, he dictated the headline each paper was to use and dispatched it by telegram.[60]

Lea's influence over the state government was a second component of his power. Through Governor Horton, he was able to dispense jobs and favors, and he used his position shrewdly to grease the machine. As a local official wrote a Lea associate: "If you will put that matter [the reference is uncertain] across as I wrote you I will personally deposit one thousand dollars guarantee that this county will go for whoever colonel dictates or the amount is hereby forfeited to the campaign fund. . . . We know our organization. It is composed of the dictators in every district except possibly one." When Lea supporters in Washington County wrote to the colonel expressing displeasure with the routing of a proposed Kingsport-Johnson City highway, Lea immediately took the matter up with Horton. He

---

59. Chattanooga *News,* July 7, 25, 1930. Chattanooga *Times,* August 5, 1930. Knoxville *News-Sentinel,* July 27, 1930. Horton to Lea, August 31, 1929, Container 50, File 2, Horton Papers. Lea to Horton, September 1, 1929, Container 13, File 1, Horton Papers.

60. Lea to Mitchell Long, June 11, 1928. Lea to George Morris, July 10, 18, 30, August 7, 13, 1928. Lea to Morris and R. H. Claggett, undated, 1928, Lea Papers.

arranged jobs for those who were politically useful and monitored the selection of candidates for office. Some would-be candidates for the legislature checked with Lea even before declaring. In early 1928, William G. Bogle of Davidson County contacted the colonel through an intermediary to say he wanted to run for the state senate, "if you [Lea] are willing."[61]

If Lea kept the machine in line through judicious use of favors, he was nevertheless capable of ruthlessness with those who crossed him. One of the most powerful small town bosses was N. B. Hardeman of Henderson, the president of Freed-Hardeman College. In exchange for his support in the 1928 primary, Lea and Horton promised that a new West Tennessee highway would be routed as he wished through Henderson. Although Austin Peay's Reorganization Act gave the governor authority to relocate all roads, Highway Commissioner Harry Berry balked. Hardeman, Berry later testified, was presented to him as "a sort of superman—a man who could provide political salvation at the polls in this world, as well as a halo and harp in the next," but the route he wanted would have increased the cost to the state by $50,000 to $60,000. Berry refused to move the road or to fire two department employees whom Lea wanted dismissed. Horton promptly demanded Berry's resignation and the commissioner complied, angrily telling the governor, "The final break between us was the result of your determination to fulfill a campaign promise which I considered a breach of public trust and an improper use of public funds." His firing, in Berry's view, was "due to the increasing friction that arose between Colonel Lea and myself." Lea had led Berry "to the door of the penitentiary, but couldn't make [him] go in." For the second time in a single year, Horton had fired his highway commissioner at the request of Luke Lea.[62]

61. Memo, T. H. Alexander to Lea, January 15, 1928, J. R. Rison, Jr. to T. H. Alexander, August 11, 1929, Lea Papers. Harry Berry to James Epps, October 15, 1928, Epps to Lea, October 18, 1929, Lea to Horton, October 19, 1928, Horton Official Papers.

62. Chattanooga *Times*, April 14, 1931. *Second Report*, pp. 25-26. Harry S. Berry to Horton, February 27, 1929, Container 49, File 1, Horton Official Papers.

Lea's power was enhanced by the reforms of Austin Peay. The administrative revolution the late governor secured, particularly the Reorganization Act, actually served as the vehicle for the colonel's emergence as the state boss. Through Governor Horton, Lea gained influence over the newly expanded executive departments. He was free to trade roads for votes, and he could secure the peremptory firing of any state official who defied him. The tremendous patronage held by the governor enabled Lea to build a large personal following around the state. He was also able to extend his influence within the legislature by offering state jobs and contracts to members who supported him. Peay's reforms made state government revolve around the chief executive, and Lea manipulated the apparatus with great ability.

Lea was able to break any local bosses who opposed him because Peay's increasing the power of state government had occurred at the expense of smaller civil units. Smaller bosses were crushed by withholding roads or schools or by giving jobs to local insurgents. Major enemies like Crump could be curbed by inquisitive state investigators with the authority to ask embarrassing questions. Although unchallenged in his own bailiwick, Crump was as vulnerable in 1930 to the greater power of the state government as he had been in 1915. "There have been many little bosses," wrote the Chattanooga *Times*, "each riding for the benefit of his particular road or school or bridge. But over and above them all there looms the figure of Col. Lea as the all powerful boss of the State and directing power of the Horton administration." With the Memphis boss pledging his fealty in mid-1929, Luke Lea became the liege lord of Tennessee's political structure.[63]

The 1930 primary involved the governor's race and two senate contests. The gubernatorial primary was a calm affair in which Horton faced a nominal challenge from L. E. Gwinn. A Shelby County attorney and farmer, Gwinn was an enemy of Crump, but he was supported by two ex-governors, Benton McMillin and A. H. Roberts, and by Hill McAlister. Lewis Pope this time

---

63. Chattanooga *Times*, April 15, 1931.

stayed out of the race to avoid splitting the anti-Horton vote. Gwinn based his campaign on Horton's connections with Lea. His newspaper supporters called Horton the "Luke-warm governor," and described voting for Horton as "reaching for a Lukey." Gwinn accused the governor of making a deal with Taylor and of raising a slush fund from state road contractors. The Gwinn forces also tried to marshall anti-Crump sentiment against Horton, warning that the latter's renomination would restore blacks to political prominence in the party. A Crump endorsement, they insisted, should be the signal for all ethical voters to switch to the other side. A cartoon entitled "Strange Bedfellows" depicted, Lea, Crump, Church, Taylor, and Horton sound asleep in a large bed.[64]

The Horton campaign, by contrast, barely acknowledged Gwinn's existence. Horton's opposition was "so negligible," his friends said, that there was little need to defend the governor. The *Tennessean* spoke vaguely about Horton's good personal qualities and his wide popularity but hardly mentioned any of the more substantial issues. "Governor Horton is Human," said the *Tennessean*, "His heart is large and filled with sympathy for his brother man. . . . Governor Horton has always been a disciple of the master. . . . Governor Horton's life is an example of Christian manhood." Lea papers used most of their editorial space to attack their Scripps-Howard competitors in Knoxville and Memphis. As the Knoxville *Journal* explained it, Scripps-Howard papers always attacked incumbent administrations, hence the opposition of the *News-Sentinel*. Lea also attempted to brand his competitors as outsiders seeking to pervert the Southern way of life. "The foreign owners of these papers," declared the *Commercial Appeal*, "are in fact parlor bolsheviks whose purpose is to work toward a socialistic scheme of government whenever possible." They were "carpetbag liberals . . . from the north side of the Ohio River" who directed their "hirelings to affront and insult the people of the south."[65]

64. Chattanooga *Times*, July 4, August 3, 1930. Chattanooga *News*, July 1, 10, 1930. Covington *Leader*, July 31, 1930.
65. Memphis *Commercial Appeal*, July 18, August 5, 1930. Nashville *Tennessean*, August 6, 1930. Knoxville *Journal*, August 3, 1930.

"Strange Bedfellows," The Chattanooga *News-Free Press*, July 1, 1930.

With the governorship apparently in his grasp, Lee also tried to influence the selection of a successor for the late Senator Lawrence Tyson. Tyson had been elected in 1924 with little help from Luke Lea or Austin Peay, and the senator in return had remained aloof from the gubernatorial primary in 1926, telling Peay, "I believe that is the attitude which you assumed toward me when I was running for the nomination for the United States Senate." After Horton's victory in the 1928 primary, however, Tyson drew close to Lea, telling his administrative assistant: "Some seem to feel that Luke Lea may be wanting to run against me two years from now, but I don't believe it, and I believe it is not wise for me to antagonize Lea with his four papers in the State."[66] When the senator died in 1929, Horton offered the seat first to Lea and then to his friend William Brock, the Chattanooga candy manufacturer.

In 1930 then, Tennessee was conducting two elections for the same seat. Brock was running against John Neal to fill the last few months of Tyson's unexpired term. The leading candidate for the full six-year term was Congressman Cordell Hull of Carthage. Hull had been an enemy of Luke Lea for nearly two decades. He had campaigned against Lea when the latter ran for the senate in 1916 labelling him a "professional mudslinger," a "chronic troublemaker," and a "political gorilla . . . with no convictions . . . and . . . no principles." Lea, said Hull, was "seized with that spirit which caused the herd of swine to run into the river and drown."[67] Lea persuaded Joseph Byrns, another long-time Tennessee Congressman, to oppose Hull, promising Byrns the backing of both the state and Shelby machines. Byrns, however, had suffered a heart attack brought on by overwork, and the strenuous primary campaign quickly proved too much for him. He withdrew and ran unopposed for the House. Both Lea and Crump then conceded the Senate race.

66. Pat Lyons to Jere Cooper, June 10, 1924; Tyson to Peay, April 20, 1926; Tyson to J. G. Sims, August 18, 1928, Lawrence Tyson Papers, unsorted, Lawson McGhee Library, Knoxville, Tennessee.
67. Cordell Hull Papers, no date, Container 1, File 3, Tennessee State Library and Archives, Nashville, Tennessee.

Crump told Hull he would back no candidate, and the Shelby County Democratic Executive Committee made no endorsement for senator. Lea's newspapers ignored the contest.[68]

The Democratic primary of 1930 was tranquil. Brock defeated Neal by more than two to one and Hull defeated former State Representative Andrew L. Todd by roughly the same margin. Governor Horton swamped L. E. Gwinn, carrying all three grand divisions and the rural, small-urban and large-urban counties (see Tables 27 and 28). There was a strong continuity in the support for Peay in 1926 and for Horton in 1930. Both men ran best in East Tennessee and in the West Tennessee counties outside Shelby. The most important difference between the two races is that in 1930 Horton carried the large-urban counties. His success with this group was due to the changed attitude in Shelby County. Shelby had gone 15,415 to 3,657 against Peay in 1926 and 24,069 to 3,693 against Horton in 1928, but after Crump's bargain with Lea, Tennessee's largest county went 27,811 to 2,227 for the governor in 1930. Gwinn drew half of his support from Middle Tennessee, reflecting the continuing close division among factions in this hotly contested section, which explains his large percentage of the small-urban vote. Like the Middle Tennessee vote, the small-urban vote usually went to the Luke Lea faction by a small percentage. Such was the case again in 1930. Gwinn's 100,000 votes represent the bedrock of opposition to both Lea and Crump in Tennessee politics. East and West Tennessee had come under Lea's sway, but Middle Tennessee, with its tradition of two strong competing factions, continued to provide a nucleus of antiadministration support.[69]

On November 5, Henry Horton easily defeated Republican C. Arthur Bruce to win reelection to the governor's chair, thus confirming Luke Lea as Boss of Tennessee. The dimensions of

---

68. Cordell Hull, *Memoirs* (New York, 1938), 1:135-38. Memphis *Commercial Appeal*, July 15, August 6, 1930. Nashville *Tennessean*, August 7, 1930. Kingsport *Times*, July 1, 3, August 6, 1930. Carthage *Courier*, July 3, 1930. Chattanooga *News*, July 1, 1930. Chattanooga *Times*, August 6, 1930.

69. *Fifty Years of Tennessee Primaries*, p. 120.

Horton's victory demonstrated the scope of Lea's power. Within three years he had made an obscure Marshall County farmer into one of the most powerful vote getters in the state. In the fall of 1930, Lea was at the apogee of his career, and the administration faction stood alone at the center of the state's political life.

5

The Emergence of Crump

On November 7, 1930, less than a week after Henry Horton was reelected Governor of Tennessee, Caldwell and Company collapsed. The Bank of Tennessee went under, taking $3,418,000 in state deposits with it. The Holston-Union National Bank and the Liberty Bank and Trust Company were quickly crushed. On November 14, Caldwell and Company, the South's greatest financial empire, went into receivership. Within a matter of days, Tennessee's state government, at the onset of the nation's worst depression, had lost $6,659,000. Luke Lea and Rogers Caldwell were destroyed.[1]

The collapse of Caldwell and Company left the state in financial shambles. Many Tennesseans believed a criminal conspiracy lay behind the disaster. On December 3, a Public Emergency Committee—the PEC—was formed to work "toward organizing the legislature to secure a disinterested examination into the causes and agencies, near and remote, that have contributed to this crisis." The new committee was headed by several important opponents of the administration: Hill McAlister, Lewis Pope, former Governor Albert H. Roberts, Kit McConnico of the Howse machine, and ousted Highway Commissioner C. Neil Bass. With the General Assembly due to convene after the first of the year, the PEC spent the intervening weeks conducting public meetings across the state. Large crowds heard the "scheming triumvirate"—Lea, Caldwell, and

1. McFerrin, *Caldwell and Company*, pp. 180-89.

Horton—denounced in Knoxville, Nashville, and Chattanooga, and smaller rallies were held in more than twenty other counties.[2]

In the midst of the clamor, Memphis remained noticeably silent. Ed Crump made no public statement on the Caldwell failure, and no mass meetings were conducted in Shelby County. Not even Crump's closest confidants were certain what he would do. Senator McKellar, for example, feared that his friend would continue to support Lea. In early December the senator wrote to Crump:

> I am intensely desirous that you gentlemen in Shelby County take no step which might prove embarrassing to you in the future. I know how loyal you are to your friends . . . but there are some things no friend should be called upon to do and one of these things that no friend should be called upon to do is to be put even into the seeming position of preventing the fullest investigation by those who desire to investigate in a situation like this. . . . For these reasons, I am giving you, unasked, the benefit of what my thoughts are on this most serious situation. I regard it as perhaps the most serious political question you have ever had to solve.[3]

Crump's support was indispensable to the success of the Public Emergency Committee. The new General Assembly would be responsible for any investigation that might be conducted and the yet-to-be-elected speakers of both houses would select the members of the investigating committee. Should Horton be impeached and convicted, the Speaker of the Senate would be the new governor. The fate of the administration might be decided by the battle to elect the speakers; thus Crump with his strength in the Democratic caucus, was a vitally important figure. As late as November 1930, the Memphis boss

2. *Ibid.*, p. 190.
3. McKellar to Crump, December 4, 1930, McKellar-Crump Correspondence, Container 2, McKellar Papers.

had been actively supporting Lea and Horton, but Crump and Lea nourished little affection for each other and it seemed likely Crump might seize this opportunity to turn on his ally.

On January 2, Crump abruptly demanded an "absolutely thorough and sweeping investigation of state affairs."[4] Two days later Crump and his chief lieutenant Frank Rice drove to Nashville to oversee the Democratic caucus. Walter Haynes, a bitter enemy of Horton, was easily elected House Speaker, but the Senate contest brought the showdown between Lea and Crump. Lea backed William K. Abernathy, a former Horton opponent who had joined the governor in 1929, allegedly in exchange for an appointment as assistant attorney general.[5] With the city buzzing over the confrontation, the administration desperately tried to round up the votes needed to nominate Abernathy before the Shelby leaders announced their candidate. Three independents—Charles L. Cornelius, Ambrose B. Broadbent, and J. Tom Durham—were also in the race, as was Hugh C. Anderson, who was backed by the PEC; but of the independents only Broadbent, Austin Peay's former campaign manager, was given any chance of success.[6]

Not until the caucus met did Crump announce that his choice for speaker would be Scott Fitzhugh, a senator from Shelby County. Abernathy showed strength on the first ballot, polling ten of the thirteen votes he needed. The votes of the Shelby delegation could have elected him, but Crump was using his position to whip administration opponents into line behind Fitzhugh. Unless they backed the Shelby senator, Crump said, he would oppose any meaningful investigation of the state's finances. As the caucus settled into a deadlock, Crump and Watkins Overton, the mayor of Memphis, prowled the senate floor talking to members and making their case. At last, on the eleventh ballot, five votes for the PEC candidate, Hu Anderson, switched to Fitzhugh, putting him within reach of the speakership. Recognizing that defeat was imminent, the administration

4. Miller, *Mr. Crump*, p. 157.
5. Chattanooga *Times*, January 1, 2, 1931.
6. Chattanooga *News*, January 5, 1931. Chattanooga *Times*, January 1, 1931.

forces abruptly switched to Fitzhugh, preferring a Crump-controlled investigation to one directed by anyone else. Since Crump was such a controversial figure in Tennessee, Lea and Horton believed that many people would support them simply to oppose Crump.[7]

Less than a week later, the assembly passed Joint Resolution Number 1 establishing an investigative committee of five speakers and seven representatives to be appointed by the speakers. Administration supporters slumped sullenly in their seats as Crump beamed from the rear of the chamber. The Chattanooga *News* proclaimed Crump as the "New Czar of Tennessee Politics," and the Chattanooga *Times* announced to its readers that "Edward H. Crump . . . climbed in the saddle and became the boss of Tennessee politics, succeeding Col. Luke Lea." In Nashville, the *Banner* agreed, saying, "E. H. Crump is the new political boss of the state." Crump, always willing to oblige a reporter, offered three rules to explain his success: "First, observe, remember, compare; second, read, listen, ask; third, plan your work and work your plan." Content with his initial victory, Crump left Nashville as the investigative committee began its work.[8]

From mid-January through mid-March, the committee focused its attention on the acts passed by the Special Session of the 1929 General Assembly and the subsequent deposit of state funds in insolvent banks. The investigation considered solely the financial aspects of the collapse, weighing who lost the money, how it was lost, and how it might be recovered. On March 16, the committee filed a unanimous interim report citing numerous instances of extreme negligence, if not fraud, on the part of Horton, the funding board members, and other high officials. With feelings running high against Lea, Horton, and Caldwell, the members also proposed an extended investigation. Administration forces tried to block the effort, but they

7. McFerrin, *Caldwell and Company*, pp. 192-93. Chattanooga *News*, January 5, 6, May 29, 1931. Memphis *Press-Scimitar*, January 7, 1931.
8. Chattanooga *News*, January 7, 1931. Chattanooga *Times*, January 7, 10, 1931. Nashville *Banner*, January 7, 1931.

lacked the votes to do so. The assembly adjourned on March 21 to reconvene on May 25. It seemed likely Horton would face impeachment in the spring.[9]

With only two months to reverse the rising sentiment against them, Lea, Caldwell, and Horton launched a multipronged attack against their encircling enemies. The reforms of Austin Peay had helped to make possible the emergence of a statewide boss like Luke Lea, and the powers in the governor's hands were stout weapons for a counterassault in this critical moment. "Every day he remains in office gives Governor Horton another opportunity to lessen the danger of impeachment," the *Press-Scimitar* warned. "This is so because of a governor's tremendous power to trade jobs, pardons, and contracts for the friendship of legislators who can throw a monkey wrench into the impeachment."[10] One of the governor's most effective tactics was awarding jobs and contracts to members of the Assembly. Senator Marshall Priest of Paris built a lucrative business selling Fords and Ford parts to the state. Representative Walter Y. Boswell found the state suddenly interested in the $50,000 farm he had been trying to sell to Brushy Mountain State Prison.[11] Representative George Chamlee got a job with the Highway Department approving titles to rights of way. An opposition representative, Harold Earthman, introduced a measure to forestall such abuses of state power, but the bill got nowhere.[12]

Department heads began to line up grass-roots support for the governor. The Tennessee National Guard under Adjutant General William Boyd was particularly active in this effort. General Boyd toured East Tennessee spreading a pro-Horton line and using guardsmen to push the administration story. In addition, the adjutant general sought the presidency of the state American Legion, hoping to mobilize its membership in defense of Horton. In mid-March, Horton announced that the 105th

---

9. Memphis *Press-Scimitar*, March 11, 17, 1931. McFerrin, *Caldwell and Company*, pp. 194-95.

10. Memphis *Press-Scimitar*, April 3, 1931.

11. Knoxville *News-Sentinel*, January 13, June 4, 1931. Chattanooga *News*, January 6, 1931.

12. Knoxville *Journal*, May 28, 1931. Chattanooga *Times*, January 8, 1931.

120 / *Tennessee in Turmoil*

Aero Squadron was being transferred from Memphis to Nashville. The squadron had been based in the capital after it returned from the war, but was moved to Memphis in 1929, allegedly as a part of the bargain between Lea and Crump. Now it was returning to Nashville.[13]

West Tennessee, where the administration faction had been strong since Austin Peay's time, was the particular target of these efforts to trade jobs and contracts for votes. J. Martin Speed, the state auditor for West Tennessee, was dismissed and his job traded for political support. West Tennessee's state elections commissioner, Grover Keaton, openly traded county elections commissionerships for Horton votes. In Lauderdale County, Senator John L. Craig, one of the few Horton friends on the Investigating Committee, was carefully wooed by the approval of his recommendation for coal oil and tobacco inspector in his senatorial district even though the local representative disliked the nominee. Rumors were whispered of members who fell in behind the governor in exchange for pardons and women, but the truth of this is uncertain.[14]

While dealing with Democrats in West Tennessee, the administration won vital support among Republicans in the East through a deal with J. Will Taylor. The minority party was particularly receptive to Horton's overtures because no Republicans had been included on the Investigating Committee.[15] The first hint of a deal came when Lea and Caldwell appeared in federal court in Knoxville to post bond on charges arising out of the collapse of the Caldwell bank in that city. Internal Revenue Collector Frank Donaldson arranged their appearance to avoid the cluster of reporters awaiting their arrival.[16] Shortly thereafter, a state textbook contract went to the Augsburg Publishing Company, an East Tennessee firm of which Donaldson was vice-president. East Tennessee's suspicion of Crump may also

13. Chattanooga *Times*, April 17, 25, 1931. Memphis *Press-Scimitar*, March 14, 1931.
14. Memphis *Press-Scimitar*, April 2, May 30, 1931. Chattanooga *Times*, April 17, June 3, 1931. Knoxville *News-Sentinel*, April 27, 1931.
15. Knoxville *News-Sentinel*, January 14, 1931. Memphis *Press-Scimitar*, March 17, 1931.
16. Memphis *Press-Scimitar*, May 26, 1931.

have played a part in Taylor's willingness to bargain with Lea. Representative J. Ed Gervin, for example, expressed fear that if Horton was impeached and removed, the University of Tennessee might be moved to Memphis and the Smoky Mountains park aborted.[17] The major item in the trade, however, seems to have been a promise of roads for East Tennessee. By May, J. Will Taylor's efficient machine was quietly working for the governor in the mountain section and among Tennessee's federal patronage holders.[18]

Lea and Horton also used friendly newspapers and bankers to line up votes in the legislature. The Lea newspapers conducted an intensive propaganda campaign against legislators who favored impeachment and they stressed the high cost of the ongoing probe. The Nashville *Tennessean* claimed the probe would cost $500,000, and the Chester County *Independent* observed that each member of the committee was getting sixteen dollars per diem, and "a fabulous account for help and other expenses."[19] Bankers who remained friendly to the administration, thanks to state deposits in their vaults, began to contact proimpeachment members whose notes and mortgages they held. Representative Gene Smith's banker, for example, threatened to call in Smith's loans if he voted for impeachment.[20]

Businesses that profited from Horton Administration policies worked actively in the governor's behalf. W. August Patton of the Tennessee Road Builders Association, a group which profited greatly from the administration's highway policy, pressured Tennessee cement contractors for a $125,000 defense fund. Both W. H. Klein of Penn-Dixie Cement and Frank G. Conkin of Signal Mountain Portland Cement admitted that they had been approached by Patton, who told them the fund was well under way and that its purpose was to save Horton and

---

17. Knoxville *News-Sentinel*, May 26, June 1, 1931.
18. Chattanooga *Times*, June 3, 1931.
19. Chattanooga *Times*, March 16, 1931. Memphis *Press-Scimitar*, March 17, 1931. Chester County *Independent*, April 16, 1931, Container 47, File 7, Horton Official Papers.
20. Chattanooga *Times*, May 28, 1931. Knoxville *Journal*, May 28, 1931.

keep the highway fund intact. Other businessmen who dealt with the state, including textbook and equipment salesmen, contributed their support to the governor. As the governor's campaign built to a climax, Crump declared in disgust that, "if some member of the legislature went to the administration and demanded a cornerstone of the capitol for their vote they would dynamite the building tonight and deliver the stone in the morning."[21]

Horton helped his own cause by mounting a slashing attack on his enemies in a series of public appearances. Speaking at a bridge dedication in Jasper on May 16, Horton lambasted his accusers for nearly two hours while a group of officeholders responded enthusiastically. State Senator Walter Faulkner, the chairman of the investigating committee, Horton declared, "violates the law every night, and he is trying to investigate me." A week later at Camden the governor described Crump as a "man who struts like a peacock with a cane on his arm and crows like a bantam rooster."[22]

Another important factor in braking the rush to impeachment was the increasing dissension among members of the Probe Committee. The reasons why the once unanimous committee divided are uncertain, but by mid-April five members were actively taking the part of the beleaguered governor. State Senator John L. Craig of Lauderdale County apparently switched after the elections commission decided in his favor in a contested election. Craig was also rumored to be jealous of the larger role some of his colleagues had played in the investigation. Representative Edmund C. Parker was heavily dependent on the support of Luke Lea's friend, utilities magnate Tom Greer, who was influential in winning Parker to Horton's cause. The motives of the other three dissenters are obscure, but very likely they too felt the hand of the state machine.[23]

Faced with internal dissension, the majority members acted quickly to suppress the renegades. As the dissenters developed

21. Chattanooga *Times*, April 23, May 28, 1931. Knoxville *News-Sentinel*, April 21, 1931. Memphis *Press-Scimitar*, May 20, 1931.
22. Chattanooga *Times*, May 17, 24, 1931.
23. Chattanooga *Times*, April 17, 1931. Knoxville *Journal*, June 9, 1931.

a pro-Horton line in their questions, the majority began to call witnesses without announcing who was coming or what they would testify to. When the dissenters persisted in supporting the governor, the proimpeachment members started examining witnesses in executive session to decide whether to continue the interrogation in public. Still unable to throttle the dissidents, the majority decided on April 10 to select a subcommittee of three to examine witnesses and report on the testimony to the whole committee in executive session. No members of the minority were named to the subcommittee. These high-handed tactics aroused antagonism not only in the committee but also in the legislature as a whole, and seemed to give credence to Horton's protests that he was being railroaded.[24]

The most important part of Horton's counterattack was an effort to make E. H. Crump himself the issue in the impeachment struggle. Crump's heavy-handed actions made him vulnerable to this strategy. After leaving Nashville in January, he said little about the investigation, but on March 4, he issued a statement saying Horton was "as dead as Barnum and Bailey" and declaring Lea and Caldwell should "go to Atlanta," meaning the federal penitentiary.[25] Two weeks later, J. W. Rankin, a Horton supporter, wrote the governor's secretary, Wallace Edwards, suggesting the contours of an anti-Crump campaign.

> I think it would be a great benefit to the administration to get as much publicity opposing the Crump control of state politics . . . and get all of this propaganda published that you can and get the charges made that it is done in order for the Memphis crowd to get control and Crump to be dictator.
>
> We have 60 days to get this through out the State and I think you ought to have some pretty good men to handle this quietly.[26]

---

24. *Minority Report of the Special Legislative Investigating Committee of the 67th General Assembly State of Tennessee*, pp. 9-10.

25. Memphis *Press-Scimitar*, March 5, 6, 1931.

26. J. W. Rankin to Wallace Edwards, March 23, 1931, Container 49, File 4, Horton Official Papers.

To this note, Edwards, who was Horton's main link to Luke Lea, replied, "I am pleased to advise that plans are now being formulated along the line of your suggestion."[27]

Through public statements and private correspondence, Horton fired volley after volley at the Memphis boss. In a letter to Memphis attorney Hunter Wilson, Horton wrote, "It is very annoying to me to have to join issue with one of Crump's character and standing; in fact, it represents everything repugnant to my convictions. . . . It is time to protest and protest vigorously when this deposed ex-mayor of Memphis boldly and brazenly announces his intention of placing the yoke of his despotic power upon the State Government of Tennessee."[28] In his speech at Camden on the eye of the climactic May session of the General Assembly, Horton told his listeners, "I hear Mr. Crump is starting out tomorrow with a brass band. He has already rented 100 rooms at a hotel. They are going to storm the legislature with the cry: 'Oust Horton.' What has Crump done in Memphis that would justify turning the state over to him?"[29]

Pro-Horton newspapers, such as the Nashville *Tennessean*, echoed the governor's charges. The *Tennessean* sneered at the "Crumped up impeachment articles" and termed the Investigating Committee's recommendations the "Crump report." Proimpeachment legislators were lumped together as "Crump's trained seals." In addition the paper began to stress Crump's links to Memphis black leader Robert Church and speculated as to why only white members of the machine had come to Nashville to lobby for impeachment.[30] Other papers like the Chattanooga *News*, more anti-Crump than pro-Horton, also gave the embattled chief executive needed support. The *News*, which had opposed Horton for renomination in 1930, caricatured Crump as a druggist preparing medicine for a character labeled "Tennessee" writhing in agony. "Hortonitis is bad," the

---

27. Wallace Edwards to J. W. Rankin, March 25, 1931, Container 49, File 4, Horton Official Papers.
28. Horton to Hunter Wilson, March 20, 1931, Container 49, File 4, Horton Official Papers.
29. Chattanooga *Times*, May 24, 1931.
30. Nashville *Tennessean*, May 10, 22, 26, June 2, 1931.

News observed, "but this cure is as bad as the disease." Many Tennesseans, the *News* remarked, were not eager to make Horton "the target of a political maneuver whose sole object was, not to clean up the state, but merely to turn its affairs over to Crump and his machine."[31]

The administration's anti-Crump campaign quickly took its toll, and the opposition was thrown back on the defensive. Senator Tyler Berry of Williamson County remarked that "in the backwoods" the people were "just as afraid of Mr. Crump as I would be alone with a lion in the wilds of Africa," and his colleague Will Clark of Washington County observed that seventy-five percent of his constituents felt "that it's nothing but a fight between two factions of the Democratic party." One anti-Horton Republican, James Snyder, said, "If it had not been that Mr. Crump projected himself into the fight and allowed himself to be made an issue, the Governor would have been impeached already."[32]

The anti-Horton press tried to downplay Crump's role in the impeachment move. "Efforts of Governor Horton to represent the contest . . . as a contest between himself and E. H. Crump are beginning to produce results," reported the Chattanooga *Times*. "The issue," the *Times* insisted, "is not one of Crump v. Horton. The issue is one of Horton versus the people and the laws of the state." The Nashville *Banner* agreed, remarking, "It is not Mr. Crump, but the people of Tennessee who are demanding the impeachment of Governor Horton." In Memphis, the *Press-Scimitar* declared that "The battle at Nashville is not between Crump and Horton, but between the self-respecting people of Tennessee, and the governor who has betrayed them."[33]

As a result of all these maneuvers, when the legislature reconvened on May 25, the future of impeachment was very uncertain. The returning legislators found on their desks a copy of the majority and minority reports of the investigating commit-

31. Chattanooga *News,* May 26, 29, 1931.
32. Nashville *Tennessean*, May 29, 1931. Knoxville *Journal*, May 31, 1931.
33. Chattanooga Times, May 12, 25, 1931. Nashville *Banner*, May 27, 1931. Memphis *Press-Scimitar*, May 19, 1931.

126 / *Tennessee in Turmoil*

tee. The majority report, signed by Chairman Walter Faulkner, Limmie Lee Harrell, Robert Alexander, Alfred F. Officer, George L. Stockton, Austin Peay Jr., John M. Payne, and ex officio members Scott Fitzhugh and Walter Haynes, was a lengthy indictment of the conduct of state government, but only the last section dealt with Horton. It condemned the governor for appointing a superintendent of banks solely on the recommendation of Luke Lea, for discharging state officials whose actions displeased Lea and Caldwell, for trading roads and pardons for political advantage, and for calling a special session of the 1929 legislature to pass laws favorable to Lea-Caldwell interests.[34]

The minority members of the committee entered a bitter dissent. Many statements in the *Majority Report*, they felt, were "stronger than the testimony justifies." The *Majority Report* assumed the "full credibility" of all witnesses although some testimony was "neither legally relevant nor competent, but largely hearsay, suspicions, general rumor and inferences of the witnesses." The minority members accused their colleagues of ignoring testimony that did not support the conclusions of the report. The *Minority Report* condemned the alleged "intolerance on the part of some members of the majority and of the public press of the rights and opinions of the minority of the committee" and declared "it was the duty of the committee to find and develop and report ALL THE FACTS, irrespective of whether or not they support our individual wishes or defeat the preformed plans of any one, either inside or outside of the committee. . . . MIGHT CANNOT MAKE RIGHT." The minority members, William W. Craig, Leighton Ewell, James A. Rush, Edmund C. Parker, and Norman H. Eubank, resented their exclusion from the subcommittee that drafted the final report. Their protest was an endorsement of Horton's insistence that Crump was using the impeachment as a vehicle to win what he had been denied at the polls.[35]

The lines were now clearly drawn, but the outcome was

34. *Second Report*, pp. 77-82.
35. *Minority Report*, pp. 2-15.

uncertain. The House took an important step toward impeachment on May 26, when it voted 71-25 to appoint a committee to draw up the formal articles. Speaker Walter Haynes named a committee of five members, all of whom opposed Horton. On May 28, however, the Senate voted 21-12 to disband the investigating committee. The impeachment forces, while seemingly strong in the House, obviously lacked a majority, much less two-thirds, in the Senate. Less than twenty-four hours after the Senate vote, Scott Fitzhugh stunned the Assembly by resigning as Speaker of the Senate, explaining that "This smokescreen has been thrown out over the state that I was anxious to get into the governor's office or that my political associates and friends were anxious to get me into the governor's office in order to capture and control the governor of the state must be put to rest." In Memphis, Crump stated that "Fitzhugh's resignation should show we are sincere and want to remove Horton for the good of the state and not to put our men in power." In other words, Crump realized that his ties to the speaker were endangering impeachment, and consequently he had ordered Fitzhugh to resign. A caucus of Democrats and proadministration Republicans then met and elected Ambrose B. Broadbent, a close friend of the late Austin Peay, as speaker. Broadbent, an independent, was not aligned with Lea although Crump considered him a "Hortonite." Senator Fitzhugh thus became the first victim of the governor's campaign to make Crump the issue.[36]

That same day, May 29, the House Committee returned the first article of impeachment against Horton. Although seven additional articles were voted on June 2, the first article carried the crux of the case. As the committee phrased it, Horton "did wrongfully, unlawfully and corruptly agree, combine, and confederate and conspire with Luke Lea and Rogers Caldwell . . . to commit acts for the perversion and obstruction of the due administration of the law." The conspiracy, explained the indictment, was carried out to secure the "pecuniary gain" of

36. Chattanooga *Times,* May 30, 1931. Chattanooga *News,* May 30, June 1, 1931. Memphis *Press-Scimitar,* May 29, 1931. Miller, *Mr. Crump,* p. 161.

128 / *Tennessee in Turmoil*

the coconspirators and to keep Horton in office to "use the power and influence of that office for his own said advantage, gain and advancement of his said confederates and coconspirators, and to the loss, detriment and disadvantage of all the people of the State of Tennessee, and the public treasury thereof."[37]

The issue was joined and both sides began lobbying furiously with the control of Tennessee at stake. Administration representatives made a bold move to unseat proimpeachment Tom Taylor as the GOP floor leader in the House. Representative Elmer E. Duncan and Representative Clyde Bogart called a secret session of the Republican caucus to try to vote the party as a bloc against impeachment. While administration Democrats nervously paced the corridors, their Republican friends lost a close vote inside the caucus room. The question still hung in the balance when on the afternoon of June 5, Tom Taylor rose and moved the impeachment of Governor Henry H. Horton "in the name of George Washington, of truth and honesty in government and of all the saints in history." As a hushed chamber looked on, the Tennessee House voted 41-58 against impeachment. A motion to reject Article I then passed 52-47. As the clerk read the result, the chamber filled with cheers and applause, and the House stood adjourned for the weekend. The proponents of impeachment made scattered efforts over the next week to bring Horton to the dock, but the two votes on June 5 had doomed their efforts.[38]

The defeat of impeachment, said the Knoxville *Journal*, showed the difficulty of "putting a political machine in jail, with its 15,000 employees and approximately $30,000,000 to disburse annually." In a more bitter mood, the *Press-Scimitar* declared that, "By a vote of 58-41 the Tennessee House of Representatives condones crookedness in politics."[39] Analysis of the roll

37. *Report of the Special Committee of the House of Representatives, 67th General Assembly State of Tennessee Relating to the Impeachment of the Governor and Submitting "Article I" of a Draft of the Articles of Impeachment*, pp. 16-17.
38. McFerrin, *Caldwell and Company*, p. 201. Chattanooga *News*, June 5, 1931. Chattanooga *Times*, May 26, 1931.
39. Knoxville *Journal*, June 6, 1931. Memphis *Press-Scimitar*, June 6, 1931.

call on impeachment reveals that Horton was saved by the usual backers of the Lea faction—rural and small-urban Democrats and East Tennessee Republicans. Thirteen of seventeen Republican members voted with Horton, providing the margin of victory. Of Horton's fifty-eight votes, twenty-four came from rural counties and twenty-three more from counties less than thirty percent urban. Twenty of the forty-one votes for impeachment came from counties more than thirty percent urban, and thirteen more came from antiadministration Middle Tennessee. The vote reflects both the strength of Luke Lea in the legislature despite the collapse of Caldwell and Company and the enduring antagonism in Tennessee politics between the large-urban areas represented by Crump and the rest of the state.[40]

With the impeachment debate behind it, the General Assembly turned to the deepening crisis in the state's finances. Despite the onset of the depression, the legislature considered no relief measures but concentrated solely on funding the money to meet the state's obligations. Tennessee's credit had been destroyed and the state could receive no more bank loans until it restored financial order in its affairs. The wrangling over a suitable plan dragged on through two extra sessions until pro- and antiadministration factions at last reached a compromise. The opposition accepted a new five million dollar bond issue to be funded by an increase in the gasoline tax, while the administration permitted $1,200,000 in Highway Department funds to be transferred to the General Fund to meet other obligations.[41]

The Lea-Horton faction remained strong in the General Assembly throughout the session (see Tables 29 and 30). Most of the legislature had been elected in the primary of 1930 when Lea was at the peak of his power. Also, many members feared the rising power of E. H. Crump and preferred the discredited administration to the Shelby boss. As a result, fifty-three members had support scores over seventy for Horton as op-

---

40. *Tennessee House Journal*, p. 1066. Joe C. Gamble interview, June 28, 1976.
41. Nashville *Tennessean*, November 21, December 17-20, 1931. Memphis *Press-Scimitar*, December 19, 1931.

posed to only thirteen with scores under thirty. Horton's coalition followed the usual contours of the Lea faction, East Tennessee, rural and small-urban areas. Forty-four of Horton's fifty-three supporters came from these three groups. The Lea faction, however, had been clearly weakened since the 1929 General Assembly. In that session, seventy-three members had support scores above seventy.

The opposition to Horton continued to center in the large-urban areas of Tennessee. Ten of the governor's thirteen opponents were from the major cities, including eight from Shelby and Davidson counties and two anti-Taylor East Tennessee Republicans. The remaining three opponents came from Middle Tennessee. In 1929, eighteen legislators had consistently opposed Horton, five more than in 1931. The opposition to Horton was reduced partly because of the Lea faction sweep in the 1930 election and partly because of the widespread distrust of E. H. Crump. Many Tennesseans, disgusted by the excesses of the Lea faction, were still unwilling to ally with the Shelby County boss.

The 1932 gubernatorial election thus loomed as a pivotal one for the future of Tennessee. Crump, in his bid to seize the state machinery, endorsed two-time loser Hill McAlister, while Luke Lea supported former Governor Malcolm Patterson (1907-11), now a Memphis judge. Once again Lewis Pope joined the race, stressing his independence of bosses. Pope drew much of his support from old friends of Austin Peay who had been alienated by the Lea-Horton regime. The three candidates conducted brutal, mud-slinging campaigns. Each tried to link his opponents to one machine or another and discredit their supporters.

McAlister identified the "overshadowing issue" in his opening statement when he asked, "Is the present administration, dominated, controlled, and guided by Horton and Lea to be continued in power in this State by the election of a candidate of their own choosing?" McAlister drew much support simply because he opposed Lea and Horton. The *Sumner County News* acclaimed him as a man who had fought the Lea machine for fifteen years and who possessed "the will and the ability to clean out and destroy the Lea-Horton regime in Tennessee." The

Clarksville *Leaf-Chronicle*, explaining that it had supported Horton in 1930 to insure the future of the Austin Peay Normal School, now condemned the governor's administration as "loose and extravagant." The paper praised Pope, yet endorsed McAlister as the strongest candidate.[42]

Patterson's administration backing made him vulnerable, and the McAlister forces gored him repeatedly. The memory of the martyred Edward Carmack still haunted Tennessee politics, and Patterson's pardoning of Colonel Duncan Cooper, who was involved in Carmack's death, remained one of the most controversial acts ever performed by a Tennessee chief executive. Pro-McAlister editors, noting that Luke Lea stood convicted in North Carolina of conspiracy to defraud and was awaiting extradition, suggested Patterson might not sign the necessary papers as governor. Crump said Patterson could have prevented Carmack's death "had he raised his finger," and condemned his "unholy alliance with the thieving, crooked Luke Lea Racketeers." Lea backed Patterson, insisted Crump, because he knew Patterson would not extradite him to North Carolina. Patterson, the Chattanooga *News* bluntly observed, "has had some experience in keeping colonels out of jail."[43]

But if Patterson bore the cross of Luke Lea, McAlister was haunted by the spector of Ed Crump. Patterson tied his opponent to the Memphis boss and worked to excite rural antagonism against urban domination. He excoriated McAlister as the "plastic puppet of Mr. Crump of Memphis" and called on country people to help him in his "lone fight" against the "city corruptionists" who were using McAlister to get control of the state. Patterson advertisements were headlined *"Don't Let Crump Extend Gangster Rule to the Rural Sections!"* and reminded readers that "when Patterson is elected governor he will owe it to the people of the small towns and rural sections more than the

---

42. Nashville *Banner*, July 1, 1932. *Sumner County News*, Gallatin, July 14, 28, 1932. Clarksville *Leaf-Chronicle*, July 16, August 3, 1932.

43. Memphis *Commercial Appeal*, July 10, 1932. Nashville *Banner*, August 2, 1932. Chattanooga *News*, June 16, 1932. Patterson pardoned Colonel Duncan Cooper for his role in the Carmack slaying.

boss-controlled cities."[44] Patterson's campaign strategy was condensed in an advertisement in the Carthage *Courier* a week before the primary: "McAlister is kept in the race by his Crump-Howse strength in the cities. . . . Most of our voters in Middle Tennessee want to rebuke the Crump-Howse city machines which herd negroes to the polls to vote in a white man's primary. . . . A vote for Patterson hits Crump straight between the eyes. . . . It was Patterson whose courageous work made this a white man's primary."[45]

Like McAlister, Patterson was at great pains to stress his independence of his controversial patrons. Asserting "I am not the candidate of anybody and I will not be controlled by anyone as governor of the state," Patterson ridiculed the idea of his being subservient to Lea: "I do not now and never have condoned the things Luke Lea has done. Lea tried and failed to control me when I was governor before and he was at the height of his power and popularity and now, in his present condition, no sane man would seek or want an alliance with him when he has passed from the picture."[46] Patterson, however, was no more convincing than McAlister in his denials, and they continued to be seen as the candidates of Lea and Crump, respectively.

The X factor in the 1932 primary was again Lewis Pope. Having no organizational support and considered a sure loser, Pope attracted a good deal of sympathy. His advertisements emphasized that he was "unbossed" and declared, "A vote for McAlister is a whole vote for Crump, the City Machines, and power companies. A vote for Patterson is a whole vote just to let things run along as they are." The issue, insisted the Pope backers, was "the issue of government by the people against government by self-serving political machines." By electing Pope, they said, the people would "end the domination of

---

44. Bolivar *Bulletin,* July 29, 1932. Chattanooga *News,* July 26, 1932. Nashville *Tennessean,* July 24, 1932. Knoxville *Journal,* July 1, 1932.
45. Carthage *Courier,* July 28, 1932.
46. Memphis *Commercial Appeal,* July 2, 1932.

bosses and machines that has for too long been the curse of Tennessee."[47]

Pope's independence was, paradoxically, both his strongest and his most vulnerable point. On the one hand it left him free to attack the boss connections of his rivals, but on the other hand most Tennesseans doubted Pope could survive as a candidate without an organization. Patterson's campaign material conceded that "Mr. Pope might make a good governor but he cannot be nominated." Independent newspapers echoed this sentiment. The Dresden *Enterprise* praised Pope's honesty and courage, but said he could only split the anti-Patterson vote. The Lawrenceburg *Democrat* admitted that both Pope and McAlister were "good competent men" but argued that Pope's candidacy could only bring about McAlister's defeat. The anti-Lea Nashville *Banner* warned its readers that "a vote for Pope will mean half a vote for Patterson." When the Chattanooga *Times* lauded Pope while urging his withdrawal from the race, the exasperated candidate asked the *Times* to withdraw from the newspaper field.[48]

Black voting soon became an important issue for Patterson. The former governor, like Peay in 1926 and Horton in 1928, accused Crump of dealing in black votes and attempted to use race to inflame voters outside Shelby County against McAlister. Patterson was joined in the effort by the Memphis *Commercial Appeal*, no longer controlled by Luke Lea, and much of the rural press. In the weeks before the election, the *Commercial Appeal* almost daily attacked black voting and ran stories and pictures of blacks at the ballot box. Its reporters prowled the black wards of Memphis, visiting houses where "ghost voters" lived and returning with stories of corruption and fraud. The paper's editorials repeatedly demanded that Patterson be given a "white man's chance" at the polls.[49] A series of advertisements ap-

47. Carthage *Courier*, July 28, 1932. Knoxville *News-Sentinel*, August 3, 1932. Columbia *Daily Herald*, July 1, 1932.
48. Carthage *Courier*, July 28, 1932. Dresden *Enterprise*, July 22, 1932. Lawrenceburg *Democrat*, July 22, 1932. Nashville *Banner*, August 3, 1932. Memphis *Press-Scimitar*, July 19, 1932. Chattanooga *Times*, July 8, 14, 1932.
49. Memphis *Commercial Appeal*, July 3, 20, 22, 23, 1931.

peared in several small county weeklies headlined, "WHITE SUPREMACY CHALLENGED." One warned that "The Crump-McAlister Machine Has Brought Us to Political Equality with the Blacks," while another accused Crump of fraudulently registering 33,500 blacks to vote in the Democratic primary and claimed the black vote in Memphis threatened to offset completely the white rural vote. Malcolm R. Patterson, the advertisements concluded, was the "white man's candidate for governor."[50] Patterson himself sponsored a bizarre contest for women and children under sixteen, offering a prize for the best picture or collection of pictures of blacks voting in the primary.[51]

McAlister angrily denied Patterson's charges of collusion with blacks and attempted to turn the issue against the former governor. In a carefully worded letter to the Memphis *Press-Scimitar*, McAlister said:

> I am emphatically and unalterably opposed to the corrupt, wrongful, or illegal voting of negroes or any other class of voters colored or white in Shelby County and in every county of Tennessee. . . .
> There is not now, there never has been, there never will be any character of agreement or understanding, secret or open, between Mr. Crump and myself. . . . Mr. Crump never has bossed or controlled me nor attempted to boss or control me.[52]

McAlister newspapers such as the Clarksville *Leaf-Chronicle* accused Patterson of raising the "smokescreen" of "negroization" when the real issues were the return of good government and a guarantee against further exploitation by the Lea machine. McAlister advertisements asked "Who is this Lily-White Ham Patterson?" and claimed he had been responsible for adding blacks to the Democratic primary during the prohibition struggle. In Chattanooga, local black leader Sid Byers said the city's

---

50. Bolivar *Bulletin*, July 22, 1932. Crossville *Chronicle*, July 28, 1932. *Jonesboro Herald and Tribune*, August 3, 1932. Clinton, *Anderson County News*, July 30, 1932.
51. Knoxville *Journal*, August 2, 1932.
52. Memphis *Press-Scimitar*, July 11, 1932.

Patterson leader had offered him $500 to deliver the black vote. Patterson officials hotly denied the story, however, charging that McAlister people had sent Byers to them to solicit the money.[53]

Conflict over the race issue exploded in a violent meeting of the Democratic State Executive Committee in late July. The session was held to consider Patterson's charges concerning black registration in Shelby. Patterson pointed to 31,000 blacks registered to vote in the county, but Crump insisted they were Church supporters and would vote in the Republican primary. In the middle of an angry speech by Shelby County Assistant Attorney General Will Gerber, a Patterson supporter rushed the podium. He was grabbed by Memphis Magistrate Lewis Morris, but Morris was immediately flattened by Rembert Moon, the sole anti-Crump member of the Shelby County Elections Commission. The meeting quickly dissolved into a brawl as National Guard Adjutant General Boyd also jumped on Morris, and State Highway Patrol Chief Joe B. Williams tackled a Crump man swinging a chair.[54] After the melee subsided, the executive committee adopted a resolution that "if the local officers . . . in Shelby . . . permit the negroes to be herded and voted by the thousands in the face of the common and universal knowledge that they belong to . . . the Republican Party . . . we . . . will deem this *prima facie* evidence of fraud." Although the *Commercial Appeal* called it a "stinging resolution," the committee could hardly have said less, given the racial mores of Tennessee in the 1930s. Moreover, it provided no machinery for enforcement of the measure. Pro-Patterson Secretary of State Ernest Haston, former Democratic state party chairman, accurately summarized the situation, saying the resolution would carry "no more weight than a similar resolution by a literary society." The action of the committee gave Patterson a meager propaganda victory at best.[55]

---

53. Clarksville *Leaf-Chronicle,* July 25, 1932. Carthage *Courier,* July 28, 1932. Nashville *Banner,* July 31, 1932. Chattanooga *Times,* July 27, 28, 1932.

54. Chattanooga *News,* July 22, 23, 25, 1932. Knoxville *News-Sentinel,* July 24, 1932.

55. Bolivar *Bulletin,* July 29, 1930. Covington *Leader,* July 21, 1932. Memphis *Commercial Appeal,* July 24, 1932.

136 / *Tennessee in Turmoil*

The gubernatorial race of 1932 was conducted against the backdrop of the nation's worst depression, and the dribble of federal funds was cynically manipulated for political advantage. Tennessee was due to receive $11,500,000 from the Reconstruction Finance Corporation, the bulk of which Horton proposed to spend on roads. The nine-man committee he appointed to supervise the operation included eight Patterson supporters. The McAlister people quickly charged that Horton was spending the money for political purposes: the RFC windfall, claimed the Chattanooga *Times,* had given the state machine the "sinews of war it lacked." Crump was outraged—particularly when his enemies were given control of the local funds in Shelby—and moved to block the dispensation of the money until Horton named an "impartial" board. The Horton forces replied that Crump's efforts were "purely a political move to bolster McAlister's candidacy." Even economic recovery, it seemed, would have to wait on the outcome of the struggle.[56]

As the campaign ran into its last days, the state machine resorted to its usual fund-raising techniques. Apparently desperate for money, it began assessing state employees, including even grass cutters, for political contributions. The machine demanded ten percent of July salaries and began shifting contracts to businesses that contributed to the Patterson campaign. When sufficient contributions were not forthcoming from the Commission of Finance and Taxation, Horton abruptly fired its head and replaced him with a man who was more willing to cooperate.[57]

At the same time, an internal struggle was raging between those who continued to favor Patterson and those who believed Patterson was doomed and wanted to throw the strength of the machine behind Lewis Pope. Joe Hatcher, political reporter for the Nashville *Tennessean,* urged *Tennessean* publisher Luke Lea to shift his support from Patterson to Pope. When Patterson refused to withdraw, however, Lea told Hatcher that he was

---

56. Chattanooga *Times,* July 23, 25, 1932. Knoxville *Journal,* July 28, 1932.
57. Chattanooga *Times,* July 22, 1932. Cookeville, *Putnam County Herald,* July 14, 28, 1932. Nashville *Banner,* August 1, 2, 1932.

committed to the former governor. Other members of the rural faction, agreeing with Hatcher that Patterson had no chance, began to lean to Pope. The Nashville *Banner* forecast July 20 as "Switch Wednesday," the day when the machine would move from Patterson to Pope. The shift did not materialize, however, and as the August primary neared, the organization remained divided on the matter.[58] The Chattanooga *Times* and Clarksville *Leaf-Chronicle*, both pro-McAlister papers, began to identify Pope as the second choice of the Lea machine.[59] The machine apparently expected Patterson to choke off support for Pope, but instead Pope was running strong in East and Middle Tennessee, while Patterson showed strength only in West Tennessee. Some sort of shift seemed likely when Patterson began ending his speeches with the injunction, "You may not like me or want to vote for me, but for God's sake don't vote for McAlister and put Crump in control of Tennessee."[60]

While the Horton-Lea machine vacillated, the McAlister campaign began to direct most of its fire at Pope. The *Banner* noted that Pope's attacks on the machine were vague and impersonal. The Chattanooga *Times* agreed, suggesting that Pope had tempered his attacks on Luke Lea because the machine was moving behind him. Former Governor A. H. Roberts, a long-time Lea opponent, published an open letter accusing Pope of playing a major part in building the state machine in the first place, and McAlister advertisements claimed that Pope had sought Lea's support for governor in 1928. As the primary neared, Pope was plainly enjoying a surge. Administration forces in the West were reportedly "sacrificing" Patterson, and the independent candidate was making gains around the state. Pope suddenly seemed a serious threat to his two rivals.[61]

---

58. Nashville *Banner*, July 15, 21, 23, 1932. Joe Hatcher interview, February 18, 1976.

59. Chattanooga *Times*, July 23, 1932. Clarksville *Leaf-Chronicle*, August 6, 1932.

60. Memphis *Press-Scimitar*, July 9, 1932. Nashville *Banner*, July 10, 1932.

61. Chattanooga *Times*, November 5, 1932. Nashville *Banner*, July 10, August 4, 1932. Manchester *Times*, July 14, 1932. Lawrenceburg *Democrat*, July 29, 1932. Clarksville *Leaf-Chronicle*, August 6, 1932.

With the race tightening, the Shelby organization intensified its efforts. Victory in 1932 was vital to Ed Crump's political future, because Patterson had a strong personal following in Shelby that could easily become the nucleus of an opposition machine if he were returned to the governorship. This threat was made all the more immediate by the fact that the new governor would be able to nominate, subject to legislative approval, a member of the state elections commission. This body in turn named the three members of each county board. One anti-Crump member already served on the Shelby board, and another hostile appointment would shift the board against the boss. In 1930, Crump had made a deal with Luke Lea to control this appointment, but in 1932 such a bargain appeared to be out of the question.[62]

Electing his candidate in 1932 would also rid Crump of the plague of unfriendly local judges. Particularly vulnerable to investigation was Frank Rice, Crump's top lieutenant, who allegedly had extensive property holdings in the Memphis vice districts. An eager grand jury could be counted on to look into "taxes" on gambling houses and "campaign donations" from Memphis prostitutes. Horton had named a strong anti-Crump man to the Shelby criminal court bench, but Crump checked the move by getting the 1929 legislature to change the method of grand jury selection. Under the old method the judge himself picked the jurors, a procedure which would have allowed the Lea machine to investigate effectively conditions in Shelby County. The new law provided that the jury would be selected by a child drawing names from a box. If Crump could control the executive chair, such threats to his machine would be ended.[63]

The Shelby machine was ready for the showdown as the primary neared. McAlister was the beneficiary of some 588 ward and district meetings in the county, 200 street corner rallies and radio talks, and the efforts of over 100 speakers. Memphis police urged registration of blacks, who eventually made up more than one-third of the 93,000 registered voters in 1932. Frank Rice kept

62. Chattanooga *News*, July 27, 1932. Nashville *Tennessean*, July 13, 1932.
63. Chattanooga *News*, July 27, 1932.

careful records on every potential voter in the county, noting who had paid the poll tax and who had registered. Nearly a month before the election he was confidently predicting 25,000 votes for McAlister, 8,000 for Patterson, and none for Pope. The Memphis underworld also responded to the battle with "campaign contributions." As local vice dens flared to new life in the depression-battered city, one newspaper headlined "Dead Prepare to Vote, Gin Flows, Dice Rolls in Memphis."[64]

Violence and corruption marred primary voting across the state. In Memphis, police smashed reporters' cameras and deliberately ignored organization toughs who were beating "troublemakers." In Lawrence County, the *Democrat* charged, "The election laws went unheeded by all. The whole procedure was a nightmare from start to finish." One of Lawrence's largest boxes was never brought in, and the final tabulation was taken from the newspaper. Lawrence County, the editor concluded, "would make any of the city machine men blush with envy." The Columbia *Daily Herald* expressed shock at the fraud in Maury County, and the Dresden *Enterprise* wrote, "Weakley County had no right to point the finger of scorn at any other county." In Nashville, according to the *Commercial Appeal*, "vote frauds took place brazenly and unashamed" as Davidson County, which normally cast sixteen thousand votes, brought in a record twenty-seven thousand.[65]

"The state," the *Banner* editorialized, "has been stirred to its depths as never before in all its annals in times of peace." The Chattanooga *Times* described the race as the most bitter since the Patterson-Carmack contest in 1908.[66] The apparent result was a narrow victory for Hill McAlister. Patterson had been soundly trounced, winning only twenty-one percent, but Lewis Pope refused to accept defeat and demanded a hearing before the state primary board. He charged fraud in Shelby, Davidson,

---

64. Memphis *Press-Scimitar*, July 22, 1932. Nashville *Tennessean*, July 17, 23, 1932. Chattanooga *News*, July 13, 1932. Chattanooga *Times*, August 7, 1932.

65. Memphis *Commercial Appeal*, August 5, 6, 1932. Lawrenceburg *Democrat*, August 12, 1932. Columbia *Daily Herald*, August 8, 1932. Dresden *Enterprise*, July 29, 1932. Knoxville *News-Sentinel*, October 14, 1932.

66. Chattanooga *Times*, August 4, 1932. Nashville *Banner*, August 3, 1932.

Lake, Obion, Unicoi, and Rutherford counties. McAlister countercharged that the Pope forces were guilty of fraud in Obion, Lauderdale, Weakley, Bledsoe, Haywood, DeKalb, Lawrence, Rhea, and Sequatchie counties and declared that the challenge was Luke Lea's idea.[67] Both sides attempted to pressure board members, but in the end, the board voted to uphold McAlister's victory. Two hours after the decision was announced, Pope issued a statement declaring that "I am the nominee of the white democrats for governor of Tennessee. My duty is plain. I cannot surrender the interests of the people to the two machines of Memphis and Nashville." Lewis Pope was bolting his party.[68]

Ed Crump and Shelby County were the keys to McAlister's success (See Tables 31 and 32.). As in 1926 and 1928, McAlister ran strongest in Tennessee's large-urban counties, winning fifty-six percent of the vote. Even excluding Shelby County, McAlister won forty-six percent of the large-urban vote. By contrast, McAlister won only thirty-one percent of the vote in the small-urban and rural counties. The usual administration strongholds, the farms and the small towns, remained heavily opposed to McAlister. Crump's contribution was clear. Shelby County went for McAlister with 31,441 votes to 8,699 for Patterson and 2,325 for Pope. McAlister barely won the nomination by 9,055 votes and actually trailed Pope by 29,000 votes in the ninety-four counties outside Shelby.

But even with Crump's support, only the split in the rural faction permitted Hill McAlister to win the 1932 nomination. A comparison of the 1932 primary with the 1930 primary shows this split clearly (See Tables 33 and 34.). In East Tennessee, where Henry Horton had won fifty-eight percent in 1930, Pope and Patterson together won sixty-one percent in 1932—but Pope, although the stronger candidate, won only forty-five percent. The rural counties, where Horton had received sixty percent of the vote in 1930, gave Patterson and Pope together sixty-nine percent, but here, too, Pope won only forty-five percent. The two anti-Crump candidates won sixty-nine per-

---

67. Memphis *Commercial Appeal*, August 24, 1932.
68. Chattanooga *Times*, August 25, 1932.

cent of the small-urban vote in 1932 as opposed to Horton's fifty-three percent two years earlier, but Pope alone received only forty-seven percent. Statewide, Pope and Patterson won fifty-nine percent of the total vote in 1932, the same percentage Horton had won, but they received only thirty-eight percent and twenty-one percent respectively.[69]

The pattern of Tennessee politics established under Austin Peay remained intact in 1932. McAlister won largely because he was able to add Shelby County to the Gwinn vote of 1930 and because the administration faction fell into total disarray (See Tables 35 and 36.). In East and Middle Tennessee, McAlister actually ran slightly behind Gwinn's total, but in West Tennessee he outpolled Gwinn 45,173 to 24,755, taking 31,441 from Shelby County. Excluding Shelby, Gwinn took 99,058 statewide to only 86,013 for McAlister. Clearly the difference between victory for McAlister in 1932 and defeat for Gwinn in 1930 was the endorsement of E. H. Crump. At the same time, however, it is reasonable to conclude that Crump's support cost McAlister approximately 13,000 votes outside Shelby. Pope, for his part, did well, but the spottiness of his strength indicates that the old machine was not willing to forgive him for his attacks on the Lea faction. Pope won a few counties in East and West Tennessee where Peay and Horton had done well, and added a cluster of votes around his native Bledsoe County, but Patterson's candidacy and Pope's past hostility to the machine ruined any chance he had to maintain the old Peay coalition. Divided and disgraced, the machine destroyed itself in the 1932 primary.

In the general election, McAlister, the Democratic nominee, and Pope, running as an independent, were joined by the Republican nominee, John McCall. A little-known Memphis attorney, McCall had held no elected offices but had gained some exposure from a year-long stint as state commander of the American Legion. As a member of the Lily-White Republican faction, McCall was bitterly opposed by the Robert Church machine in his home county and by J. Will Taylor in East Tennessee. He had won the nomination largely because Taylor

69. *Fifty Years of Tennessee Primaries*, pp. 114-15.

had a still greater hatred for his opponent, Hal Clement. McCall's campaign was destitute, he could raise little money locally, and funds from the national headquarters were funnelled through Taylor. With inadequate funds and his party divided, McCall plainly had little chance.[70]

The general election campaign was a bitter affair, with Crump's enemies desperately trying to block him from gaining control of the governor's mansion. Pope made Crump his main target and warned that the Memphis boss sought to control the choice of senators, congressmen, and even county officeholders. His newspapers warned, "Don't Move the Capitol to Memphis," and excoriated McAlister's ties to Crump. The independent Knoxville *News-Sentinel* praised Pope as an opponent of both Horton and Crump and demanded that McAlister repudiate Crump and his methods. The Chattanooga *News* lamented, "One man has dictated to Tennesse whom it shall accept as the Democratic nominee for governor," and urged Tennesseans not to replace Lea with Crump. The Memphis *Press-Scimitar,* also independent, attacked the alleged manipulation of black votes in Shelby and said that in Pope's candidacy the people of the rural districts "have recorded their protest against machine rule in Tennessee." "The people of Tennessee chose Pope," said the Columbia *Daily Herald,* "but Crump named McAlister." By electing Pope in November, the paper continued, the voters could "end the domination of bosses and machines that has for too long been the curse of Tennessee."[71]

McAlister and Crump tried to brand Pope with the Luke Lea label and accused him of trying to stir rural antagonism against the cities. In another of his celebrated newspaper advertisements, Crump called Pope "An Eminent Demagog [sic] and a Compound Falsifier" and charged that the Lea machine was funding Pope's campaign. Crump speculated that Lea and

---

70. Chattanooga *News,* October 24, 1932. Knoxville *News-Sentinel,* November 2, 3, 9, 1932. Memphis *Commercial Appeal,* October 16, 1932.

71. Nashville *Tennessean,* October 27, 1932. Knoxville *Journal,* November 8, 1932. Knoxville *News-Sentinel,* November 2, 1932. Chattanooga *News,* August 6, 1932. Memphis *Press-Scimitar,* August 5, 1932. Columbia *Daily Herald,* July 1, August 5, 1932.

Horton had shifted fifteen to twenty thousand votes from Patterson to Pope on primary day and condemned Pope's "desperate effort to arouse hatred and prejudice among the good people in the rural sections of Tennessee against the equally good people of the splendid cities of the state." Other McAlister backers echoed Crump's charges. The Nashville *Banner* deplored the "bitter attacks made by Mr. Pope upon the largest counties in the state," and the Putnam County *Herald* accused Pope of not acting with "decent fairness in attempting to make the country people of Tennessee hate the city people."[72]

The rural faction was weakened and divided. Luke Lea supported Pope, but the press of indictments and business failures took most of his time, and, as one associate has observed, "His stinger was more or less pulled." State officials were divided in their loyalty. P. L. Harned, commissioner of education, sent pro-Pope letters to all the teachers in the state, and General W. C. Boyd threw the National Guard into Pope's campaign, but Secretary of State Ernest Haston and Highway Commissioner Robert Baker supported McAlister.[73] George Dempster of the Finance and Taxation Department endorsed Pope and used the department to further Pope's effort.[74] Horace Frierson, chairman of the state Democratic Executive Committee, charged that state employees were being instructed to vote for Pope, and in Knox County, the machine-controlled elections commission mailed instruction cards with absentee ballots that showed Pope as the Democratic nominee.[75] Horton, perhaps realizing he could only hurt Pope, stayed out of the race.

Charges surrounding reports of a Pope-Lea deal came to a climax in early November when the *Banner* reported a secret meeting in Nashville's Andrew Jackson Hotel between adminis-

---

72. Memphis *Commercial Appeal*, August 26, 1932. Memphis *Press-Scimitar*, November 2, 1932. Cookeville, *Putnam County Herald*, November 3, 1932. Nashville *Banner*, October 26, 1932. Chattanooga *Times*, October 31, 1932.

73. Chattanooga *News*, November 3, 1932. Chattanooga *Times*, November 6, 1932. Joe Hatcher interview, February 18, 1976.

74. Chattanooga *Times*, October 17, 1932.

75. Chattanooga *Times*, October 23, November 6, 1932. Chattanooga *News*, October 22, 1932.

tration representatives George Dempster and Wallace Edwards and Pope's campaign manager, James Ezell. Dempster and Edwards, Horton's secretary, were considered Lea's main links to the state government. According to the *Banner* the meeting lasted an hour and a half and was apparently tied to the mysterious burning of five thousand "unexplained" Davidson County poll tax receipts. Pope vehemently denied any alliance with Lea, claiming they had not spoken to each other in five years. Anyone who declared otherwise, he snapped, was a "damnable liar." Dempster said he had never talked politics with Pope, but he angrily told a *Banner* reporter, "I shall continue to attend any meetings I so desire without performing the ceremony of obtaining the consent of your scandal sheet."[76]

Lea's involvement, however slight, was sure to generate antagonism and Pope was soon at pains to stress his independence of the state machine. The *Sumner County News* and the Knoxville *News-Sentinel* accused Pope of relenting in his attacks on Lea while maintaining the pace against McAlister and Crump. The Chattanooga *News* said Pope was now under a burden equal to McAlister's in having the support of a machine. In fact, the *News* speculated, Crump might be the lesser of the two evils because he was too "heavy-handed" to be an effective state boss.[77] Pope was clearly being hurt in some quarters by Lea's support, and his repeated denials could not repair the damage.

Pope was also hurt by the opposition of powerful business leaders, organized labor, and blacks. McAlister's attorneys in the contest before the State Primary Board in August were Ed Seay, chief counsel of the Louisville and Nashville Railroad; Walter Armstrong, counsel for Memphis Power and Light; and K. T. McConnico, a leader of the Howse machine in Nashville and attorney for Standard Oil and the American National Bank.[78] Pope agreed with Franklin D. Roosevelt that East

---

76. Chattanooga *News*, November 4, 1932. Chattanooga *Times*, November 4, 1932. Knoxville *Journal*, November 8, 1932.
77. Gallatin, *Sumner County News*, October 13, 1932. Knoxville *News-Sentinel*, October 16, 1932. Chattanooga *News*, November 5, 1932.
78. Memphis *Press-Scimitar*, August 26, 1932.

Tennessee water power should be publicly rather than privately developed. His stand generated much antagonism among Tennessee businessmen, and the utility companies led a major effort against him in power-conscious East Tennessee.[79] Organized labor, including the Tennessee Federation of Labor and the state's railroad brotherhoods, endorsed McAlister over Pope largely on the issue of tax rates for commercial trucks. The truckers were offering formidable competition to railroads for the state's shipping business, and labor wanted the truckers heavily taxed. Pope was willing to compromise the issue, but McAlister's position was more favorable to the railroad workers' cause. Pope's willingness to use convict labor was another factor in labor's opposition. "McAlister is a friend of labor," concluded the TFL, "and Pope is not."[80]

The state's black vote also seemed likely to go overwhelmingly for McAlister. The Republican candidate, John McCall, was a Lily-White leader in Memphis, while Lewis Pope had made several strident attacks on black voting. Thus black organizations in Chattanooga and Knoxville endorsed McAlister, as did most Nashville blacks, although a splinter group stayed with McCall. Memphis blacks were likely to go solidly for McAlister too. Crump and local Republican boss Robert Church were plainly working together, as sample ballots were passed among blacks marked for Herbert Hoover and McAlister. George W. Lee, a Church lieutenant, rallied the nominally Republican troops, urging, "We should vote for Hill McAlister who has sympathy for us."[81]

Nineteen thirty-two was a depression year, but, as the Memphis *Commercial Appeal* noted, "So intense has it [the gubernatorial race] become by virtue of charges made openly by nearly every faction that national issues have been partially obscured."[82] Franklin Roosevelt was extremely popular in Ten-

---

79. Knoxville *News-Sentinel*, November 8, 1932. Memphis *Press-Scimitar*, November 9, 1932.

80. Chattanooga *Times*, July 22, 1932. Knoxville *News-Sentinel*, July 25, 1932. Memphis *Commercial Appeal*, October 21, 1932.

81. Chattanooga *News*, October 25, 1932. Knoxville *News-Sentinel*, November 6, 1932.

82. Memphis *Commercial Appeal*, November 6, 1932.

nessee, however, and both Pope and McAlister were eager to win his endorsement, but Roosevelt had nothing to gain by getting caught between two feuding factions and, working through James Farley and Senator Cordell Hull, he carefully circumvented the Tennessee election. In Roosevelt's only campaign appearance in the state, his train stopped for fifteen minutes in Knoxville, where the candidate greeted a responsive crowd with, "I just wanted to say 'Howdy!' and I'll be back to see you soon."[83] Hull best conveyed the attitudes of the national leadership in a letter to FDR aide Louis Howe, writing, "I have kept entirely aloof from this State controversy, and am giving all possible attention to safeguarding the national ticket in particular."[84] Roosevelt leaders nevertheless feared the Pope-McAlister battle would split the Democratic vote. In late October, therefore, James Farley explained to State Chairman Horace Frierson that, "I could not permit myself to be put in the position of seeming to oppose any candidate who has the regular Democratic nomination. . . . So far as our records are concerned, therefore, he [McAlister] is the Democratic candidate." Senator Hull also finally endorsed McAlister.[85]

If the national Democratic leadership stayed aloof from the Pope-McAlister campaign, state Republicans were eager to participate. A time-honored political device in East Tennessee was a system known as "trading." Under this arrangement Republicans would vote for a Democrat for one office in exchange for Democratic votes for their candidate for another office. Trading was most extensive in the hotly contested First District Congressional race. B. Carroll Reece, a five-term veteran, had lost his seat in 1930 to dissident Republican O. B. Lovette. These two faced each other again in 1932 in a race considered a toss-up. The tangled politics of the mountains took on a byzantine cast as both the Reece and Lovette factions made bargain and counter-bargain with Pope and McAlister Demo-

---

83. Knoxville *Journal*, October 23, 1932. Memphis *Press-Scimitar*, October 15, 1932.
84. Hull to Louis Howe, August 13, 1932, Container 2, File 9, Hull Papers.
85. Nashville *Banner*, October 26, 29, 1932.

crats on the county level and below. Both Republican factions hoped to trade their votes for governor for Democratic votes in the Congressional race. Such trades were usually of the simplest variety, each group agreeing to vote for the candidate of the other, and did not involve lavish payoffs. Whistling in the dark, McCall declared, "I do not believe the leaders of either of the Congressional factions would sacrifice a Republican nominee for governor."[86]

Election Day brought a solid victory for Franklin Roosevelt and Hill McAlister. Roosevelt carried the state better than two to one over Hoover, winning in both the urban and rural areas. Even in heavily Republican East Tennessee, Hoover led by only 2,774 out of 159,128 votes cast (See Tables 37 and 38). In the gubernatorial race, McAlister won; John McCall, thanks to the large vote in East Tennessee, finished second; and Lewis Pope ran a poor third (See Tables 39 and 40.). As expected, McAlister was strong in the large-urban counties, winning fifty-two percent of their vote, and also edged Pope by a narrow margin in the small-urban counties. Even excluding Shelby County, McAlister won the large-urban vote with forty-two percent, compared to thirty-five percent for McCall and twenty-three percent for Pope, despite the fact that nine of the remaining fourteen large-urban counties were in heavily Republican East Tennessee. McAlister also won a heavy majority in West Tennessee (though only thirty-seven percent outside Shelby County) and took a strong plurality in Middle Tennessee. McCall won half of the vote in East Tennessee, the grand division with the largest turnout, and won a plurality of the rural votes, but the Republicans, as usual, generated little support west of the mountains. McAlister's victory was impressive—he ran much stronger in the general election than in the primary. He won pluralities in two of three grand divisions, both the small- and the large-urban counties, and ran ahead of Pope in East Tennessee and the rural counties, areas where the admin-

---

86. Chattanooga *News*, October 22, November 3, 1932. Knoxville *News-Sentinel*, November 9, 1932. Memphis *Commercial Appeal*, October 28, 1932. Joe C. Gamble interview, June 28, 1976.

istration faction was usually strong. The Memphis *Press-Scimitar* neatly summarized the outcome, observing that even though McAlister owed his nomination to the bosses, he had been truly elected by the people.[87]

Pope's campaign simply collapsed. He won virtually nothing in East Tennessee, and his strength in Middle and West Tennessee had also weakened since the primary. The administration faction depended heavily on a large vote in East Tennessee, but McCall's presence drew much of this away. McCall's strength in the rural counties also cut into a prime source of potential administration support. Only in the small-urban counties did the old state machine push Pope close to the front-running McAlister. Pope simply could not shake the label of bolter. As T. H. Alexander of the Nashville *Tennessean* wrote, Pope could not overcome the habit of party regularity in the South. His task was further complicated by the fact that 1932 was a presidential election year when the Democrats looked like sure winners. After twelve years in the patronage wilderness, few party members cared to risk their job prospects on a bolter. Furthermore, the Crump machine could generate funds to pay the poll tax for McAlister backers, while Pope had no such organization and two dollars was a large sum in depression-ridden Tennessee.[88] The opposition of the power companies hurt him in East Tennessee, and the mountain Republicans seem to have done most of their trading with McAlister. The Democratic congressional candidate in the first district won only 7,950 votes, but Pope won 9,475, and McAlister 20,817 for a total of 30,292. Reece and Lovette, both avowed Republicans, got a total of 58,224, but McCall got only 32,461.[89]

The election of 1932 closed an era in Tennessee politics. The state machine built by Luke Lea was shattered as E. H. Crump succeeded the colonel as Boss of Tennessee. Sixteen years after

---

87. *Fifty Years of Tennessee Elections*, p. 87. Memphis *Press-Scimitar*, November 9, 1932.
88. Nashville *Tennessean*, November 9, 1932. Nashville *Banner*, November 1, 1932. Chattanooga *Times*, November 10, 1932. Will R. Manier, Jr. to James Farley, no date, Container 1, File 9, Hull Papers.
89. *Fifty Years ot Tennessee Elections*, pp. 84-86.

his ouster as Mayor of Memphis, Crump had at last established his hold on state government. For most of the next two decades, he remained the most important politician in the state. Nineteen thirty-two witnessed a similar change in the leadership of the Republican Party. Taylor and Church had held their positions in the 1920s because they managed federal patronage, but the Democrats were again in power in Washington and fewer favors would be forthcoming in the future. For ten years the state had echoed with the clash of rival political machines, but now only one survived in Boss Crump's Tennessee.

6

All Idols Were Clay

One of the most persistent debates in American political analysis has centered on the proper relationship among the three branches and among the three levels in our system of government. For more than two centuries Americans have been of a divided mind on the matter, but in the early twentieth century, in response to the rising complexity of society, power began to flow rapidly upward to the state and federal levels and to shift from the diffuse deliberative arena of the legislature to the single hand of a chief executive. Tennessee in the 1920s provides a microcosm of this process, and its particular experience provides some insight into the relationship between social change and political structure, the dangers of consolidated power, and the irony of reform.

Tennessee state government was faltering in the early 1920s: roads were unpaved, schools were inadequate, and the tax structure was failing. The changing social and economic scene in the state—the emergence of cities and industry—and the subsequent demand for increased public services were straining the state's existing governmental structure and underlining the need for a new one. The specific contours of the new system, however, were not dictated by these changes. The governor was elevated to his new place almost by default. The alternative of leaving the main responsibility for governing with the legislature was not seriously considered because the legislature had persistently failed to handle problems in the past. Also, one important organized interest, business, was ready with a plan to make the governor the center of responsibility. No counterplan was forthcoming. Discredited and without spokesmen, the legislative branch docilely surrendered to the executive.

The new state government that emerged during Austin Peay's tenure as governor (1923-1927) made tremendous strides in bettering conditions in the state. Paved highways replaced strips of mud and an eight-month school term was instituted across the state. The tax system was redesigned, making it more equitable. Higher education flourished and beautiful parks were created at Reelfoot Lake and in the Great Smoky Mountains. Peay, a physical manifestation of moral recitude, ran the government with an iron hand, and chicanery during his administration was at a minimum. The very system that, under Peay, produced these accomplishments, however, also became the vehicle for the creation of a state political machine. Peay's successor, Henry Horton, with virtually no state-wide personal following, needed Luke Lea and Rogers Caldwell in order to survive as governor. Using Caldwell's money, Horton's authority, and Lea's newspapers, the machine quickly came to dominate the state. Road and school construction was used to influence factional squabbles at the local level in order to topple the administration's enemies and to boost its friends. Jobs and contracts rewarded supporters and enticed the wavering. Officials who refused to cooperate in dispensing the largesse were dismissed. Lea's three newspapers, the Knoxville *Journal,* the Nashville *Tennessean,* and the Memphis *Commercial Appeal,* extolled Horton and damned his foes. Buttressed by this potent array of forces, the machine ran Tennessee in the late 1920s. Their power was destroyed, however, when Caldwell and Company failed and they were accused of using state money in a vain attempt to save the conglomerate.

The pattern of Tennessee politics in these years was set by the clash of two highly personal factions. The administration faction emerged gradually during the five years of the Austin Peay governorship. First elected in 1922 with the support of the state's urban areas and his native Middle Tennessee, Peay's backing altered drastically as his term progressed. Although the Reorganization Act was popular with the governor's original constituency, his emphasis on expanded public services benefited the state's rural areas. Moreover, Peay's tax measures weighed heavily on the cities. As a consequence, the Peay faction came to include the rural and small-urban areas across the state. In addition, Peay carefully cultivated Republican East Tennessee which, by 1926, was providing him with important votes at the polls and in the General Assembly.

Because the state's urban areas were driven into opposition by Peay's taxation and public service programs, the conflict between the two factions became basically urban-rural in nature. The opposition faction included an amorphous collection of smaller machines scattered across the state, but it had as its base the Hilary Howse machine in Nashville and the personal following of E. B. Stahlman and his Nashville *Banner* in Middle Tennessee. The wide circulation of the *Banner* was extremely important in building opposition strength in the middle part of the state. To this core was added, except in 1924 and 1930, the E. H. Crump machine in Shelby County, an increasingly important element in Tennessee politics.

Tennessee in the twenties was an eager participant in what George Tindall has characterized "business progressivism" in Southern state governments. This particular brand of progressivism, at least in the Volunteer State, was demanded, supported, and enacted largely by the people from the farms and small towns that comprised the administration faction. The major urban areas provided the most determined opposition to these programs. Just as the "rednecks" had sparked much reform legislation in Mississippi and the "Southern Agrarians" had contributed to moving President Woodrow Wilson "toward a dynamic, positive program of federal actions," so the farmers of Tennessee also backed important reform moves. Tindall's implication that "business progressivism" in the twenties was an urban movement does not seem to apply to Tennessee.[1]

The basic organizational unit in Tennessee politics prior to 1920 was the personal faction. Tennessee actually contained two

---

1. Tindall, "Business Progressivism," pp. 92-106.

separate one-party systems. The Republicans controlled the eastern one-third of the state, and the Democrats held Middle and West Tennessee. Since neither party was seriously challenged in its own bailiwick, both tended to split into collections of quarreling groups centered on local bosses or courthouse cronies. Like most Southern states, Tennessee thus suffered from a serious disorganization of leadership. Candidates for statewide offices won election by building coalitions based on their own personal appeal. Such jerry-built structures usually could not be willed to potential successors, so the state's politics were in constant upheaval.

The "business progressive" measures of the Austin Peay years, however, changed this pattern. As power shifted from the local to the state level, and from the legislature to the executive, the governor became a more potent political force. The legislation of the twenties moved the tools of coalition-building, particularly road and school construction, from the local leaders to the governor. The result was a concentration of leadership in the administration faction headed by Austin Peay and Luke Lea. With their new powers, they could control the Democratic Party and through it, the state government.

Had Lea not become involved in the Caldwell affair, he might have enjoyed a long reign as Boss of Tennessee. The main challenge to his position came from Edward Crump in Memphis. In the late twenties, Shelby County's percentage of the state's Democratic vote was growing rapidly, and Crump's gubernatorial candidates were nearly successful in 1926 and 1928; nevertheless, Lea's control of state government had enabled him to bring Crump into line in 1930. Crump was a controversial man who inspired intense hatred in many parts of Tennessee, thus his intervention against Horton in the impeachment episode paradoxically may have saved the governor. No other man could have touched Lea in 1930. The scandals of 1931, however, destroyed Lea and shattered his machine. With the election of Hill McAlister as governor in 1932, Boss Crump proceeded to build his own state machine and to become invincible in Tennessee for the next sixteen years.

Tennessee politics in the 1920s is a study in the irony of

reform. Staid institutions were rearranged and bold legislation was passed, but the measures designed to pull the state into the twentieth century also permitted political chicanery on a scale that scandalized and embarrassed its citizens. The strong executive office and strong state government that gave Tennessee new roads, parks, and schools, also permitted a tangle of deals and bargains. The Peay legislation poured the old wine of corruption into the new skins of reform. Perhaps more than anything else, the workings of Tennessee politics in the twenties is a reminder that reform, like most human efforts, trails both good and ill in its wake.

TENNESSEE IN TURMOIL

APPENDICES
TABLES
BIBLIOGRAPHY
INDEX

APPENDICES
TABLES
BIBLIOGRAPHY
INDEX

Appendix A

Definition of Urban and Rural

For the purposes of this study, Tennessee's ninety-five counties were divided into three categories based on the urban population within their boundaries. Following the practice of the United States Bureau of the Census, a town was defined as urban if it contained at least 2500 people. Rural counties were those containing no urban population at all. Small-urban counties were those in which less than thirty percent of the total population of the county lived in urban areas. Counties in which more than thirty percent of the total population lived in urban areas were considered large-urban counties.

During the years 1920 to 1930, certain counties changed categories. To compensate for these population shifts, the percentage change between the 1920 and 1930 censuses, or between the 1930 and 1940 censuses, was divided by ten and added by increments to the base 1920 or 1930 figure. If, for example, a county was twenty-five percent urban in 1920, and thirty-five percent urban in 1930, then at some point it must be moved from the small-urban to the large-urban category. The percent of change was ten points over ten years, or one percent per year. Hence the county is assumed to have become thirty percent urban in 1925. Below is the categorization of Tennessee counties over the period 1920-1932.[1]

Rural Counties, 1920-32

Anderson	Cheatham	Cumberland	Franklin	Hardin
Benton	Chester	Decatur	Grainger	Hawkins
Bledsoe	Claiborne	DeKalb	Grundy	Henderson
Cannon	Clay	Fayette	Hancock	Hickman
Carroll	Crockett	Fentress	Hardeman	Houston

1. U.S., Department of Commerce, Bureau of Census, *Fifteenth Census of the United States: 1930, Population*, vol. 3, pt. 2, pp. 891-896.

Humphreys	Lewis	Moore	Rhea	Trousdale
Jackson	McNairy	Morgan	Scott	Union
Jefferson	Macon	Overton	Sequatchie	Van Buren
Johnson	Marion	Perry	Sevier	Wayne
Lake	Meigs	Pickett	Smith	White
Lauderdale	Monroe	Polk	Stewart	

Small-Urban, 1920-32

Bedford	Dyer	Lawrence	Putnam	Unicoi
Campbell	Gibson	Lincoln	Robertson	Warren
Carter	Giles	Marshall	Rutherford	Weakley
Cocke	Greene	Maury	Sumner	Williamson
Coffee	Haywood	Obion	Tipton	Wilson
Dickson				

Large-Urban, 1920-32

Bradley	Hamblen	Knox	Roane	Sullivan
Davidson	Hamilton	Madison	Shelby	Washington

Counties changing from small-urban to large-urban between 1920-1932:

Blount, 1930   Loudon, 1924   Montgomery, 1932
Henry, 1930   McMinn, 1928

In addition, Henry County dropped from the large-urban class to the small-urban class in 1932.

Appendix B

The Grand Divisions of Tennessee

East

Anderson	Cocke	Hawkins	Monroe	Scott
Bledsoe	Cumberland	Jefferson	Morgan	Sevier
Blount	Grainger	Johnson	McMinn	Sullivan
Bradley	Greene	Knox	Polk	Unicoi
Campbell	Hamblen	Loudon	Rhea	Union
Carter	Hamilton	Marion	Roane	Washington
Claiborne	Hancock	Meigs	Sequatchie	

Middle

Bedford	Fentress	Lawrence	Overton	Sumner
Cannon	Franklin	Lewis	Perry	Trousdale
Cheatham	Giles	Lincoln	Pickett	Van Buren
Clay	Grundy	Macon	Putnam	Warren
Coffee	Hickman	Marshall	Robertson	Wayne
Davidson	Houston	Maury	Rutherford	White
DeKalb	Humphreys	Montgomery	Smith	Williamson
Dickson	Jackson	Moore	Stewart	Wilson

West

Benton	Dyer	Hardin	Lake	Obion
Carroll	Fayette	Haywood	Lauderdale	Shelby
Chester	Gibson	Henderson	Madison	Tipton
Crockett	Hardeman	Henry	McNairy	Weakley
Decatur				

Appendix C

Support Scores

Support scores were used to measure the support individual legislators gave to the administration faction. I derived these scores through a simple form of roll call analysis. Since Austin Peay and Henry Horton were closely identified with Luke Lea, legislators who supported their positions are considered pro-Lea. I established the governor's attitude toward bills before the legislature by reading his messages as published in the House and Senate *Journals*. I made no attempt to group roll calls on the basis of issue content or any other criteria, simply including all measures on communication to the legislature. Using this information, I constructed an index of support modeled on the *Congressional Quarterly's* index of support for the president. I divided the number of times a member voted with the governor by the number of times he voted. This percentage, multiplied by 100 to give a whole number, was the index of support for each member. Following are the support scores for each legislator and the roll calls used in compiling those scores.

1923 GENERAL ASSEMBLY

Senate

A. Anderson	66	H. Flowers	44	W. Overton	55
W. Ausmus	17	F. Gailor	38	J. Perry	75
D. Barger	75	W. Gant	88	J. Reid	100
H. Bennett	75	W. Hake	86	I. Remine	22
S. Breazeale	44	S. Hill, S.	63	G. Rhodes	75
C. Brown	89	L. Hill, L.	56	F. Scates	25
E. Bryan	75	C. Larsen	38	R. Swink	55
E. Butler	25	S. Maiden	75	I. Warren	25
W. Clayton	56	L. Mayo	33	W. Washington	75
J. Durham	89	Z. Massey	22	H. Whitfield	100
T. English	78	P. Moffitt	43	J. Wiseman	56

House

A. Adams	63	O. Fox	88	J. Odle	87
J. Allen	89	R. Ginn	00	M. Owens	67
W. Barry	13	J. Gordon	88	A. Park	100
W. Bass	88	M. Griffin	63	J. Peal	71
I. Beasley	38	R. Greene	25	G. Peek	33
L. Bejach	33	S. Grindstaff	25	I. Peterson	89
W. Bogle	29	W. Grubb	67	W. Prince	67
S. Bratton	89	F. Hale	71	W. Rackley	78
G. Buckner	71	G. Hall	99	J. Rowsey	100
W. Burton	00	J. Hamilton	88	R. Russell (Knox)	40
J. Butler	78	J. Hamner	33	W. Russell (Maur)	86
H. Candler	63	W. Hatcher	100	J. Shea	17
C. Carothers	100	J. Haynie	88	W. Sloan	44
G. Choate	63	W. Haynes (Fran)	67	E. Smith	75
C. Claiborne	100	G. Haynes (Unic)	37	J. Sparks	100
W. Clark	78	R. Hilliard	100	J. Spencer	67
W. Clarke	25	J. Jacobs	71	F. Sperry	80
D. Coleman	75	E. Jeter	33	J. Stewart	75
W. Cooper	50	A. Johns	67	W. Stone	78
H. Crawford (Fay)	44	T. King	88	D. Street	100
C. Crawford (Law)	89	J. Kivette	100	J. Sullins	100
R. Croskery	44	J. Lay	100	R. Swann	100
J. Cunningham (Shel)	55	W. McClanahan	67	E. Tatum	100
		N. McDaniel	78	J. Terry	33
E. Cunningham (War)	100	H. McMillen	100	J. Thomas	100
		H. Major	75	J. Thompson	38
C. Dean	50	J. Marshall	50	T. Tyne	55
A. Drinnon	33	A. Matthews	100	J. Wade	13
J. Durham	88	T. Maxey	50	W. Walton	75
O. Easterly	25	W. Miles	100	C. Willett	100
J. Edwards	78	R. Moore	71	I. Williams	13
G. Ellis	75	R. Neely	100	B. Wilson (Andr)	50
J. Fielder	50	E. Norvell	00	C. Wilson (Coff)	29
		T. Nuchols	14	J. Yoakley	100

1923 General Assembly—Roll Calls (Yea-Nay-Present) (One independent voter is included in the total vote but not in the party subtotals.)

Senate		Dems	Reps	Total
HB 183,	Reorganization Act—to alter the structure of state government. Administration favored	25-0-1	0-3	25-4-1
HB 1103,	Enlarge state board of elections commission from three to five members. Administration favored.	16-11	0-3	16-15

164 / *Tennessee in Turmoil*

SB 508,	Eads Veto—jurisdictional dispute between Shelby County and the town of Eads. Administration opposed motion to override pro-Shelby measure	13-5-8	4-0	18-5-8
SB 899,	To finance road building through bond issues. Administration opposed.	19-7	3-0	23-7
HB 541,	Distribute auto tax fees back to counties. Administration opposed.	18-11	3-1	21-12
HB 462,	Place a two cent per gallon tax on gasoline to finance road building. Administration favored.	25-2	2-1	27-4
HB 443,	Impose three percent excise tax on corporate profits. Administration favored.	25-2	2-2	27-5
HB 259,	Return power to regulate utilities from state commission to local governments. Administration favored. (Vote is on motion to table.)	13-12	4-0	18-12

House		Dems	Reps	Total
HB 183,	Reorganization Act—to alter the structure of state government. Administration favored.	67-3-3	6-13-1	73-16-4
HB 1103,	Enlarge state board of elections commission from three to five members. Administration favored.	55-15	2-15	57-30
SB 508,	Eads Veto—jurisdictional dispute between Shelby County and the town of Eads. Administration opposed. Motion to override pro-Shelby measure.	16-47-5	8-10-1	24-57-6
SB 899,	To finance road building through bond issues. Administration opposed.	27-30-1	18-2	45-32-1

HB 541,	Distribute auto tax fees back to counties. Administration opposed.	31-21-1	8-5-3	39-26-4
HB 443,	Impose three percent excise tax on corporate profits. Administration favored.	66-9	10-10-2	76-19-2
HB 259,	Return power to regulate utilities from state commission to local governments. Administration favored.	64-1	8-13	72-14
HB 45,	To cut the ceiling on interest rates from eight to six percent. Administration favored.	40-26	9-10	49-36
HB 1135,	Miscellaneous Appropriations Bill. Administration favored.	53-14	7-2	60-16

1925 GENERAL ASSEMBLY

Senate

H. Bennett	75	W. Grubbs	67	J. Shields	44
S. Breazeale	67	L. Hill	56	C. Simonton	56
J. Brown	33	D. Humphreys	63	C. Sims	56
E. Butler	83	T. King	40	J. Spencer	14
S. Carothers	50	T. Locke	75	J. Trice	100
S. Doty	71	S. Maiden	63	O. Underhill	56
G. Evans	33	H. McGinness	38	J. Vanzant	44
F. Fuller	56	W. Monroe	55	A. Vincent	50
W. Fuqua	22	W. Overton	14	R. Wallace	56
W. Furlow	25	J. Owen	22	I. Warren	60
A. Graves	78	J. Shelton	100	H. Whitfield	89

House

J. Acuff	33	C. Brooks	43	A. Cooper (Maur)	83
E. Allen	50	T. Brown (Blnt)	55	T. Cooper (Coff)	14
T. Anthony	86	B. Brown (Warr)	55	S. Davis (Dav)	60
F. Armstrong	71	C. Bushart	60	A. Davis (Knox)	67
T. Atkins	50	J. Butler	33	H. Dowell	50
H. Barger	55	W. Carter	50	T. Driver	55
W. Barry	100	G. Chamlee	83	J. Durham	00
W. Bogle	60	G. Choate	71	T. Early	67
R. Boyd (Monr)	80	D. Coleman	100	N. Eubank	67
M Boyd (Shel)	50	W. Clark	50	J. Edwards	60
C. Boyer	40	D. Conaster	83	J. Fielder	55
S. Bratton	86	R. Cook	50	O. Fox	43

166 / *Tennessee in Turmoil*

H. Frank	29	C. Larsen	50	W. Rackley	29
F. Gemmill	50	J. Lee	50	W. Riggins	33
R. Gallimore	55	J. Lewis	55	D. Sewell	29
R. Gleaves	67	W. Loveless	33	B. Ruffin	100
W. Gray	80	W. Lowe	60	J. Shoun	71
A. Greene	25	W. Lyle	100	A. Simms	40
C. Gwinn	50	J. Marshall	100	E. Sparks	50
W. Hatcher	67	J. Moran	20	E. Spiceland	100
W. Haynes	29	J. McCleish	75	J. Stalcup	55
J. Haynie	50	F. McDaniel	43	G. Stockton	83
J. Hamilton	100	A. McKnight	60	L. Stroup	100
J. Hallberg	100	L. Miller (Hard)	83	J. Summer	71
J. Henard	50	W. Miller (Laud)	75	J. Thompson	50
D. Hill	43	R. Neely	60	O. Tindall	80
A. Holland	83	W. Overton	43	P. Wallace (Shel)	50
J. Howard	83	E. Parker	55	W. Wallace (McNa)	80
R. Hutchings	17	S. Patton	86	B. Ward	86
B. James	67	J. Peal	80	J. White	86
W. Jennings	33	J. Perry	100	W. Whitwell	75
S. Johnson	33	I. Peterson	60	C. Willett	80
C. Key	86	R. Poston	20	J. Yoakley	100

1925 General Assembly—Roll Calls

Senate			Dems	Reps	Total
HB 12,	Tax on processed tobacco products. Administration favored.		20-8	3-1	23-9
HB 780,	General Education Act—to centralize and upgrade the state educational system. Administration favored.		23-4	2-2	25-6
SB 1028,	Miscellaneous Appropriations Act. Administration opposed motion to override Peay veto of this bill.		15-11	2-1	17-12
SB 831,	To establish board to decide disputes with highway contractors. Administration opposed.		12-14-1	3-0	15-14-1
HB 64,	To create a commission to establish Reelfoot Lake State Park. Administration favored.		20-7-1	3-0	23-7-1

Appendix C / 167

SB 524,	To obtain Little River tract to establish Great Smoky Mountains Park. Administration favored.	16-12	4-0	20-12
SJR 20,	To establish committee to weigh Miscellaneous Appropriations and General Revenue bills. Administration opposed.	19-7	3-0	22-7
SB 219,	To return power to regulate utilities from state commission to local governments. Administration favored.	13-13	4-0	17-13
SB 355,	To curb "loan sharks" but permit interest rates of 42%. Administration opposed	16-9	1-2	17-11
House		**Dems**	**Reps**	**Total**
HB 12,	Tax on processed tobacco products. Administration favored.	59-13-3	9-13-1	68-26-4
HB 780,	General Education Act to centralize and upgrade the state educational system. Administration favored.	41-21-7	14-5-3	55-26-10
SB 1028,	Miscellaneous Appropriations Act. Administration opposed motion to override Peay's veto	37-26-5	15-1-2	52-27-7
SB 831,	To establish board to decide disputes with highway contractors. Administration opposed.	37-26-5	15-1-2	52-27-7
SB 524,	To obtain Little River tract to establish Great Smoky Mountains park. Administration favored.	36-36-3	22-0	58-36-3
SJR 20,	To establish committee to weigh Miscellaneous Appropriations and General Revenue bills. Administration opposed.	17-31-5	4-9	21-40-5

168 / *Tennessee in Turmoil*

| SB 355, | To curb "loan sharks" but permit interest rates of 42%. Administration opposed. | 23-48-1 | 14-6 | 37-54-1 |

1927 GENERAL ASSEMBLY

Senate

J. Albright	43	J. Chrisman	100	D. Layne	38
T. Atkins	78	T. Cummings	00	S. Lewis	75
W. Barry	67	E. Fitzhugh	17	T. Locke	00
D. Bramley	75	A. Greaves	88	A. McKnight	22
S. Bratton	100	J. Hallberg	50	W. Miller	60
S. Breazeale	86	G. Harris	44	W. Moody	67
W. Brown (Bed)	00	D. Henry	11	W. Overton	11
J. Brown (Shel)	11	W. Hensley	13	I. Remine	22
E. Butler (John)	100	L. Hill	88	J. Shelton	100
J. Butler (McNa)	100	H. Horton	100	A. Wiggs	38
L. Chambers	33	T. Keaton	38	C. Willett	83

House

E. Allen	25	T. Driver	38	J. Lankester	38
W. Anderson (Knox)	63	N. Eubank	75	C. Larsen	25
W. Anderson (Put)	38	J. Finch	50	A. Lipscomb	14
E. Arnold	33	W. Foster	38	C. Love	88
H. Avery	40	O. Fox	63	M. Lumpkins	55
F. Barton	25	H. Franks	38	E. Luther	13
T. Bean	50	S. Frazier	29	W. McClanahan	17
R. Beck	14	J. Fugate	20	J. McCleish	86
W. Bell	14	R. Gallimore	55	W. McDonough	14
J. Blevins	50	J. Gammon	75	R. McReynolds	80
W. Bogle	60	J. Gillum	14	S. Maiden	88
M. Boyd	38	R. Gleaves	50	O. Malone	43
A. Brown	43	J. Gordon	75	J. Mantooth	50
C. Bushart	25	J. Hale	50	G. Mitchell	25
R. Caldwell	43	E. Hall	29	C. Mooney	25
C. Campbell	50	S. Hames	86	A. Moose	88
Z. Carrey	17	J. Hamilton	83	B. Murphree	67
G. Chamlee	43	W. Haynes	00	R. Neely	83
W. Clark (Dav)	29	R. Hickey	75	H. Nichol	38
J. Clark (McMn)	33	A. Holland	55	J. Pettyjohn	50
D. Coleman	100	J. Hooker	38	R. Potter	40
R. Cook	50	L. Hughes	29	J. Pratt	60
C. Cortner	60	R. Hutchings	25	W. Prince	13
J. Cowley	29	L. Jetton	50	J. Riley	55
P. Cox	29	F. Johnson	43	P. Roach	50
J. Craig	60	J. Jones (Knox)	86	N. Robinson (Cart)	71
L. Culbreath	38	G. Keaton	71	W. Robinson (Ruth)	63
J. Dannel	63	D. Kemmer	50	H. Savage	71
S. Davis	80	C. Key	75	R. Seaton	25

J. Sloan	88	J. Thompson	83	W. Wilkinson	50
E. Spiceland	55	J. Trotter	63	B. Williams (Knox)	55
G. Stockton	38	W. Wallace	60	E. Williams (Shel)	25
B. Taylor	38	J. White	14	C. Wrinkle	67

1927 General Assembly—Roll Calls (One independent voter is included in the total vote but not in the party subtotals.)

Senate		Dems	Reps	Total
SB 263,	To provide funds for the construction of new buildings at the University of Tennessee. Administration favored.	20-4	4-0	25-4
SJR 11,	Constitutional amendment to permit the taxation of intangible property. Administration favored.	16-9-1	4-0	20-10-1
SB 288,	To raise state gasoline tax by one cent and divide the proceeds equally among the counties. Administration faction voted no on a motion to override Peay's veto.	11-13	2-2	13-16
HB 583,	To issue ten million dollars in short term notes to finance roads. Administration favored.	15-7	4-0	20-7
SB 835,	To permit showing motion pictures on Sunday. Administration faction voted no on a motion to override Peay's veto.	17-7	0-3	18-10
HB 246,	General Appropriations Bill. Administration faction voted no on a motion to override Peay's veto.	17-9-1	2-1-1	20-10-2
SB 771,	Urban sponsored bill that virtually gave away transportation franchises. Administration voted no on a motion to override Peay's veto.	16-3	0-2	17-5

SB 26,	To increase Confederate pensions. Administration faction voted no on a motion to override Peay's veto.	19-7	0-3	20-10
HB 348,	To permit open fishing season in Warren County. Administration faction voted no on a motion to override Peay's veto.	9-13-1	0-2	10-15-1

House		Dems	Reps	Total
SB 14,	To tax processed tobacco products. Administration favored.	68-6	14-5	82-11
SJR 263,	To provide funds for the construction of new buildings at the University of Tennessee. Administration favored.	50-22-1	13-4-1	63-26-2
SB 288,	To raise state gasoline tax by one cent and divide the proceeds equally among the counties. Administration faction voted no on a motion to override Peay's veto.	63-14	18-1	81-15
HB 835,	To permit showing motion pictures on Sunday. Administration faction voted no on a motion to override Peay's veto.	40-17-6	5-13	45-30-6
HB 246,	General Appropriations Bill. Administration faction voted no on a motion to override Peay's veto.	43-28	14-5	57-33
SB 26,	To increase Confederate pensions. Administration faction voted no on a motion to override Peay's veto.	66-10-1	11-6	77-16-1
HB 348,	To permit open fishing season in Warren County. Administration faction voted no on a motion to override Peay's veto.	41-20-5	9-6-2	50-26-7

1929 GENERAL ASSEMBLY

Senate

W. Abernathy (Grun)	42	H. Candler	85	C. Larsen	31
W. Abernathy (McNa)	100	W. Clarke	77	J. Lee	33
		J. Cummings	100	W. Love	58
J. Adams	77	J. Durham	50	J. Parks	78
J. Avery	100	S. Fitzhugh	30	T. Poe	90
W. Barry	33	J. Gordon	58	T. Pratt	70
J. Bean	69	A. Gray	92	C. Rainey	67
T. Beasley	91	W. Grubb	83	T. Schlater	11
S. Bratton	67	F. Hall	38	J. Toomey	77
C. Brown (Giles)	54	W. Hensley	92	A. Wiggs	83
J. Brown (Shel)	30	L. Hill	75	C. Willett	31
		J. Keefe	8		

House

A. Adams	87	W. Haynes	38	S. Reid	100
R. Alexander	44	B. Henderson (Mad)	89	J. Riley	86
W. Anderson (Put)	63	G. Henderson (Car)	67	J. Robbins	86
W. Anderson (Knox)	83	J. Hicks	00	N. Robison (Cart)	100
H. Baker	75	H. Holman	78	W. Robison (Ruth)	78
J. Biggs	75	W. House	100	P. Scott	67
A. Blakeney	22	R. Huffman	100	R. Seaton	71
H. Blanken	88	L. Hughes	17	E. Simpson	88
W. Bogle	89	I. Human	100	J. Sloan	100
H. Brooks	75	R. Hutchings	67	G. Smith	78
B. Brown (War)	75	C. Jackson	67	G. Snoddy	88
R. Brown (Hick)	89	C. Johnson	83	J. Spencer	100
A. Brown (Uni)	44	J. Jones (Knox)	83	H. Spivey	100
D. Byrge	100	J. Jones (Hend)	71	T. Stevenson	100
E. Carter	22	W. Latham	78	G. Stockton	25
G. Chamlee	56	J. Levine	71	B. Taylor (Dav)	25
T. Chapman	88	R. Lewis	100	T. Taylor (McMn)	25
F. Cohn	22	C. Love	100	W. Thompson	71
D. Coleman	100	W. Lowry	56	C. Toler	71
W. Cook	14	R. McReynolds	25	H. Tull	25
F. Copeland	100	J. McWherter	78	H. Vance	78
C. Crabtree	22	R. Miles	67	H. Veal	71
L. Creasy	38	C. Moore	86	W. Ward	100
J. Crosby	55	A. Moose	75	R. Ware	50
C. Denton	88	C. Morse	67	F. Warren (Croc)	40
J. Dykes	50	H. Naylor	89	N. Warren (Hrdn)	25
E. Eblen	50	R. Neeley	67	G. Warren (Hump)	33
L. Ferguson	89	R. Orr	22	J. White	63
S. Fitzpatrick	71	R. Overton	89	C. Wilkes	89
W. Foster	40	F. Parrott	100	B. Williams	75
R. Gooch	50	J. Pettyjohn	75	R. Wilson (VanB)	33
J. Greer	56	W. Phillips	100	W. Wilson (Fay)	100
C. Hardin	75	M. Priest	100	J. Wolfe	71
L. Harrell	56	K. Rayner	14		

1929 General Assembly—Roll Calls

Senate		Dems	Reps	Total
HB 161,	To raise the state gasoline tax to five cents. Administration favored.	18-6	8-0	26-6
HB 268,	To create a board to review applications for pardons. Administration favored.	15-5	5-2	20-7
HB 43,	To amend the natural gas inspection act, Chapter 33, Public Acts of 1927. Administration favored.	11-12-1	8-0	19-12-1
SB 397,	To tax liquid carbonic acid gas. Administration favored.	15-7	6-1	21-8
HB 162,	To amend Chapter 21, Public Acts of 1923. Administration favored.	7-13	1-6	8-19
SB 26,	To establish a commission to codify state laws. Administration faction voted no on a motion to override Horton's veto.	11-10-1	8-1	19-11-1
SB 90,	To register the operations of motor vehicles—the "bus bill." Administration faction voted no on a motion to override Horton's veto.	14-10	4-3	18-13
SB 311,	To require the highway department to pay certain costs. Administration voted no on a motion to override Horton's veto.	13-10-1	0-8	13-18-1
SR 15,	To investigate the operations of the highway department. Administration faction voted yes on a motion to table this resolution.	12-13	6-1	18-14
HB 38,	To authorize the Funding Board to borrow ten million dollars for the construction of roads. Administration favored.	16-8-1	7-1	23-9-1

HB 29,	To extend from five to ten years the time for maturity of bonds previously issued for highway construction. Administration favored.	17-5	6-1	23-6
HB 114,	To authorize the Funding Board to approve the selection of depositories for state highway funds. Administration favored.	14-9	7-1	21-10
HB 26,	To abolish the state property tax. Administration favored.	19-4-1	6-1	25-5-1

House		Dems	Reps	Total
HB 468,	To amend the tax on processed tobacco. Administration favored.	49-17	16-7-4	65-24-4
SB 397,	To tax liquid carbonic acid gas. Administration favored.	36-17-1	16-7-2	52-24-3
HB 162,	To amend Chapter 21, Public Acts of 1923. Administration favored.	46-14-1	16-5-2	62-19-3
SB 26,	To establish a commission to codify state laws. Administration faction voted no on a motion to override Horton's veto.	38-31	15-8-3	53-39-3
SB 90,	To register the operation of motor vehicles—the "bus bill." Administration faction voted no on a motion to override Horton's veto.	47-20-1	13-13-1	60-33-2
HB 38,	To authorize the Funding Board to borrow ten million dollars for the construction of roads. Administration favored.	45-20	20-4	65-24
HB 26,	To abolish the state property tax. Administration favored.	45-18	17-4-2	62-22-2

1931 GENERAL ASSEMBLY

Senate

W. Abernathy	92	H. Clements	67	C. Jackson	79
J. Albright	91	T. Coleman	79	C. Kennedy	50
R. Alexander	55	C. Cornelius	64	C. Larsen	36
H. Anderson	78	W. Craig	77	O. Mahon	75
G. Ault	86	L. Doak	58	W. Monroe	83
T. Berry	92	J. Durham	64	A. Officer	85
A. Broadbent	92	L. Ewell	86	M. Priest	86
J. Brown	31	W. Faulkner	44	J. Riley	79
H. Candler	73	S. Fitzhugh	50	J. Spencer	92
J. Chambliss	73	A. Graves	67	J. Todd	64
W. Clarke	92	T. Hoppel	82	C. Vaughan	91

House

C. Alexander	89	J. George	50	J. Murphy	50
J. Atchley	11	J. Gervins	50	R. Murray	67
W. Bell	78	L. Gilbert	56	H. Naylor	88
C. Bogart	100	J. Gillum	67	R. Neely	33
W. Boswell	75	M. Goodwin	60	B. Nixon	43
E. Bradshaw	33	W. Green (Wil)	75	K. Nuckolls	55
R. Brown (Hick)	50	J. Geer	38	R. Overton	75
A. Brown (Unic)	88	W. Griggs	63	E. Parker	88
R. Campbell	60	J. Hamilton	89	L. Payne (Dav)	22
D. Canale	33	L. Harrell	44	J. Payne (Ham)	38
E. Carter	29	G. Harris	71	A. Peay	44
G. Chamlee	55	C. Haston	78	J. Pettyjohn	86
F. Cohn	38	W. Haynes	22	J. Ridley	78
D. Coleman	71	G. Henderson	75	J. Rush	63
W. Cook	25	J. Hicks	33	E. Sanders	33
A. Cooper	63	H. Holman	44	E. Shaw	60
C. Crabtree	25	J. Holtsinger	71	J. Shutts	60
L. Creasy	50	L. Hughes	20	J. Siler	55
G. Cross (Dav)	44	W. Hunt	75	G. Smith	71
G. Cross (Rone)	44	G. Jaynes	67	G. Snoddy	66
W. Crawley	75	O. Johnson	55	D. Sparkman	60
J. Cummings	50	W. Jones (Giles)	67	J. Sprouse	50
S. Daniel	88	J. Jones (Hend)	33	T. Stevenson	50
C. Denton	38	W. Lowery	100	G. Stockton	56
W. Draper	55	W. Matthews	44	L. Stone	83
E. Duncan	78	B. Maxwell	38	W. Story	44
W. Durham	63	A. Maysilles	67	W. Swallows	78
W. Dyer	80	H. McCory	75	T. Taylor	29
H. Earthman	50	J. McMurray	88	J. Tipton	75
N. Eubank	78	J. McWherter	43	C. Toler	71
H. Franks	43	J. Moneyhun	50	H. Tull	40
J. Gamble	56	C. Mooney	33	R. Wilson (VanB)	50
T. Gaines	75	A. Moose	78	W. Wilson (Fay)	33

1931 General Assembly—Roll Calls

Senate		Dems	Reps	Total
SB 940,	To relieve counties of providing the right of way for highways. Administration favored.	24-3	4-0	28-3
HB 667,	To appoint an assistant attorney general for the sixth district, including Davidson County. Administration faction voted no on a motion to override Horton's veto.	18-2-6	2-2-1	20-4-7
HB 679,	To terminate the offices of two investigators for the attorney general in the sixth district. Administration faction voted no on a motion to override Horton's veto.	20-1-4	2-2	22-3-4
SB 481,	To increase the state gasoline tax. Administration favored.	16-12	4-1	20-13
HB 1283,	To renew the obligation of nine million dollars in short term highway notes. Administration favored.	16-6	5-0	21-6
SJR 43,	To dissolve the Probe Committee. Administration favored.	17-11	4-1	21-12
HB 251,	To transfer funds from the highway department to the General Fund. Administration opposed.	22-3	3-1	25-4
HB 1,	To authorize the Funding Board to borrow money to meet state debts. Administration favored.	19-6	4-0	23-6
SB 4,	To authorize counties to levy taxes. Administration favored.	21-5-1	4-0	25-5-1

SB 13,	To tax stocks and bonds. Administration favored.	20-5	1-1	21-6
SB 43,	To levy a general income tax. Administration favored.	21-6	2-1	23-7
SB 63,	To amend the tobacco tax act. Administration favored.	23-3	3-0	26-3
HB 179,	To give the state treasurer custody of funds allocated to the highway department. Administration favored.	18-7	4-0	22-7
HB 74,	To repeal the Fort Negley Appropriation. Administration favored.	19-3	4-0	23-3

House		Dems	Reps	Total
HB 679,	To terminate the offices of two investigators for the attorney general in the sixth district. Administration faction voted no on a motion to override Horton's veto.	53-11-1	9-2-2	62-13-3
SB 481,	To increase the state gasoline tax. Administration favored.	49-28-1	12-2-1	61-30-2
HB 761,	To validate a school board contract with two teachers. Administration faction voted no on a motion to override Horton's veto.	51-14-8	13-0	64-14-8
HB 1283,	To renew the obligation of nine million dollars in short term highway notes. Administration favored.	42-33-1	11-3	53-36-1
SJR 43,	To dissolve the Probe Committee. Administration favored.	50-26	12-1-1	62-27-1
SB 4,	To authorize counties to levy taxes. Administration favored.	53-22	11-2	64-24
SB 13,	To tax stocks and bonds. Administration favored.	62-9-1	7-2-1	69-11-2

SB 43,	To level a general income tax. Administration favored.	50-23	6-8	56-31
	To impeach the Governor of Tennessee.	37-45	4-13	41-58

Tables

TABLE 1: Raw Vote, 1922
Democratic Gubernatorial Primary

	Peay	McMillin	Hannah	Gwinn
TOTAL	63,954	59,938	24,033	15,143
Grand Division				
East	10,008	14,195	12,889	343
Mid	33,166	33,740	6,783	2,433
West	20,780	12,003	4,361	12,367
Rural-Urban				
Rural	15,073	20,660	10,305	3,736
Small-Urban	25,931	22,641	7,898	7,327
Large-Urban	22,950	16,637	5,830	4,080

TABLE 2: Percentage Vote, 1922
Democratic Gubernatorial Primary

	Peay	McMillin	Hannah	Gwinn
TOTAL	39%	37%	15%	9%
Grand Division				
East	27	38	34	1
Mid	44	44	9	3
West	42	24	9	25
Rural-Urban				
Rural	30	42	21	7
Small-Urban	41	36	12	11
Large-Urban	46	34	12	8

TABLE 3: Raw Vote
1922 Gubernatorial Election

	Peay	Taylor
TOTAL	141,012	102,586
Grand Division		
East	36,620	51,988
Mid	65,147	29,089
West	39,245	21,509
Rural-Urban		
Rural	46,249	43,115
Small-Urban	56,717	47,400
Large-Urban	38,046	12,071

TABLE 4: Percentage Vote
1922 Gubernatorial Election

	Peay	Taylor
TOTAL	58%	42%
Grand Division		
East	41	59
Mid	69	31
West	65	35
Rural-Urban		
Rural	52	48
Small-Urban	53	47
Large-Urban	75	25

TABLE 5: Support and Opposition for Austin Peay's Program
Sixty-third General Assembly, 1923 (Raw Totals)

	Supporters	Opponents	Independents	Total
Grand Division				
East	12	13	11	36
Mid	36	3	16	55
West	19	4	18	41
Rural-Urban				
Rural	22	6	15	43
Small-Urban	34	7	13	54
Large-Urban	11	7	17	35
TOTAL	67	20	45	132

180 / Tennessee in Turmoil

TABLE 6: Support and Opposition for Austin Peay's Program Sixty-third General Assembly, 1923 (Percentages)

	Supporters	Opponents	Independents	Total
Grand Division				
East	33	36	31	100
Mid	65	5	30	100
West	49	10	41	100
Rural-Urban				
Rural	50	14	36	100
Small-Urban	63	13	24	100
Large-Urban	31	20	49	100
TOTAL	51	15	34	100

TABLE 7: Raw Vote, 1924 Democratic Senatorial Primary

	Bachman	Shields	Tyson
TOTAL	50,946	54,990	72,497
Grand Division			
East	17,711	9,979	17,205
Mid	17,335	28,337	29,815
West	15,900	16,674	25,477
Rural-Urban			
Rural	14,383	15,791	19,874
Small-Urban	13,635	21,038	27,706
Large-Urban	22,928	18,161	24,917

TABLE 8: Percentage Vote, 1924 Democratic Senatorial Primary

	Bachman	Shields	Tyson
TOTAL	29%	31%	40%
Grand Division			
East	39	22	39
Mid	23	38	39
West	27	29	44
Rural-Urban			
Rural	29	31	40
Small-Urban	22	34	44
Large-Urban	35	28	37

TABLE 9: Raw Vote
1924 Presidential Election

	Coolidge	Davis	LaFollette
TOTAL	130,728	158,679	10,510
Grand Division			
East	79,892	45,294	4,539
Mid	28,516	64,263	2,865
West	22,320	49,122	3,106
Rural-Urban			
Rural	52,309	48,162	2,244
Small-Urban	33,953	56,146	1,781
Large-Urban	44,466	54,371	6,485

TABLE 10: Percentage Vote
1924 Presidential Election

	Coolidge	Davis	LaFollette
TOTAL	44%	53%	3%
Grand Division			
East	62	35	3
Mid	30	67	3
West	30	66	4
Rural-Urban			
Rural	51	47	2
Small-Urban	37	61	2
Large-Urban	42	52	6

TABLE 11: Raw Vote
1924 Senatorial Election

	Lindsay	Tyson
TOTAL	109,863	147,744
Grand Division		
East	68,704	45,322
Mid	24,500	57,589
West	16,659	44,833
Rural-Urban		
Rural	43,652	43,369
Small-Urban	27,540	51,493
Large-Urban	38,671	52,882

182 / *Tennessee in Turmoil*

TABLE 12: Percentage Vote
1924 Senatorial Election

	Lindsay	Tyson
TOTAL	43%	57%
Grand Division		
East	60	40
Mid	30	70
West	27	73
Rural-Urban		
Rural	50	50
Small-Urban	35	65
Large-Urban	42	58

TABLE 13: Raw Vote
1924 Gubernatorial Election

	Peay	Peck
TOTAL	162,003	121,228
Grand Division		
East	49,788	72,169
Mid	59,547	30,431
West	52,668	18,628
Rural-Urban		
Rural	45,735	48,649
Small-Urban	56,796	32,827
Large-Urban	59,472	39,752

TABLE 14: Percentage Vote
1924 Gubernatorial Election

	Peay	Peck
TOTAL	57%	43%
Grand Division		
East	41	59
Mid	66	34
West	74	26
Rural-Urban		
Rural	48	52
Small-Urban	63	37
Large-Urban	60	40

TABLE 15: Support and Opposition for Austin Peay's Program Sixty-fourth General Assembly, 1925 (Raw Totals)

	Supporters	Opponents	Independents	Total
Grand Division				
East	15	2	20	37
Mid	9	12	33	54
West	20	2	19	41
Rural-Urban				
Rural	21	8	20	49
Small-Urban	15	6	25	46
Large-Urban	8	2	27	37
TOTAL	44	16	72	132

TABLE 16: Support and Opposition for Austin Peay's Program Sixty-fourth General Assembly, 1925 (Percentages)

	Supporters	Opponents	Independents	Total
Grand Division				
East	41%	5%	54%	100%
Mid	17	22	61	100
West	50	5	45	100
Rural-Urban				
Rural	43	16	41	100
Small-Urban	33	13	54	100
Large-Urban	22	5	73	100
TOTAL	33	12	55	100

TABLE 17: Raw Vote, 1926 Democratic Gubernatorial Primary

	Peay	McAlister
TOTAL	96,546	88,403
Grand Division		
East	29,731	13,831
Mid	41,503	40,994
West	25,312	33,578
Rural-Urban		
Rural	33,533	22,597
Small-Urban	38,012	31,458
Large-Urban	25,001	34,348

184 / *Tennessee in Turmoil*

TABLE 18: Percentage Vote, 1926 Democratic Gubernatorial Primary

	Peay	McAlister
TOTAL	52%	48%
Grand Division		
East	68	32
Mid	50	50
West	43	57
Rural-Urban		
Rural	60	40
Small-Urban	55	45
Large-Urban	42	58

TABLE 19: Support and Opposition for Austin Peay's Program Sixty-fifth General Assembly, 1927 (Raw Totals)

	Supporters	Opponents	Independents	Total
Grand Division				
East	12	7	20	39
Mid	12	15	25	52
West	11	11	19	41
Rural-Urban				
Rural	14	8	22	44
Small-Urban	14	10	26	50
Large-Urban	7	15	16	38
TOTAL	35	33	64	132

TABLE 20: Support and Opposition for Austin Peay's Program Sixty-fifth General Assembly, 1927 (Percentages)

	Supporters	Opponents	Independents	Total
Grand Division				
East	31%	18%	51%	100%
Mid	22	29	49	100
West	27	27	46	100
Rural-Urban				
Rural	32	18	50	100
Small-Urban	28	20	52	100
Large-Urban	19	39	42	100
TOTAL	27	25	48	100

TABLE 21: Raw Vote, 1928 Democratic Gubernatorial Primary

	Horton	McAlister	Pope
TOTAL	97,333	92,047	26,849
Grand Division			
East	24,487	17,625	7,642
Mid	42,871	36,126	15,273
West	29,975	38,296	3,934
Rural-Urban			
Rural	34,617	19,027	9,600
Small-Urban	40,756	25,022	10,404
Large-Urban	21,960	47,998	6,845

TABLE 22: Percentage Vote, 1928 Democratic Gubernatorial Primary

	Horton	McAlister	Pope
TOTAL	45%	43%	12%
Grand Division			
East	50	35	15
Mid	45	38	17
West	42	53	5
Rural-Urban			
Rural	55	30	15
Small-Urban	53	33	14
Large-Urban	31	60	9

TABLE 23: Raw Vote 1928 Presidential Election

	Smith	Hoover
TOTAL	156,169	195,195
Grand Division		
East	41,176	109,021
Mid	62,037	53,234
West	52,956	32,940
Rural-Urban		
Rural	44,657	68,013
Small-Urban	50,542	45,790
Large-Urban	60,970	81,392

186 / *Tennessee in Turmoil*

TABLE 24: Percentage Vote 1928 Presidential Election

	Smith	Hoover
TOTAL	44%	56%
Grand Division		
East	27	73
Mid	54	46
West	62	38
Rural-Urban		
Rural	40	60
Small-Urban	52	48
Large-Urban	43	57

TABLE 25: Support and Opposition for Henry Horton's Program, Sixty-sixth General Assembly, 1929 (Raw Totals)

	Supporters	Opponents	Independents	Total
Grand Division				
East	28	1	8	37
Mid	26	7	22	55
West	19	10	12	41
Rural-Urban				
Rural	34	3	16	53
Small-Urban	25	1	14	40
Large-Urban	14	14	12	40
TOTAL	73	18	42	133

TABLE 26: Support and Opposition for Henry Horton's Program, Sixty-sixth General Assembly, 1929 (Percentages)

	Supporters	Opponents	Independents	Total
Grand Division				
East	76%	3%	21%	100%
Mid	47	13	40	100
West	46	24	30	100
Rural-Urban				
Rural	64	6	30	100
Small-Urban	63	3	34	100
Large-Urban	35	35	30	100
TOTAL	55	14	31	100

TABLE 27: Raw Vote, 1930 Democratic Gubernatorial Primary

	Horton	Gwinn
TOTAL	144,991	101,285
Grand Division		
East	34,257	25,186
Mid	55,611	51,344
West	55,123	24,755
Rural-Urban		
Rural	46,172	30,798
Small-Urban	44,320	38,857
Large-Urban	54,499	31,630

TABLE 28: Percentage Vote, 1930 Democratic Gubernatorial Primary

	Horton	Gwinn
TOTAL	59%	41%
Grand Division		
East	58	42
Mid	52	48
West	69	31
Rural-Urban		
Rural	60	40
Small-Urban	53	47
Large-Urban	63	37

TABLE 29: Support and Opposition for Henry Horton's Program, Sixty-seventh General Assembly, 1931 (Raw Totals)

	Supporters	Opponents	Independents	Total
Grand Division				
East	18	2	18	38
Mid	20	5	28	53
West	15	6	20	41
Rural-Urban				
Rural	22	1	21	44
Small-Urban	18	2	24	44
Large-Urban	13	10	21	44
TOTAL	53	13	66	132

188 / *Tennessee in Turmoil*

TABLE 30: Support and Opposition for Henry Horton's Program, Sixty-seventh General Assembly, 1931 (Percentages)

	Supporters	*Opponents*	*Independents*	*Total*
Grand Division				
East	47	5	48	100
Mid	36	9	55	100
West	37	15	48	100
Rural-Urban				
Rural	50	2	48	100
Small-Urban	41	5	54	100
Large-Urban	30	23	47	100
TOTAL	40	10	50	100

TABLE 31: Raw Vote 1932 Democratic Gubernatorial Primary

	McAlister	*Pope*	*Patterson*
TOTAL	117,454	108,399	60,522
Grand Division			
East	26,203	30,459	10,499
Mid	46,078	52,328	22,166
West	45,173	25,612	27,857
Rural-Urban			
Rural	26,396	37,903	20,208
Small-Urban	27,531	41,212	19,764
Large-Urban	63,527	29,284	20,550

TABLE 32: Percentage Vote, 1932 Democratic Gubernatorial Primary

	McAlister	*Pope*	*Patterson*
TOTAL	41%	38%	21%
Grand Division			
East	39	45	16
Mid	38	44	18
West	46	26	28
Rural-Urban			
Rural	31	45	24
Small-Urban	31	47	22
Large-Urban	56	26	18

TABLE 33: Raw Vote, Rural Faction
1930 and 1932 Democratic Gubernatorial Primaries

	Horton	Pope	Patterson
TOTAL	144,991	108,399	60,522
Grand Division			
East	34,257	30,459	10,499
Mid	55,611	52,328	22,166
West	55,123	25,612	27,857
Rural-Urban			
Rural	46,172	37,903	20,208
Small-Urban	44,320	41,212	19,764
Large-Urban	54,499	29,284	20,550

TABLE 34: Percentage Vote, Rural Faction
1930 and 1932 Democratic Gubernatorial Primaries

	Horton	Pope	Patterson
TOTAL	59%	38%	21%
Grand Division			
East	58	45	16
Mid	52	44	18
West	69	26	28
Rural-Urban			
Rural	60	45	24
Small-Urban	53	47	22
Large-Urban	63	26	18

TABLE 35: Raw Vote, Antiadministration Faction
1930 and 1932 Democratic Gubernatorial Primaries

	Gwinn	McAlister
TOTAL	101,285	117,454
Grand Division		
East	25,186	26,203
Mid	51,344	46,078
West	24,755	45,173
Rural-Urban		
Rural	30,798	26,396
Small-Urban	38,857	27,531
Large-Urban	31,630	63,527

TABLE 36: Percentage Vote, Antiadministration Faction 1930 and 1932 Democratic Gubernatorial Primaries

	Gwinn	McAlister
TOTAL	41%	41%
Grand Division		
East	42	39
Mid	48	38
West	31	46
Rural-Urban		
Rural	40	31
Small-Urban	47	31
Large-Urban	37	56

TABLE 37: Raw Vote, 1932 Presidential Election in Tennessee

	Roosevelt	Hoover
TOTAL	259,450	126,806
Grand Division		
East	78,205	80,979
Mid	96,397	27,122
West	84,848	18,705
Rural-Urban		
Rural	76,219	48,625
Small-Urban	74,509	26,413
Large-Urban	108,722	51,768

TABLE 38: Percentage Vote, 1932 Presidential Election in Tennessee

	Roosevelt	Hoover
TOTAL	67%	33%
Grand Division		
East	49	51
Mid	78	22
West	82	18
Rural-Urban		
Rural	61	39
Small-Urban	74	26
Large-Urban	68	32

TABLE 39: Raw Vote
1932 Gubernatorial Election

	McAlister	*McCall*	*Pope*
TOTAL	169,075	117,797	106,990
Grand Division			
East	51,988	79,055	27,733
Mid	58,797	24,034	45,599
West	58,290	14,708	33,658
Rural-Urban			
Rural	42,814	49,228	32,707
Small-Urban	41,167	24,776	38,583
Large-Urban	85,094	43,793	35,700

TABLE 40: Percentage Vote
1932 Gubernatorial Election

	McAlister	*McCall*	*Pope*
TOTAL	43%	30%	27%
Grand Division			
East	33	50	17
Mid	46	19	35
West	55	14	31
Rural-Urban			
Rural	34	40	26
Small-Urban	39	24	37
Large-Urban	52	27	21

Bibliography

Manuscript Collections

Knoxville, Tennessee. Calvin M. McClung Historical Collection, Lawson McGhee Library. John C. Houk Papers.
Knoxville, Tennessee. Calvin M. McClung Historical Collection, Lawson McGhee Library. Lawrence Tyson Papers.
Nashville, Tennessee. Mrs. Cromwell Tidwell. Luke Lea Papers.
Nashville. Tennessee State Library and Archives, Archives and Manuscript Section. Figuers Family Papers.
Nashville. Tennessee State Library and Archives, Archives and Manuscript Section. Henry Horton Official Papers.
Nashville. Tennessee State Library and Archives, Archives and Manuscript Section. Cordell Hull Papers.
Nashville. Tennessee State Library and Archives, Archives and Manuscript Section. Austin Peay Official Papers.
Nashville. Tennessee State Library and Archives. Untitled account of his attempt to kidnap the Kaiser, by Luke Lea.
Memphis, Tennessee. Memphis-Shelby County Public Library and Information Center. Kenneth Douglas McKellar Papers.
Memphis, Tennessee. Memphis-Shelby County Public Library and Information Center. "Gordon Browning: An Oral Memoir." Interviews with Joseph Riggs.
Joe C. Gamble, Republican member of 1931 Tennessee House of Representatives, interview with the author, June 28, 1976, Maryville, Tennessee.
Joe Hatcher, Nashville *Tennessean* reporter, 1919-1976, interview with the author, February 18, 1976, Nashville, Tennessee.
Mrs. Cromwell Tidwell, daughter of Luke Lea, interviews with the author, January 26, March 11, 1976, Nashville, Tennessee.

Newspapers, 1922-1932

Bolivar *Bulletin*
Camden *Chronicle*
Carthage *Courier*
Chattanooga *News*
Chattanooga *Times*
Clarksville *Leaf-Chronicle*
Clinton, *Anderson County News*
Columbia *Daily Herald*
Cookeville, *Putnam County Herald*
Covington *Leader*

Dresden *Enterprise*
Fayetteville *Observer*
Jonesboro *Herald and Tribune*
Gallatin, *Sumner County News*
Kingsport *Times*
Knoxville *Journal and Tribune*
Knoxville *News-Sentinel*
Lawrenceburg *Democrat*
Manchester *Times*
Maryville *Enterprise*
Memphis *Commercial Appeal*
Memphis *News-Scimitar* to 1926, then *Press-Scimitar*
Nashville *Banner*
Nashville *Tennessean*
Selmer, *McNairy County Independent*

State Publications

Allred, C. E. "Human and Physical Resources of Tennessee." *Tennessee Agricultural Experimental Station Report 50.*
Biographical Directory of Tennessee State Legislators. Collected in Tennessee State Library and Archives.
Second Report of the Special Legislative Investigating Committee of the 67th General Assembly, State of Tennessee.
Minority Report of the Special Legislative Investigating Committee of the 67th General Assembly, State of Tennessee.
Report of the Special Committee of the House of Representatives, 67th General Assembly, State of Tennessee, Relating to the Impeachment of the Governor and Submitting "Article I" of a Draft of the Articles of Impeachment.

Tennessee House and Senate Journals

Fifty Years of Tennessee Elections, 1916-1966. Compiled by Shirley Hassler, State Election Coordinator, under the direction of Joe C. Carr, Secretary of State.
Fifty Years of Tennessee Primaries, 1916-1966. Compiled by Shirley Hassler, State Election Coordinator, under the direction of Joe C. Carr, Secretary of State.

Books

Alexander, T. H. *Austin Peay, Governor of Tennessee: A Collection of State Papers and Public Addresses with a Biography by T. H. Alexander.* Kingsport: Southern Publishers, 1929.
Allen, Robert S., ed. *Our Fair City.* New York: Vanguard Press, Inc., 1947.
Baker, Thomas Harrison. *The Memphis Commercial Appeal: The History of a Southern Newspaper.* Baton Rouge: Louisiana State University Press, 1971.
Brownlow, Louis. *A Passion for Anonymity: The Autobiography of Louis Brownlow.* Chicago: University of Chicago Press, 1958.
Buck, A. E. *The Reorganization of State Government in the United States.* New York: Columbia University Press, 1938.

Burt, Jesse C. *Nashville: Its Life and Times.* Nashville: Tennessee Book Company, 1959.
Catledge, Turner. *My Life and the Times.* New York, Evanston, and London: Harper and Row, 1971.
Dykeman, Wilma. *Tennessee: A Bicentennial History.* New York and Nashville: W. W. Norton and the American Association for State and Local History, 1975.
Folmsbee, Stanley, and Corlew, Robert, and Mitchell, Enoch. *History of Tennessee.* New York: Lewis Historical Publishing Company, Inc., 1960.
Goodman, William, *Inherited Domain: Political Parties in Tennessee.* Knoxville: Bureau of Public Administration, University of Tennessee Record Extension Series 30, No. 1, 1954.
Greene, Lee S. and Avery, Robert S. *Government in Tennessee,* 2nd Edition. Knoxville: University of Tennessee Press, 1966.
Hall, Charles. *Negroes in the United States.* New York: Arno Press and the New York Times, 1969.
Holt, Andrew D. *Struggle for a State System of Public Schools in Tennessee, 1903-1936.* New York: Bureau of Publications, Teachers College, Columbia University, 1938.
Hull, Cordell. *Memoirs of Cordell Hull.* New York: Macmillan, 1948.
Isaac, Paul. *Prohibition and Politics: Turbulent Decades in Tennessee.* Knoxville: University of Tennessee Press, 1965.
Jackson, Kenneth T., *Ku Klux Klan in the City, 1915-1930.* New York: Oxford University Press, 1967.
Key, V. O. *Southern Politics in State and Nation.* New York: Vintage Books, 1949.
Kirwan, Albert. *Revolt of the Rednecks: Mississippi Politics, 1876-1925.* New York: Harper and Row, 1965.
Knox, John B. *The People of Tennessee: A Study of Population Trends.* Knoxville: University of Tennessee Press, 1949.
Lee, George W. *Beale Street: Where the Blues Began.* New York: Robert Ballou, 1934.
Lewinson, Paul. *Race, Class, and Party. A History of Negro Suffrage and White Politics in the South.* New York: Russell and Russell, 1964.
McFerrin, John. *Caldwell and Company: A Southern Financial Empire.* Nashville: Vanderbilt University Press, 1969.
McGill, Ralph. *The South and the Southerner.* Boston and Toronto: Little Brown and Company, 1964.
McIlwanie, Shields. *Memphis Down in Dixie.* New York: E. P. Dutton and Company, 1948.
Martin, Harold. *Ralph McGill, Reporter.* Boston and Toronto: Little, Brown and Company in association with the Atlantic Monthly Press, 1973.
Miller, William D. *Mr. Crump of Memphis.* Baton Rouge: Louisiana State University Press, 1964.
Moore, John Trotwood and Foster, Austin. *Tennessee: The Volunteer State, 1769-1923.* Chicago and Nashville: S. J. Clarke Publishing Company, 1923.
Scott, Mingo, Jr. *The Negro in Tennessee Politics and Governmental Affairs, 1865-1965: The Hundred Years Story.* Nashville: Rich Printing Company, 1964.

Talley, Robert. *One Hundred Years of the Commercial Appeal: The Story of the Greatest Romance in American Journalism, 1840-1940*. Memphis: Memphis Publishing Company, 1940.

Thorogood, James E. *A Financial History of Tennessee*. Nashville: Tennessee Industrial School, 1949.

Tindall, George B. *Emergence of the New South, 1913-1945*. Baton Rouge: Louisiana State University Press, 1967.

Tucker, David. *Lieutenant Lee of Beale Street*. Nashville: Vanderbilt University Press, 1971.

Waller, William, ed. *Nashville, 1900-1910*. Nashville: Vanderbilt University Press, 1972.

Articles

Bridges, Lamar. "Editor Mooney Versus Boss Crump." *West Tennessee Historical Society Papers* 20 (1966):77-107.

————. "The Fight Against Boss Crump: Editor C. P. J. Mooney of Memphis." *Journalism Quarterly* 44 (1967):245-249.

Eberling, Ernest J. "Social Interpretation: Tennessee." *Social Forces* 5 (1926):19-31.

Hicks, Bobby Eugene. "The Great Objector: The Life and Public Career of Dr. John R. Neal." *East Tennessee Historical Society Publications* 41 (1969):33-66.

Kitchens, Allen H. "Ouster of Mayor Edward H. Crump, 1915-1916." *West Tennessee Historical Society Papers* 19 (1965):105-120.

Macpherson, Joseph T. "Democratic Progressivism in Tennessee: The Administrations of Governor Austin Peay, 1923-1927." *East Tennessee Historical Society Publications* 40 (1968):50-61.

Rouse, Franklin. "The Historical Background of Tennessee's Reorganization Act of 1923." *East Tennessee Historical Society Publications* 8 (1936):104-120.

Reichard, Gary. "The Aberration of 1920: An Analysis of Harding's Victory in Tennessee." *Journal of Southern History* 36 (1970):33-49.

————. "The Defeat of Governor Roberts," *Tennessee Historical Quarterly* 30 (1971):94-110.

Tindall, George B. "Business Progressivism: Southern Politics in the Twenties." *South Atlantic Quarterly*, 62 (1963):96-102.

Ward, Frank. "Industrial Development in Tennessee." *Annals of the American Academy of Political and Social Sciences* 153 (1931):141-147.

Theses and Dissertations

McCorkle, Charles H. "Taxation in Tennessee." M. A. thesis, Vanderbilt, 1932.

Macpherson, Joseph T. "Democratic Progressivism in Tennessee: The Administration of Governor Austin Peay." Ph.D. dissertation, Vanderbilt, 1969.

Reichard, Gary W. "The Republican Victory in Tennessee: An Analysis." M. A. thesis, Vanderbilt, 1966.

Index

Abernathy, William K., 100, 117
Administrative Reorganization Act, 41-42, 46, 49, 59, 61, 64, 108, 151
Agriculture, 1, 3, 6, 8, 9, 15, 20, 21, 22-23, 25-27, 28, 29, 36, 43, 48, 77
Alabama, 8, 17, 37
Alexander, Robert, 126
Alexander, T. H., 102, 148
American Legion, 119, 141
American National Bank, 144
Anderson County News, 31
Anderson, Harry, 29
Anderson, Hugh C., 117
Andrew Jackson Hotel, 143
Arkansas, 62
Armstrong, Walter, 144
Arn, Fred, 18
Augsburg Publishing Company, 120
Austin Peay Normal School, 131

Bachman, Nathan, 47-48
Back Tax Act, 8, 25, 27, 28, 30, 31
Baker, Robert, 143
Bank of Tennessee, 105, 115
Barry, William F., 51
Bass, C. Neil, 67, 81-83, 88-90, 93-94, 115
Bass, Ed, 14, 46, 67
Bean, James, 100, 101
Benton County, 66

Berry, George L., 72
Berry, Harry S., 83, 89, 108
Berry, Tyler, 125
Birmingham, Alabama, 37
Black-and-Tan Republicans, 15, 18, 49
Blacks, 2, 5, 15-18, 70-74, 91-92, 99, 132-35, 138, 142, 145. *See also* Racism; Church, Robert, Jr.
Bledsoe County, 97, 140, 141
Bogart, Clyde, 128
Bogle, William G., 108
Bolivar *Bulletin*, 79
Boswell, Walter Y., 119
Boyd, H. T., 58
Boyd, William, 119, 135, 143
Bramley, Dorsey, 59
Bratton, Sam R., 42, 44, 100, 103
Breazeale, Sam, 44
Broadbent, Ambrose B., 117, 127
Brock, William, 93, 112, 113
Browning, Gordon, 12, 59
Bruce, C. Arthur, 113
Bryan, William Jennings, 57
Buck, Arthur E., 41
Business Progressives, 59-60, 152-53
Businessmen, 20, 25-27, 28, 36, 41, 43, 46, 59, 72, 77, 95, 144-45
Byers, Sid, 134-35
Byrns, Joseph, 112
Byrd, Harry F., 37-38

Caldwell and Company, 81, 84, 96, 115, 116, 129, 151, 153
Caldwell, Rogers, 58, 81, 84, 85, 86-89, 95-96, 105, 115, 118, 119, 120, 123, 127, 151
Camden *Chronicle*, 66
Camden, Tennessee, 122, 124
Capers, Gerald, 62
Carey, John C., 43-44
Carmack, Edward Ward, 10, 27, 31, 131, 139
Carr, Herbert, 88, 89
Carr, Horace, 82
Carthage *Courier*, 21, 88, 132
Carthage, Tennessee, 112
Catholics. *See* Roman Catholics
Catledge, Turner, 73
Chamber of Commerce, 26, 41
Chamlee, George, 119
Chattanooga *News*, 21, 28, 53, 84, 94, 95, 96, 118, 124-25, 131, 144
Chattanooga, Tennessee, 3, 14, 18, 22, 29, 46, 47, 67, 112, 116, 134, 145
Chattanooga *Times*, 74, 106, 109, 118, 125, 133, 136, 137, 139
Chester County Independent, 121
Church, Robert R., Jr., 15-18, 70, 73, 91, 99, 106, 110, 124, 135, 141, 145, 149. *See also* Blacks
Church, Robert R., Sr., 16
Civil War, 1, 2, 47-48, 63, 74, 99. *See also* Veterans
Clark, Will, 125
Clarksville *Leaf-Chronicle*, 95, 132, 134, 137
Clarksville, Tennessee, 27, 34, 41, 62, 93
Clay County, 35
Clements, Hal, 142
Clinchfield Railroad, 4
Colton, Henry, 77
Columbia *Daily Herald*, 26, 139, 142
Confederacy. *See* Civil War; Veterans
Conkin, Frank G., 121

Coolidge, Calvin, 17, 50-51
Cooper, Duncan, 10, 31, 131
Cooper, Robin, 10, 31
Cornelius, Charles L., 117
Crabtree, William Riley, 21, 23
Craig, John L., 120, 122
Craig, William W., 126
Creveling, James G., 67
Crump, Edward H., 29, 43-44, 65, 76-77, 85, 86, 99, 152-54; background of, 13-14; and impeachment, 116-118, 122-29; and Lea, 100-106, 109; and 1922 general election, 31-36; and 1924 primary, 46; and 1926 primary, 70-74; and 1928 primary, 90-92, 95-96; and 1930 primary, 110-113; and 1932 primary, 130-41; and 1932 general election, 142-49; opposes Peay, 60-63
Cummins Faction, 106
Curtis, A. D., 77

Davidson County, 4, 22, 23, 34, 49, 55, 61, 66, 77, 78, 92, 100, 102, 105, 108, 130, 139. *See also* Nashville
Davidson County Court, 9
Davis, John, 50, 100
Dayton, Tennessee, 57
DeKalb County, 140
Democrats, 2, 10, 11, 13, 14, 21, 22, 27-31, 42, 43, 45, 46, 47, 48, 49, 51, 53, 56, 68, 71, 73, 75, 76, 78, 92, 98-100, 102, 113, 116, 117, 120, 127, 128, 129, 134, 140, 141, 146, 153
Dempster, George, 143, 144
Depression, 136, 145, 148
Donaldson, Frank, 120
Dresden *Enterprise*, 133, 139
Durham, J. Tom, 117

Earthman, Harold, 119
East Tennessee, 1-4, 15, 18, 22, 23, 28, 29, 30, 44, 48, 50, 51, 54, 56, 62, 74-75, 78, 79, 89, 93, 97-98, 101-102,

105-106, 113, 119, 120-21, 129, 130, 136, 140, 141, 142, 144-45, 146-48
East Tennessee State Teachers College, 56
Edgerton, John E., 72, 95
Education, 7, 24, 37, 52-53, 59, 61, 66, 67, 94, 109, 143, 151-54. *See also* General Education Act
Edwards, Wallace, 123-24, 144
Elections: 1908 primary, 27, 139; 1916 primary, 11, 112; 1920 primary, 20-22; 1920 general election, 22-23; 1922 primary, 27-30, 74-75; 1922 general election, 30-35, 50; 1924 primary, 46-48; 1924 general election, 48-51, 100; 1926 primary, 64-75, 86, 93, 94, 95, 97-98, 104, 113, 140; 1926 general election, 76; 1928 primary, 86-98, 104, 107, 112, 113, 140; 1928 general election, 98-100; 1930 primary, 109-113, 129, 140-41; 1930 general election, 113-114; 1932 primary, 130-41; 1932 general election, 141-49
English, Thomas Y., 44
Eubank, Norman H., 126
Ewell, Leighton, 126
Ezell, James, 144

Factionalism, 10, 14, 18, 24-25, 28-29, 30, 44, 53, 54, 60-61, 65, 75, 98-100, 100-106, 109, 113, 125, 140, 142-43, 147-49, 151-53. *See also* Rural-urban conflict
Faulkner, Walter, 122, 126
Farley, James, 146
Fayetteville, Tennessee, 49
Fitzhugh, Guston T., 29
Fitzhugh, Scott, 102, 117, 126, 127
Fly, Joe, 95
Ford automobiles, 37, 119
Fourth and First National Bank, 105
Fowler, James, 98
Frierson, Horace, 143, 146

Gailor, Frank, 73
Garrett, Finis T., 86, 97
General Assembly, 23-25, 26, 27, 31, 38-40, 62, 75; 62nd, 23-25, 41, 49, 108, 109, 152; 63rd, 40, 45, 50, 52, 53; 64th, 46, 51-55, 78; 65th, 59, 76-79; 66th, 100-107, 118, 126, 138; 67th, 115-30
General Education Act, 52-53, 64
General Telephone Company, 35
Gerber, Will, 96, 135
Gervin, J. Ed, 121
Gillenwaters, Ed. M., 67, 72
Grady, Henry, 1
Great Smoky Mountains National Park, 49, 52, 54, 56, 61, 77, 121, 151
Greer, Thomas, 101, 122
Gwinn, L. E., 28, 109-114, 141

Hamilton County, 4, 22, 23, 54, 78. *See also* Chattanooga, Tennessee
Hannah, Harvey, 28
Hardeman, N. B., 108
Harding, Warren G., 17, 23, 98
Harned, Perry L., 143
Harrell, Limmie Lee, 126
Harris, Isham G., 63
Haston, Ernest, 135, 143
Hatcher, Joe, 81, 136
Hawkins County, 79, 102
Haynes, Walter, 117, 126, 127
Hays, Will, 17
Haywood County, 140
Heflin, J. Thomas, 17
Henderson, Tom, 58
Highway Department, 30, 31, 58-59, 81-83, 88-90, 108, 119, 129. *See also* Public services; Roads
Hill, Graham, 41
Hill, Lucius D., 51
Holland, 11
Holston-Union National Bank, 105, 115
Hoover, Herbert, 98-100, 145

Hopkins, Raleigh, 98
Horton, Henry, 76, 100, 101, 103, 104, 105, 151, 152, 153; and impeachment, 116-129; and Lea and Caldwell, 81-85; and Lea machine, 106-109; and 1928 election, 85-98; and 1930 election, 109-114; and 1932 primary, 130, 136, 138, 140-41; and 1932 general election, 143
Houk, John C., 24
Howe, Louis, 146
Howse, Hilary, 12, 14, 19, 29, 60, 67, 132, 152. See also Howse-McConnico-Stahlman faction
Howse-McConnico-Stahlman faction, 12-13, 14, 19, 29, 36, 64, 115, 144. See also Howse, Hilary; McConnico, Kit T.; and Stahlman, Edward B.
Hughes, Thomas, 101
Hull, Cordell, 112, 113, 146
Huston, Claudius H., 18

Impeachment, 116-29, 153
Industrialism, 1, 3, 5, 8, 18
Insull, Samuel, 101
Interest rates, 25, 28, 31, 59
International Printing Pressman's Union of America, 72

Jackson County, 35
Jasper, Tennessee, 122
Jews, 6

Johnson City, Tennessee, 107
Keaton, Grover, 101, 104, 120
Kentucky, 4, 8, 27, 71
Kentucky Rock Asphalt Company, 82, 84, 88-90, 96. See also Kyrock
Key, V. O., 14
Kilby, Thomas, 37
Kingsport, Tennessee, 4, 37, 88, 107
Klein, W. H., 121
Knox County, 23, 78, 143. See also Knoxville

Knoxville *Journal*, 25, 81, 89, 92, 101, 110, 128, 151
Knoxville *News-Sentinel*, 56, 88, 94, 95, 110, 142, 144
Knoxville, Tennessee, 4, 5, 24, 47, 52, 56, 93, 106, 110, 116, 120, 145, 146. See also Knox County
Ku Klux Klan, 5, 37, 71
Kyrock, 58, 82, 84, 90. See also Kentucky Rock Asphalt Company

Labor, 67, 72, 95, 145
LaFollette, Robert, 50
Lake County, 140
Land tax repeal League, 93
Lauderdale County, 120, 122, 140
Lawrence County, 139, 140
Lawrenceburg *Democrat*, 133, 139
Lea, Luke, 29, 31, 34, 35, 54, 55, 61, 65, 151-53; and Austin Peay, 56-59; background of, 10-12, 13; establishes power, 100-106; and Horton transition, 80-84; and impeachment, 115-29; and 1928 primary, 85-96; and 1928 general election, 99-100; and 1930 primary, 109-114; and 1932 primary, 130-141; and 1932 general election, 142, 143, 144, 148; power of, 106-109, 120, 129-30, 138
League of Nations, 47
Lee, George, 145
Levine, Jake, 101
Lewinson, Paul, 15
Liberty Bank and Trust Company, 115
Lily White Republicans, 15, 18, 141-42, 145
Lincoln League, 17
Lindsay, Hal, 48, 50
Little River, 56
Littleton, Jesse, 22, 24
Louisville and Nashville Railroad, 5, 144
Louthan, A. V., 49, 70

Love, Charlie, 100
Lovette, O. B., 146-48
Lowden, Frank, 48

Maiden, Sheldon, 76
Manhattan Savings Bank and Trust Company, 85
Manier, Will, 41
Maryville, Tennessee, 3
Maury County, 26, 27, 44, 139
McAlister, Hill, 59, 64-65, 68-75, 85-98, 104, 109, 115, 130-41, 142-48, 153
McCall, John, 141-42, 147-48
McConnico, Kit T., 12, 14, 19, 29, 77, 115, 144. *See also* Howse-McConnico-Stahlman faction
McGill, Ralph, 5, 32
McKellar, Kenneth, 11, 29, 34-35, 46, 62-63, 85, 86, 97, 98, 99, 100, 102, 104, 116
McMillin, Benton, 27, 29, 30, 109
Memphis *Commercial Appeal*, 17, 34, 71-74, 77, 81, 85, 89, 96, 99, 103, 110, 133, 135, 139, 145, 151
Memphis *News-Scimitar* (later *Press-Scimitar*), 34, 85, 86, 90, 95, 96, 104, 119, 125, 128, 134, 142, 148
Memphis Power and Light Company, 144
Memphis, Tennessee, 2, 6, 14, 28, 29, 31, 32, 33, 46, 60, 62, 64, 65, 70-75, 85, 86, 91-92, 95, 106, 110, 116, 117, 120, 121, 123, 124, 125, 127, 130, 131, 133-35, 138, 139, 140, 141, 142, 145, 153. *See also* Shelby County
Mencken, H. L., 37
Middle Tennessee, 2, 10, 12, 13, 29, 35, 44, 45, 48, 49-51, 54, 55, 62, 67, 71, 75, 77, 78, 79, 97-98, 106, 113, 129, 137, 141, 151, 153
Milton, George Fort Jr., 53, 84
Milton, George Fort Sr., 28
Miser, Hugh D., 67
Mississippi, 62, 99, 152

Mr. Bowers stores, 95
Montgomery County, 26-27
Moon, Rembert, 135
Mooney, Charles P. J., 71-74, 85
Morris, Lewis, 135
Mulcahy, Jim, 70, 96

Nashville *Banner*, 5, 12, 13, 29, 31, 32, 40, 42, 45, 48, 49, 53, 54, 61, 67, 68, 74, 86-90, 93, 118, 125, 133, 137, 139, 143, 144, 152
Nashville *Tennessean*, 10, 31, 34, 49, 54, 55, 56-57, 61, 66, 68, 70-71, 81, 92, 93, 110, 121, 125, 136, 148, 151
Nashville, Tennessee, 2, 5, 10, 12, 13, 18, 31, 39, 41, 46, 52, 53, 60-61, 64, 67, 72, 75, 77, 79, 102, 104, 106, 116, 117, 118, 120, 123, 124, 125, 139, 140, 143, 144, 145, 152. *See also* Davidson County
National Guard, 28, 119-20, 135, 143
National Republican Advisory Board, 17
Neal, John Randolph, 46-48, 112, 113
Neil, D. R., 82, 88-89
New York Bureau of Municipal Research, 41
Nineteenth Amendment, 22
Nolan, John, 76
North Carolina, 37, 131

Obion County, 42, 100, 140
O'Brien, M. J., 11
Officer, Alfred F., 126
"Old Limber," 22
105th Aero Squadron, 119-20
114th Field Artillery Regiment, 11
Orange Mound Booster Club, 71
Overton County, 35, 44, 66
Overton, Watkins, 85, 86, 117
Overton, William, 44

Paine, Rowlett, 14, 71
Paris *Partisan*, 20
Parker, Edmund C., 122, 126

Patronage, 29, 58, 99, 107, 120, 121, 148, 149, 151
Patterson, Malcolm R., 7, 10, 27, 130-41
Patton, W. August, 121
Payne, John M., 126
Peay, Austin, 21, 82, 84, 85, 86, 88, 92-95, 97-98, 100, 103, 104, 105-106, 108, 112, 117, 119, 120, 127, 130, 141, 151-52, 154; background of, 27; constituency of, 55-60, 79; and Horton, 79-81; and 1922 primary, 28-31; and 1922 general election, 31-35; and 1924 primary, 46-48; and 1924 general election, 46, 48-51; and 1926 primary, 64-75, 113; and 63rd General Assembly, 41-45; and 64th General Assembly, 51-55; and 65th General Assembly, 59.
Peay, Austin Jr., 126
Peay, Sallie (Mrs. Austin), 93-94, 95
Peck, Grover C., 44
Peck, Thomas, 24, 48-51
Penn-Dixie Cement, 121
Perry, Ralph, 40
Pershing, John J., 11, 12
Piggly Wiggly, 29, 33, 65, 90. *See also* Saunders, Clarence
Police, 71, 138, 139
Polk County, 102
Poll tax, 16, 70, 139, 148
Pope, Lewis, 85, 89, 109, 115; and 1928 primary, 93-98; and 1932 primary, 130-41; and 1932 general election, 141-48
Porteous, Clark, 70
Priest, Marshall, 119
Progressive Party, 50
Prohibition, 7, 11, 14, 31, 98, 134
Public Emergency Committee, 115, 116, 117
Public services, 7, 18, 35, 50, 55, 56, 61, 64, 151-52. *See also* Education; Highway department; Roads

Putnam County, 35
Putnam County Herald, 143

Racism, 71, 91-92, 99, 124, 132-35. *See also* Blacks
Radio; first political use, 35
Rankin, J. W., 123
Reconstruction, 99
Reconstruction Finance Corporation, 136
Redistricting, 101-102
Reece, B. Carroll, 18, 79, 146-48
Reelfoot Lake, 52, 151
Remine, Ingersoll Osea, 42
Reorganization Act. *See* Administrative Reorganization Act
Republicans, 1, 10, 11, 14-18, 21-25, 29, 42, 43, 45, 48-51, 54, 56, 62, 68, 70, 75, 76, 79, 90, 98-102, 106, 113, 120, 125, 128, 129, 130, 135, 141-42, 145-49, 152, 153. *See also* Black-and-Tan-Republicans; Lily White Republicans
Rhea County, 140
Rice, Frank, 70, 117, 138
Roads, 7, 24, 32, 33, 37, 43, 50, 52, 59, 61, 62, 64, 66, 67, 81-84, 103, 105, 106, 109, 121, 126, 136, 151-54. *See also* Highway department; Public services
Roberts, Albert H., 19-25, 28, 68, 109, 115, 137
Rockwood Times, 8
Roman Catholics, 5, 6, 98-100
Roosevelt, Franklin D., 144-47
Roosevelt, Theodore, 16
Rural-urban conflict, 45, 50-51, 54-56, 59-63, 64-65, 66-67, 75, 77, 78-79, 93, 97-98, 129, 131-32, 140-41, 142-43, 147-49, 151-53. *See also* Factionalism
Rush, James, 126
Rutherford County, 140
Rye, Thomas, 7, 9, 14, 19, 24

Sanders, Newell, 29, 34
Saunders, Clarence, 29, 33, 35, 44, 46, 65, 71, 90-92. *See also* Piggly Wiggly; Sole Owner of My Name
Schools. *See* Education
Scopes Trial, 37, 57-58
Scripps-Howard newspapers, 110
Seay, Ed, 144
Sequatchie County, 140
Shelby County, 4, 13, 14, 17, 22, 23, 29, 30, 32, 33, 34, 43-44, 46, 50, 61, 62, 65, 70-75, 77, 78, 79, 85, 86, 90-92, 96, 98, 100-101, 102, 104, 105, 106, 109, 112, 113, 116, 117, 129, 130, 133, 135, 138, 139-41, 142, 147, 152, 153. *See also* Memphis
Shelby County Democratic Executive Committee, 113
Shelbyville, Tennessee, 77
Shields, John K., 47-48
Signal Mountain Portland Cement, 121
Smith, Al, 98
Smith, Gene, 121
Snyder, James, 125
Sole Owner of My Name, 65. *See also* Clarence Saunders
South, 1, 14, 15, 17, 23, 37, 38, 59-60, 115, 148, 152, 153
Southern Agrarians, 152
Southern Railway, 5
Southern Utilities Corporation, 101
Speed, J. Martin, 120
Springfield, Tennessee, 100
Stahlman, Edward Bushrod, 12-13, 14, 19, 29, 31, 34, 46, 48-49, 61, 67-68, 76, 86, 100, 152. *See also* Howse-McConnico-Stahlman faction
Standard Oil, 144
State Board of Elections Commission, 43-45, 46, 77, 100-101, 104, 122, 135, 138
State Board of Equalization, 19, 28

State Democratic Executive Committee, 102, 135, 143
State government, 18, 30, 35, 36, 37; concentration of power in, 42, 52-53, 55, 60, 61-62, 64, 75, 109, 119, 151-54; efficiency in, 24, 26, 28, 45; reorganization of, 26-27, 31, 37, 38-42, 109
State highway patrol, 135
State legislature. *See* General Assembly
State Railroad Commission, 19, 21, 22, 24, 28, 101, 103
Stockton, George L., 126
Sullivan County, 102
Sumner County News, 35, 99, 130, 144

Taft, William Howard, 16
Tammany Hall, 98
Taxes, 7-8, 9, 19-21, 22, 25, 27, 28, 30, 31, 32, 33, 37-38, 41, 43, 45, 46, 50, 51, 52, 55, 59, 61, 62, 64, 66, 72, 77, 78, 93-95, 103, 145, 151, 153. *See also* Back Tax Act; Poll tax; Tobacco tax
Taylor, Alfred A., 15, 22-25, 27, 29-34
Taylor, J. Will, 15, 18, 29, 49, 79, 101-102, 106, 110, 120-21, 130, 141-42, 149
Taylor, Robert Love, 13, 22
Taylor, Tom, 128
Tennessee, 1, 3, 10, 15, 16, 18, 27, 29, 33, 34-36, 47, 50, 53, 57-58, 60, 62, 63, 66, 73, 75, 78, 81, 83, 88, 92, 97, 98-100, 105, 107, 112, 113, 115, 118, 124, 125, 128, 129, 130, 131, 133, 135, 137, 140-41, 142-43, 145-46, 148-49, 150
Tennessee Eastman Corporation, 4
Tennessee Electric Power Company, 101
Tennessee Federation of Labor, 72, 95, 145
Tennessee Manufacturers Association, 26, 41, 72, 95

Tennessee River, 54, 97
Tennessee Road Builders Association, 121
Tenure of Office Act, 24
Thorogood, James, 7
Tindall, George B., 37, 59, 152-53
Tobacco Tax, 52-53, 62, 64, 66, 67
Todd, Andrew L., 113
"Trading," 146-48
Trenton *Herald-Democrat*, 20
Trenton, Tennessee, 66
Trezevant and Crump Insurance Company, 90
Tyson, Lawrence, 21, 27, 47, 50, 107, 112

Unicoi County, 140
University of Tennessee, 46, 47, 54, 56, 94, 106, 121
Urban-rural conflict. *See* Rural-urban conflict
Urbanization, 3, 4, 15, 16, 18

Vanderbilt University, 41

Veterans: Confederate, 47, 99; Union, 47; World War I, 47, 68
Vice, 5, 6, 70, 71, 138-39
Virginia, 37

"War of the Roses," 22
Washington County, 107, 125
Washington, D. C., 52, 149
Washington, George, 128
Water power, 1-2, 101-102, 144-45, 148
Weakley County, 76, 139, 140
Webb, William Robert (Sawney), 13
West Tennessee, 2, 29, 30, 31, 43-45, 48, 50, 51, 53, 55, 62, 75, 78, 79, 97-98, 100-101, 106, 108, 113, 120, 137, 141, 153
White County, 35
White primary, 16
White, Walter, 76
Wilhelm II, 11, 12
Williams, Joe B., 135
Wilson, Hunter, 124
Wilson, Woodrow, 11, 22, 47-48, 152
World War I, 1, 3, 7, 11, 47, 68, 83, 120